HEALTH AND WELLBEING:
A READER

This Reader forms part of the Open University course *Health and Well-being* (K258), a core course for the Diploma in Health and Social Welfare. The selection of items is therefore related to other material available to students. It is designed to evoke the critical understanding of students. Opinions expressed in it are not necessarily those of the Course Team or of The Open University. If you are interested in studying the course or working towards the Diploma, please write to the Information Officer, Department of Health and Social Welfare, The Open University, Walton Hall, Milton Keynes MK7 6AA, UK.

Also published by Macmillan in association with The Open University

COMMUNITY CARE
Edited by Joanna Bornat, Charmaine Pereira, David Pilgrim and Fiona Williams

HEALTH AND WELLBEING: A READER

Edited by

Alan Beattie, Marjorie Gott, Linda Jones
and Moyra Sidell
The Open University

313256914

MACMILLAN in association with

First published 1993 by
THE MACMILLAN PRESS LTD
Houndmills, Basingstoke, Hampshire RG21 2XS
and London
Companies and representatives
throughout the world

ISBN 0–333–58716–2 hardcover
ISBN 0–333–58717–0 paperback

A catalogue record for this book is available
from the British Library.

Printed in Great Britain by Mackays of Chatham PLC
Chatham, Kent

Contents

List of Figures and Tables

Figures

Tables

Foreword

As the influential Black Report commented in 1980, 'an understanding of "health" will always be evolving'. This volume of articles, and the associated Open University course K258, *Health and Wellbeing*, is not only a documentation of this evolution, but also an important contribution to the continuing process.

When ordinary people are asked what they understand by 'health', or what they believe causes them to fall into illness, or what determines their struggle to cure it or cope with it, they always express very complex ideas of wholeness, happiness and wellbeing. Health is more than the absence of disease. As these articles make clear, it is now widely recognised that medicine's role, however important, is limited; it cannot hope to consider, much less solve, all the social, economic and cultural problems which impinge on wellbeing.

Thinking about health, as readers of this book will find, soon raises questions about different aspects of social life – from homelessness to transport policies, from childrearing to the nature of unequal power relationships. Essentially, 'health' is about the quality of human life. People know this, but perhaps we need encouragement to be confident that this knowledge is legitimate and part of the evolutionary process; that the health agenda is wide and has room for many viewpoints. This is perhaps the particular value of a carefully chosen collection of articles such as this. Readers are presented with informational papers about policies and structures associated with health, findings from academic research, and the reality of individual experience. These areas are commonly kept apart, and their juxtaposition is thought-provoking. In particular, care has been taken to include the voices of those not often heard – poor people, those whose roots are in other cultures, and those approaching the 'third age'.

This book is not, as so many volumes on health and illness tend to be, a catalogue of dangers and problems. It is very positive. It provides, to quote the title of one of the articles, 'resources for a journey of hope'.

MILDRED BLAXTER
University of East Anglia

x

Acknowledgements

The authors and publishers wish to thank the following for permission to use copyright material:

Ashgate Publishing Ltd for material from James Robertson, 'Possible Futures for Work' in *Future Work*, ed. Smith, Gower/Temple, 1985; Basil Blackwell Ltd for material from Simon Chapman and Garry Egger, 'Myth in Cigarette Advertising and Health Promotion' in *Language, Image and Media*, eds H. Davis and P. Walton, 1983; British Sociological Association for material from N.D. Jewson, 'The Disappearance of the Sick Man from Medical Cosmology, 1770–1870', *Sociology*, Vol. 10, 1976; Edinburgh University Press for material from Sonja M. Hunt, 'The Public Health Implications of Private Cars' in *Readings for a New Public Health*, eds C. Martin and D. McQueen, 1989; Faber & Faber Ltd for material from Stephen Bayley, *Sex, Drink and Fast Cars*, 1988; Falmer Press for material from Nicki Thorogood, 'Caribbean Home Remedies and their Importance for Black Women's Health Care in Britain' in *New Directions in the Sociology of Health*, eds P. Abbott and G. Payne, 1990; Victor Gollancz Ltd for material from Patrick Pietroni, 'The Return of the Spirit' in *The Greening of Medicine*, 1990, and Ursula LeGuin, 'The Space Crone' in *Dancing at the Edge of the World*, 1989; HarperCollins Publishers for material from Cynthia Enloe, 'Women in Banana Republics' in *Bananas, Beaches and Bases*, Pandora Press, 1989, and Norma Pitfield, 'Making Gardens from Wildernesses' from *A Wealth of Experience: The Lives of Older Women*, ed. Susan Hemmings, Pandora Press, 1985; David Higham Associates Ltd on behalf of the author for material from Rosalind Coward, 'The Myth of Alternative Health' in *The Whole Truth*, Faber & Faber, 1990; Mayer Hillman for material from 'Social Goals for Transport Policy' in *Transport in Society*, Proceedings of the Conference of the Institution of Civil Engineers, 1975; Macmillan Education Ltd for material from Gillian Dalley, 'Familist Ideology and Possessive Individualism' in *Ideologies of Caring*, 1988; Joseph D. Matarazzo for material from Aaron Antonovsky, 'The Sense of Coherence as a Determinant of Health' in *Behavioural Health: an Overview*, eds J.D. Matarazzo et al.,

1984, John Wiley Inc.; MIND for material from Suman Fernando, 'Mental Health for All' in *Mental Health, Race and Culture*, 1991; Ann Oakley for material from 'The Limits of the Professional Imagination' in *Telling the Truth about Jerusalem*, Part 2, revised edition to be published by Edinburgh University Press, 1993; Open University Press for John Ashton and Howard Seymour, 'The Setting for a New Public Health' in *The New Public Health*, 1988; Oxford University Press for material from Alison Watt and Sue Rodmell, 'Community Involvement in Health Promotion', *Health Promotion*, Vol. 2, 1988, and Helen Rosenthal, 'Neighbourhood Health Projects', *Community Development Journal*, Vol. 18, 1983; Pergamon Press for material from C.W. Aakster, 'Concepts in Alternative Medicine', and Health Education Unit, WHO, 'Life-styles and Health', *Social Science and Medicine*, Vol. 22, No. 2, 1986; Random House UK Ltd for material from Raymond Williams, 'Resources for a Journey of Hope' in *Towards 2000*, Chatto & Windus, 1983; Routledge for material from Robert Crawford, 'A Cultural Account of Health: Control, Release and the Social Body' in *Issues in the Political Economy of Health Care*, ed. J.B. McKinlay, Tavistock, 1984; Sage Publications, Inc. for material from Robert Dingwall and Kathleen M. Robinson, 'Policing the Family?' in *The Homecare Experience: Ethnography and Policy*, eds J.F. Gubrium and A. Sankar, 1990; Virago Press for material from M. Llewelyn Davies (ed.), *Maternity: Letters from Working Women*, 1978; Paul E. Willis for material from 'The Expressive Style of Motor-Bike Culture' in *The Body as a Medium of Expression*, eds J. Benthall and T. Polhemus, 1975, Institute of Contemporary Arts; World Futures Society for material from J. Popay, J. Griffiths, P. Draper and J. Dennis, 'The Impact of Industrialization on World Health' in *Through the '80s: Thinking Globally, Acting Locally*, ed. F. Feather, 1980.

Every effort has been made to trace all the copyright-holders, but if any have been inadvertently overlooked the publishers will be pleased to make the necessary arrangement at the first opportunity.

General Introduction

Academic research and popular interest in health have grown dramatically in recent years, but there is still considerable progress to be made in conceptualising and delineating 'health' as an area for study, and for practical intervention. Much of the recent literature, exemplified by the valuable collection of research papers edited by Caroline Currer and Margaret Stacey (1986), is still largely dominated by studies of illness rather than health. This Reader is committed to the view that health is a territory yet to be fully explored, a 'discourse' still in the process of fabrication. Moreover, any explorers of this terrain must listen to the multiple voices that speak today for lay experience and beliefs about health, as well as acknowledging the vital contributions to debate that come from a range of academic disciplines. What is needed is a fundamental re-examination of health and wellbeing within the framework of cultural studies. To accomplish this we have to draw upon insights and theories from diverse intellectual traditions – popular, literary, academic, political. The articles brought together here begin to sketch out and develop this new field, and will, we hope, inform and stimulate debate about health issues.

Increasing dissatisfaction with the dominant model of health offered by biomedicine has been voiced by professional workers in the field of health as well as by a range of lay groups and interests. Such critics have advanced a 'social model' of health with which to challenge the claims of biomedicine to encompass the study of health. They argue that a preoccupation with disease, illness, suffering and discomfort has rendered biomedicine incapable of developing health as a positive concept. In its place they wish to develop a new paradigm of health which recognises the dynamic interaction between individuals and their environment, and attempts to promote health-enhancing social and material conditions of life and work.

This is one view among many represented in this Reader. Although the 'social model' would be endorsed by some health professionals and academics it is an 'umbrella' concept which conceals significant differences of emphasis. It must be set alongside a growing enthusiasm for various versions of holistic health medicine among both traditional and alternative medical practitioners, and an increasing interest in alternative therapies – on ideological and practical grounds – by the general public. It must also be evaluated against the ideas of the New Public Health movement and the current preoccupation within the health field with engineering 'lifestyle' changes in individuals and populations. At the same time emergent social groupings – the women's movement, black and minority ethnic groups, gay and lesbian groups, 'green' environmentalists – are raising popular consciousness about health matters and developing new and often more radical agendas for action.

Dissatisfaction with dominant models of health has been expressed on conceptual and epistemological grounds. The claims to truth of biomedical discourse have been weakened not least by the loss of faith in science which has accompanied the mounting attack from the social sciences, and from within science itself, on scientific objectivity and detachment. No longer is medicine shored up by its close association with scientific method; on the contrary its attachment to what are seen as oversimplified normative criteria and mechanistic methods to measure health has produced a humanistic backlash. Life histories, ethnomethodology, reminiscence work and cultural analysis represent alternative research traditions which challenge the epistemological dominance of the 'one true science'. They help to expose the rich tapestry of lay health beliefs and the multiple and complex interactions between individual health experiences and the shared explanations and collective practices that characterise specific social, cultural and religious groups, including those of professionals. In doing so, they have helped to create a different account of health, one that emphasises its social construction. They draw attention to the debates and decisions in everyday life which influence perceptions and interventions regarding health. All this makes it increasingly clear that health has become a contested concept and an arena for fierce debate about principles and values. Such debates about health, this Reader contends, are essentially 'healthy', for they fuel the development of new research, fresh insights and leaps of imagination. By its very title, the editors indicate a need to move beyond traditional and dominant concepts of health, by linking the study of health to an exploration of wellbeing. If health is examined as a positive state then criteria other than 'absence of disease' become relevant. The term 'wellbeing' focuses attention on the exploration of good health, whether by statistical models and surveys or through qualitative research. Recognising that a sense of wellbeing is intensely subjective does not mean abandoning the attempt to investigate it; the Reader includes several personal, philosophical and political visions of what makes for 'a healthy future' and 'a healthy society'.

If, for the foreseeable future, contestation and pluralism in health are to be the rule, students will need a cross-section of accounts and interpretations of health from which to make their own assessment of the debate. Consequently the material collected into this Reader is drawn from a variety of traditions and disciplines to reflect the wide-ranging nature of the health debate. It includes articles which have been valuable in initiating or moving on debate, others which represent a significant or central tradition in discussions about health, and yet others which speak for hitherto silent voices in the health debate.

The articles are grouped within three sections: health as a contested concept; debates and decisions in everyday health; and health on wider agendas. These represent three key themes in the book and reflect the editors' assessment of the current state of debates about health and wellbeing. Some of the articles in Section 1 explore and appraise the health beliefs and values of contemporary social groups and movements which are attempting to move their ideas higher up the health agenda. Others chart the ebb and flow of official accounts of health across cultures and through time, and raise fundamental questions about health priorities today.

In Section 2 the articles have been chosen to reflect debates and decisions in 'everyday health'. From several different standpoints the authors examine how opportunities and constraints operate in contemporary society to influence the realisation of health and wellbeing. Some address the question of how wellbeing might be realised; others focus on the powerlessness of some groups to realise health at all. Finally, in Section 3 the Reader turns to examine the prospects for putting this broader view of health and wellbeing onto current social welfare agendas. Through an examination of debates about lifestyles and transport the section raises key issues about the future direction of health. A series of articles, from literature, philosophy, politics and the health field itself, offers diverse visions of health and wellbeing in contemporary society.

Each section has a short introductory guide to its central theme and issues, and some guidance on the articles. The articles within each section demonstrate the diversity and vitality of current writing about aspects of health, as well as the continued significance of earlier insights and observations. Several of the articles have a general relevance beyond their particular section; indeed, the section themes are inter-connected rather than exclusive preserves. The Reader is best viewed as an evolving dialogue about health and wellbeing, and not as a sequential narrative. The main objective throughout the Reader is to prompt debate rather than to offer ready answers; to encourage the reader to think about health and wellbeing in new ways rather than merely to revisit traditional themes.

Over thirty articles have been selected including journal articles, extracts from books, published texts of lectures and newly commissioned papers. We would like to thank the authors for their co-operation in reviewing and agreeing the sometimes extensive edits, amendments and revisions. With their help, we think the substance and style of the original papers has been largely retained.

The Reader has been developed to accompany an Open University second level course and pack K258 'Health and Wellbeing', which is one of two compulsory core courses in the Health and Social Welfare Diploma. It reflects and underpins a major aim of that course, which is to 'encourage students to gain greater awareness of current issues and controversies in health and wellbeing, and to move as appropriate towards principled social commitments as citizens and/or as professionals'. It is hoped that the Reader will also support another, complementary course aim, which is to introduce the students to new voices in contemporary debates about health and wellbeing, to help them to see previously unacknowledged contexts for health, and to grasp the new critical perspectives that are central in the growing debate about personal and public health. While the Reader stands as an essential element in the 'Health and Wellbeing' course, it is also intended to be a coherent and wide-ranging source book for those interested in debates about health. The book will be of value to all those engaged in health work as health or welfare professionals, to a wider lay audience of volunteers and campaigners, to students of undergraduate courses in social and behavioural sciences, and to the general public. The editors hope that this collection of articles will not just inform and stimulate debate but help to widen its terms of reference, so that hitherto marginalised groups and hidden voices, in particular, will feel more able to play an active part in setting future health agendas.

For more information on the course and pack contact The Information Officer, Department of Health and Social Welfare, The Open University, Walton Hall, Milton Keynes MK7 6AA.

Part I

HEALTH AS A CONTESTED CONCEPT

Introduction

The articles in this first section report on explorations of the many different ways in which people talk about health and wellbeing. Some document the recent emergence of voices which speak for lay experiences and beliefs related to health; others examine key phases in the development of 'official' discourses on health – including systems of thought both from earlier times in Europe, and from non-Western cultures.

'Lay' voices have hitherto not been heard so clearly as have professional and official voices on matters of health; and a feature of the current health scene is the number of groups and projects which are trying to get more of a hearing for lay people's views about health. So in the first section of this Reader, we start with a cluster of articles which show that exploring lay accounts of health is crucial in rethinking health and in developing new ways of working.

The articles by Watt and Rodmell, and by Rosenthal, offer interpretations of the significance of the recent growth of the community health movement in working for health and wellbeing. These authors note that the community health movement has grown in spite of the fact that it has had little official recognition or backing. They argue that, in comparison to the media attention that is paid to the National Health Service (NHS), community health projects are (officially) almost invisible. They suggest that a principal reason for the rise of the movement is public dissatisfaction with the dominant authority of medicine within formal health care. A powerful source of this dissatisfaction is dissonance between lay people's lived experience of health, and official accounting for health. People feel that their personal stories of health are not heard, or, if they are, they are marginalised or seen as illegitimate. The two articles show how local initiatives have given a hearing to accounts of health by lay people that stand uneasily alongside official accounts of health. When these new lay voices for health encounter the official health system, an uneasy set of negotiations and conflicts ensues.

The conflict between lay and official accounts of health can be documented for all levels and sectors of society, but is particulary marked in the experience of black and minority ethnic people in Britain. Thorogood describes some of the tensions that arise for British Afro-Caribbean families as they attempt to take care of their own health while living in a culture that devalues the beliefs about health that are part of their personal identity and their cultural heritage.

A source of conflict for all social groups when faced with the biomedical account of health as THE official account is not only its sometimes limited relevance to the experience of their day-to-day lives, but its presentation as the sole and exclusive form of reliable knowledge. The article by Stainton Rogers points out that people commonly draw upon multiple, rather than single, accounts of health, depending on the story they are telling and the context in which they are speaking. The article recommends the useful term 'sympatricity' to indicate that alternative accounts are not fixed and static, but rather that they compete with one another and shift over time.

A second cluster of articles in this section examines various aspects of 'official' accounts of health. The article by Jewson explores the transition to modern medicine in Europe and identifies the social conditions and consequences of significant shifts in medical cosmologies. The article by Armstrong offers an interpretation of the emergence into dominance of the biomedical account as the official – in many domains the only – account of health in Western society today, arguing that it itself is a very particular way of constructing an understanding of illness and health. Both Jewson and Armstrong cite the rise of scientific reductionism as being responsible for the reconceptualisation of the human body, and for the demise of earlier views. Both these articles challenge us to reflect upon why the biomedical account has enjoyed such precedence to date.

Further aspects of the power of current official accounts are identified in the article by Fernando, which draws our attention to the way in which the reductionist stance and associated social values lead to an ethnocentric approach to mental health, which is highly prejudicial to black and minority ethnic people. He also points to the irony of the way in which the Western (biomedical) account of health is exported to, and adopted by, Third World countries. The article by Anionwu reveals that genetic health is another area in which there are severe conflicts of perspective between health professionals and their lay clients, and where the accumulation of medical knowledge has often served to reduce the opportunity for families to discuss health and wellbeing in their own terms. In this case also, the threats to the rights of minorities are exacerbated by ethnocentrism and racism.

Holistic practices have been, until recently, seen as 'alternative medicine' (to be used as a last resort rather than as a complement to, or true alternative to, biomedicine). But this is now changing; the concept is rapidly gaining popularity in professional health circles, and several alternative therapies are now incorporated within NHS services. The article by Aakster explores the contrasts between the conventional medical model and the alternative holistic model. He suggests that what is at stake is a shift from the technical to the human, from complex to simple – and from a preoccupation with health as a deviation from disease to a view of illness as a deviation from health. The article by Coward gives a powerful warning that the incorporation of alternative therapies into mainstream NHS practices may change the nature and value of their contribution to meanings of health and wellbeing. She argues that holism is yet another attempt at blaming the victim – the individual who suffers – rather than the circumstances which precipitate suffering. Coward believes that embracing holism, as part of the quest for natural health, colludes with the emergence of a new individualistic morality, and alleges that the search for health is becoming a personal quest to avoid the ills of modern society.

The question of personal responsibility for health and ill health is an issue that we will return to in Section 3 of this Reader. Here we raise it in the context of debates surrounding the 'New Public Health'. The article by Ashton and Seymour describes the origins of both the Victorian and the New Public Health movements, and identifies the similarities and the differences between these two ideologies. The most obvious contrast relates to responsibility for protecting health and wellbeing. In the Victorian era protecting health was seen as a public concern, whereas nowadays, they argue (as Armstrong does in his article), it is seen as a private one: the New Public Health makes people responsible for maintaining and monitoring their own bodies.

A final pair of articles in this section focuses on women's accounts of health. The extracts of 'Letters from working women' present poignant and graphic stories about experiences of childbirth and parenting in the nineteenth century. The article by Oakley documents the devaluing of women's experience and testimony both in encounters between doctors and patients, and in the construction of expert accounts of childbirth and parenting. She argues that professional paradigms of pregnancy need to be seen as part of a 'cultural project' which seeks to reshape commonsense understandings of women and motherhood. Both of these articles testify to the particular significance of women's voices in contesting official and dominant concepts of health.

Taken together, the articles in this section of the Reader show that to contest ideas about what health is, or how it may be achieved or maintained, has long been an important aspect of social change – it is one of the ways in which a society moves on. They show some of the main dimensions of the debate between competing ideas.

1

Community Involvement in Health Promotion: Progress or Panacea?*

ALISON WATT and SUE RODMELL

Introduction

The community health movement is vast; well over ten thousand initiatives exist, yet they are little known. When the movement is discussed in health promotion literature, surprisingly loose typologies and typecasting predominate. In sharp contrast, there has been a large number of attempts to define health promotion. All of these attempts (regardless of their resulting definitions) indicate that health promotion will not succeed without the engagement of the community. Given this dependence on the community, it is curious that so few attempts have been made to uncover and analyse the nature and significance of existing community health activities.

As a gloss to these observations, it is particularly interesting to note, within certain aspects of health promotion, a concern with addressing the concept of medical dominance. Medical dominance has been of central interest to medical sociologists since the earliest days of the discipline (Ehrenreich, 1978; Friedson, 1970; Navarro, 1976; Parsons, 1972). Latterly, this interest has spread to a wider range of disciplines and professions, perhaps with less theoretical focus, but certainly with a surprising degree of consensus on the major imperatives within the

*This is an abridged version of an article that was first published in *Health Promotion*, Vol. 2, No. 4, Oxford University Press, pp. 359–67, 1988.

concept. Indeed, the concept has achieved popularity to the extent that, wittingly or not, a fundamental reason for the existence of the thousands of community health initiatives is as a response to the recognition of medical dominance. In other words, the general public, as well as professional and occupational groups, is aware that the organization of the medical profession most commonly makes for uncomfortable consultations. Further, there is an increased understanding that the medical profession can be seen as a significant health hazard in itself. This substantial public recognition of medical dominance stands in sharp contrast to the current failure of those who are formally concerned in the politics of health to take account of a social movement that holds the potential to challenge and perhaps overturn medical dominance.

The community health movement

Most community health initiatives are invisible to the National Health Service (NHS). Groups of people meet in community halls, factory canteens, women's centres, their own homes, church halls, and a large number of other venues. Only a small minority meet in general practitioners' premises, in health centres, or in the meeting rooms of the district health authority. This invisibility both protects and undermines the community health movement. The protection comes from the unwillingness or structural inability of most health professionals to participate in or support community health initiatives. While this is in itself a regrettable observation on the state of formal health care, it ironically allows space for the initiatives to generate their own agendas without the risk of being captured and controlled by a number of health professions accustomed to, and respectful of, the concept of medical dominance. The undermining that comes from the invisibility of the community health movement is, again, a reflection on the formal practice of health care. There is almost a tautology in the movement's invisibility. It is invisible because it is invisible – because it is beyond the limits of the medical remit and therefore insignificant, invalid, and inconsequential in the medical model.

As long as the concept of medical dominance remains strong within formal health care, the community health movement must therefore struggle with its most difficult contradiction. It needs independence to create the space for an imaginative and useful collective response to health and sickness, yet it also needs to be able to affect the medical profession if the inappropriateness of much medical care is to be challenged. Once people begin to understand how the medical profession can also be a purveyor of sickness both through its practice and its social organization, then it will be imperative to call a halt to the unhealthy aspects of the profession. The profession, however, remains impervious because it needs to be so, to retain its dominance.

One strategy for entering this cycle is to work from within. Within the community health movement there is frequent debate on the role of health professionals. Similarly, health professionals – some more than others – are beginning to show a well developed interest in participating in the movement. At the moment there is more interest than action. Yet much of the commendable uncertainty expressed by some health professionals about their role in the movement could be assuaged if the focus were shifted away from what professionals can do in the community – that is, how they can take action in the community – to what they can do within the NHS to erode medical dominance. Although the answer to such a question is beyond the scope of this article, the task may begin through a sharper analysis of the community health movement.

The three major sections of this movement are: self-help groups; community health groups; and community development health projects.

Self-help groups

Self-help groups form around conditions that are recognized by the medical profession as falling within its remit. Groups are usually initiated by sufferers themselves, or relatives or friends of a sufferer. The groups attempt to provide support for each other that would be inappropriate to seek from the formal health care system. So, for example, a person who has psoriasis may advertise in the local paper for other sufferers to come to a support group. Within the group, people would exchange experiences of the condition, swap treatments, and offer coping strategies. Perhaps most importantly, they would draw strength from the loss of stigma that comes from being with people who share a common, socially ascribed misfortune, deviance, or failing. Such groups exist in their thousands, and many are sufficiently well organized to have national networks and paid workers. The groups may function as a lobby for changes in both health care provision and societal attitudes to, for example, mental illnesses and physical disabilities. Many such self-help groups are well regarded by the medical profession because they do not challenge the profession's power base.

Other self-help groups challenge the medical profession, where, in addition to providing mutual support, such groups exist because they are critical of the nature and extent of NHS provision for their shared condition. Hence groups of women who meet to see each other through the menopause are angry both about their own experience of care within the NHS and on behalf of other women who may experience a similar paucity of respect, knowledge and interest.

Community health groups

These differ little from self-help groups in their structure and organization. The fundamental difference is the issue around which they are organized. People in community health groups address health issues that the medical profession considers to be beyond its remit. Take, as an example, the maintenance of adequate safety standards in council housing. If a woman with small children is aware of safety hazards in her home such as the lack of safety catches on windows, unprotected electric sockets, and the absence of a stair gate, yet is unable to extract any response from the people responsible for maintenance and repairs on the estate, she faces a double problem: the actual danger her children are in, and the effects on her own health from cumulative anxiety and annoyance at the council's failure to take remedial action. On talking to other residents, she decides that the only solution to these health problems is to exert collective pressure and perhaps embarrass the council into a response.

People meet, therefore, to tackle problems that have a direct bearing upon their health, but to which the medical profession typically makes one of two responses. Either the profession considers the problem to be outside its remit, or it treats the manifestations of the problem rather than its source. Currently, however this section of the community health movement is the most invisible to the medical profession and therefore evokes little response. Where there is awareness, the medical profession tends to regard the activities as supplementary rather than oppositional.

Community development health projects

Community development health projects are neighbourhood based. Paid community health workers cover a geographical patch and try to assist residents of that neighbourhood to identify their health needs and interests, and to organize themselves collectively to attempt to get these needs met. Such projects emerge through the efforts of small numbers of people committed to the concept of community development in health. These people attract funding from government schemes such as the Community Programme, from their local authority, a trust or foundation, or, very occasionally, their district health authority. Upon receipt of a grant, one or more workers are employed. At some stage in these proceedings, local residents become formally involved in managing the project.

The principles underpinning community development health work are generally similar to those of community development. There is a stated concern with identifying and tackling the roots of ill health in areas where structural inequalities are seen to be responsible for ill health. This emphasis upon structural inequalities in health prompts a specific interpretation of the word community. It means a geographical neighbourhood whose residents suffer most from inequalities produced by society. It refers therefore to people who have the least amount of power. The capacity of powerless people to control their housing, employment status, income and personal relationships is minimal. Their capacity to control their health is therefore equally minimal.

Community development health workers encourage powerless people to find ways of gaining control of their health. Again, there is an important distinction between being held responsible for one's health, and wishing to take control of it. The former negates any societal responsibility for ill health, while the latter places health firmly into the political arena of allocation of limited resources. This emphasis upon control has significant implications for the medical profession. Professional dominance relies upon professional control and any challenge to that control is staunchly resisted. For this reason, community development health projects have attracted disproportionate attention in relation to the other two sections of the community health movement.

Community development health workers devise methods of practice that equip people to deal more assertively with the medical profession, and to learn how to affect decision-making processes. This section of the community health movement is obviously seen in oppositional terms by the profession.

Different sections of the community health movement clearly offer different challenges to medical hegemony. For this reason, anyone intending to support the movement must understand where pressure might most usefully be applied. For example, work by a health visitor with a 'supplementary' slimming self-help group, can be seen as less effective in challenging medical dominance than work, by that same health visitor, with an 'oppositional' anorexia self-help group. Similarly, work by a health education officer with a 'supplementary' smoking cessation self-help group can be seen as less challenging to medical dominance than the same officer's attempts to have tobacco advertisements removed from council hoardings.

Health promotion and medical dominance

In recent years interest has increased in the concepts, policies and programmes devised under the label of health promotion. Documents about health promotion invariably recognize the importance of community involvement. Statements refer to the needs of the community, and seek to employ a community development approach in the implementation of health promotion strategies. It is hoped that the above typology of the community health movement will make some contribution to the necessary development of sensitive professional involvement in the movement. Moreover, three additional points should be borne in mind in considerations of the potential of health promotion to challenge medical dominance.

First, evidence from a number of studies shows consistently that the medical profession remains a curative profession and does not give any major priority to the promotion of health (Stott and Davis, 1979; Royal College of General Practitioners, 1981; Anderson, 1984; Boulton and Williams, 1983; Calnan *et al.*, 1986). Doctors in the acute services cannot be expected to perceive themselves as having a significant role in the promotion of health. General practitioners (GPs), however, can be described as being at the sharp end of community-based health care, and as such are more likely to redefine their role in terms of promotion of health.

The second point concerns a lack of congruence between statutory and non-statutory sectors. Anderson (1984) notes that, within the diversity of views and understandings of health promotion, many health professionals (especially health educators, community nurses and community physicians) are more familiar with the term than are the people who work outside the health sector but are involved in health-enhancing, community-based activities. Thus, for example, play group workers, sports instructors or welfare rights workers do not typically recognize the term, and, more importantly, they do not always recognize their work as health-enhancing. This is the case despite a growing awareness amongst health promotion strategists that such workers may play a more important role than many health professionals in the improvement of health. This gap in perception should be borne in mind in any discussions of the promotion of health within communities. It illustrates the need for the careful use of the labels that are becoming commonplate in health action networks, particularly, as Jacob (1986) points out, with the addition of 'the new public health' to the repertoire.

Third, governments have recently shown interest in health promotion. Over the last five years the involvement of government in strategic planning for health promotion has significantly increased. In Britain, regional health authorities are expected to include details of health promotion programmes in their regional review process and to have made appropriate strategic plans. This in itself has given health professionals an impetus to generate health promotion programmes. In addition, the creation of a national Health Education Authority heralds a new era in the involvement of government in the promotion of health. Although government interest in health promotion can provide legitimacy and credibility for health professionals who undertake health promotion work, it does not in itself guarantee that health authorities need do any more than make token gestures towards community involvement.

Nevertheless, the opportunity to involve communities fully in enhancing health has increased greatly with the generation of new plans and programmes under the rubric of health promotion. The community health movement challenges medical dominance, and has the potential, if supported, radically to alter the nature of health care delivery. There is, at the same time, an awareness of the need for community involvement through health promotion, and, already, some professional support for community health initiatives. Given the call for community involvement in health promotion projects and programmes, any approaches by professionals should be based on, at the very least, an understanding of the different sectors within the movement. This will allow strategic decisions to be made about creating a health care system based on, and responsive to, people's health needs. The challenge to medical dominance from the community health movement is obvious. The challenge for health professionals is to be prepared to take on the implications of empowering ordinary people to take control of their health.

References

Anderson, R. (1984) *Health Promotion: an overview*, Edinburgh, Scottish Health Education Group, pp. 1–126 (European Monographs in Health Education Research, No. 6).

Boulton, M. and Williams, A. (1983) 'Health education in the general practice consultation', *Health Education Journal*, **42**(2), 57–63.

Calnan, M., Boulton, M. and Williams, A. (1986) 'Health education and general practitioners: a critical appraisal', in Rodmell, S. and Watt, A. (eds) (1986) *The Politics of Health Education: raising the issues*, London, Routledge and Kegan Paul, pp. 183–203.

Ehrenreich, J. (1978) *The Cultural Crisis of Modern Medicine*, New York, Monthly Review Press.

Friedson, E. (1970) *The Profession of Medicine*, New York, Dodd Mead and Co.

Jacob, M. (1986) 'Use language with care', *Health Education Journal*, **45**(3), 126.

Navarro, V. (1976) *Medicine under Capitalism*, New York, Prodist.

Parsons, T. (1972) 'Definitions of health and illness in the light of American values and social structure, in Gently Jao, E. (ed.) *Patients, Physicians and Illness*, New York, Free Press.

Royal College of General Practitioners (1981) *Health and Prevention in Primary Care*, London, Royal College of General Practitioners.

Stott, N.C.H. and Davis, R.H. (1979) 'The exceptional potential in each primary care consultation, *Journal of the Royal College of General Practitioners*, **29**, 201–208.

2

Neighbourhood Health Projects – Some New Approaches to Health and Community Work in Parts of the United Kingdom*

HELEN ROSENTHAL

Introduction

As part of its broad concern with health care in London, the King Edward Hospital Fund for London in 1978 began considering the scope for new initiatives which address the major problems of primary and community care, particularly in the least well-off areas. Strategies to tackle these problems were a high priority for the Health and Local Authorities as well as being a central preoccupation of those Community Health Councils, voluntary organisations and community groups who were struggling to mobilise fresh thinking and action around health needs, often as part of a critique of existing statutory services. The King's Fund Centre was also working with other London organisations

---

*This is an abridged version of an article that was first published in *Community Development Journal*, Vol. 18, No. 2, pp. 120–31, 1983.

including the London Voluntary Services Council (LVSC), to identify ways of using different experiences and networks to foster improved collaboration in community care, that is, not just better collaboration between Health and Local Authority services but also more effective relationships between professional services and the informal caring resources of the community itself.

There was a growing interest amongst community groups in health and social service care and a consequent spread of neighbourhood health projects with a 'community development' orientation. It appeared that, at a time when major changes in London's health services were taking place, these projects were exploring fundamental questions which included the relationships between patients and health professionals, neighbourhood support for collective action on health and social problems, community influence in the planning of public services, and how the concept of 'health' itself can best be understood. In 1979 the King Edward's Hospital Fund commissioned a short survey of what was broadly described as 'Alternative Approaches to Primary Care in Big Cities'. This article is based upon that survey and draws heavily on the experience of two community health projects in South London.

The search for some new approaches to health in the community

In 1977 the City and Hackney Community Health Council (CHC) was beginning to establish an active role for itself in an inner-city working class borough with a long tradition of political and community activity. Hackney's health service provision was beginning to be dramatically affected by the 'rationalisation' programme of the Resource Allocation Working Party, by a history of continuous underfunding, and by the drain on those decreasing resources caused by the presence of a major teaching hospital in the District. The CHC quickly developed a position and style of work which has often been militant, e.g. campaigning for day-care abortion facilities, improved maternity and ante-natal care, and more recently against cutbacks in acute hospital provision and community health services. But there was increasing awareness that the work was often only responsive in character. It was defined by the demands of the National Health Service (NHS) itself for a response by the CHC, and by individuals approaching the CHC with problems and complaints. Accordingly, a good deal of time was spent responding to District, Area and Regional Plans which were often incomprehensible and frequently bore little relationship to developments forced on the local health services by more immediate economic and political considerations.

ations. There was plenty of contact of a limited kind with the public, through casework, through organising stalls and displays at local events, and through often packed public meetings. But the connection between this public work, and comments on District proposals for Community Hospitals was sometimes hard to perceive.

Much of the CHC's work was conducted in small working groups which met to discuss specific issues – mental handicap, women's health, children's health, etc. This way of working was adopted in order to involve more people in the CHC in a more active way, but there was also awareness that only a small number of middle-class people were being attracted. Hackney is a working class borough with all the hallmarks of urban decay and social and environmental deprivation. It was realised that the roots of sickness and health lay in the surrounding social conditions, that the local health services were poor in contrast to those in more affluent areas, and that there was a higher incidence of every disease and health risk amongst people from the lower social classes. It was felt that the health and health services of the people of Hackney could only begin to improve when the people themselves were engaged in an informed dialogue with the providers and practitioners in the health and medical services. That local people cared about their health and the NHS there was no doubt.

Community development: some definitions, contradictions and applications

Although 'community development' is a much used term, it has a host of differing definitions. The meaning of community development used here is the process by which a community, defined geographically, is aided by community workers in defining the needs that it has. With the continued help of community workers, a dialogue is then entered into with the controllers and providers of services to bring about change. A community worker is usually someone employed by a voluntary group or public authority, but may be an unpaid person working with a community interest or project. Community workers are sometimes, though not necessarily, trained and qualified.

In Britain, community development has grown mainly since the late 1960s. At this time, poverty was 'rediscovered,' especially in the inner cities. The Child Poverty Action Group was set up, and the Welfare Rights Movement was established. Local authorities were reorganised into larger, more hierarchical structures, with new ideas of corporate management being introduced, and more power being invested in the State. The grand visions of the Town Planners were crumbling with the realisations of the disastrous reality of their vast new housing estates and tower blocks.

This climate generated extensive localised political and community activity, which not surprisingly was often perceived as a threat to the State. For national and local government, encouragement of the idea and practice of 'participation' was to become important in preparing the public to accept plans and proposals, and gaining public co-operation. Some kinds of community action encouraged by community workers (e.g. militant housing campaigns, rent strikes, Women's Aid work) and the conclusions of some Community Development Projects indicate the need for radical changes in our society, and it can become a contradiction for the State to continue its support of certain kinds of community action.

In spite of these inherent contradictions, community workers have increased rapidly in number in this country. Throughout the 1970s, their emphasis was on housing and tenants association work, nursery and play facilities for children, youth work, work with pensioners, neighbourhood care schemes, etc. All were issues linked to services provided (or not provided) by local authorities or district councils.

In the last few years, however, health and health service provision have become areas of importance for community workers. The Women's Movement, the unionisation of health and hospital workers, the reorganisations and cutbacks in the National Health Service, and the radical movements in public and environmental health have all become important forces in creating new awareness that health and illness are indeed issues for public and collective concern. Community workers have both responded to and helped to create this awareness.

Neighbourhood health projects

The earliest established projects in South London all grew out of existing local community or action centres where a range of other community activities take place. All of them have very closely involved support groups made up largely of local people and local health workers. The workers all have previous experience of community work and were part of a team of other workers and volunteers. One of them was already employed as a community worker at the Centre. Her work came to be increasingly involved with health issues, and thus the health project grew out of her everyday work.

The projects have certain common features. All are based in deprived working class, inner-city areas. All try to counter the predominant individual and disease-based models of ill-health on which our health services are organised, recognising that ill-health is actually created by society in various ways. Several of the projects use the World Health Oganisation definition of health as a primary reference point for their activities – i.e. 'a state of complete mental and social well-being and not merely the absence of disease.' Their activities reflect a recognition of the relationship between social class, poverty and health, and the inequalities in health provision that exist between deprived and more affluent areas. All of the projects employ workers trained and experienced in community work rather than in medicine, nursing or health education, to work on health issues in small, defined geographical areas. This is often a housing estate. The workers are usually supported by an advisory or support group of both local people and sympathetic health professionals, who decide collectively on the direction and initiatives the project should take.

Examples of neighbourhood health projects in the early 1980s

Work with the elderly

In the Waterloo Health Project work with the elderly has combined a regular health input into discussions and activities at old people's clubs and groups already in existence in the neighburhood, and initiating new groups and projects. In one club, a series of discussions were held on topics including relaxation and exercise, diet (a local dietician was invited), uses and dangers of drugs, and massage. Another old people's club was already running a course put on by the local Health Education Unit, and invited the worker to provide a follow-up session on local health services. There has been work on health rights, as part of a welfare rights course for old peple organised at a nearby Settlement. There have been discussions on 'Going to the Doctor,' followed by a meeting with a local GP at the Settlement Sheltered Workshop for psychiatrically ill and physically handicapped people. The elderly people who have been involved in these initiatives were the main participants in a public meeting on rheumatism. Arising out of the public meeting a regular relaxation and exercise class has been set up at an Adult Education Centre.

Work with women

Work on women's health developed from a small women's group which met regularly. The aims of the group were to improve women's health by increasing social contact and providing the opportunity for mutual support, enabling a sharing of knowledge and increase in confidence, in turn leading to the group bringing about changes in factors influencing both health and health service provision. Discussions varied from pregnancy, slimming, smoking, sex, family planning, the estate, to bringing up children in flats. The group met a GP to discuss contraception, made bread, saw films on breast examination, the Leboyer birth method, and drugs. The group had an active role in obtaining funding for a local 'Drop-in' Centre for Mothers with toddlers and in fighting for provision for play space for children on the estate. It also stimulated the setting up of a keep fit group and yoga group at an Adult Education Centre.

A group for menopausal women was established, which has met monthly for the women to share their experience, and collect and share information. The ante-natal work with pregnant women has included a survey of women on the estate to find out about facilities used and the women's attitudes and feelings about the local facilities. The health clinic on the estate currently houses family planning, the school dentist, a baby clinic, and audiology, but no ante-natal provision. It is hoped that an ante-natal group could be set up there to enable local pregnant women to think and talk together about their needs, and eventually to establish some kind of ante-natal clinic which would meet the specific needs of women in the locality.

Advice and information work

Advice and information work is carried out as part of the Waterloo Action Centre's general work, and in a weekly 'Drop-in' session in the Tenants Association's flat. The Action Centre opens on to a busy street with a street market, and is open for members of the public to walk in. The community health workers take their turn with the other community workers at the Centre to ensure that the shop front is staffed. The Drop-in session allows people the opportunity for a lengthier and more private discussion of their problems. The advice and information work is used to indicate particular health issues and concerns that can be taken up more widely – e.g. the need for group work on the menopause was spotted after several women had come to the Action Centre wanting advice and information. The advice work at the Action Centre led to an increase in the number of enquiries about health and to other advice workers in turn learning more about health. A health information sheet has also been produced for distribution via the shop front.

The community health projects: characteristics, achievements and constraints

The number of range of community health initiatives continues to grow. There is now quite a recognisable community health movement in Britain, the main characteristics of which are:

— that it is based firmly *outside* the health professions
— that it is concerned with inequalities in health and health care
  provision
— an understanding that the achievement of a healthy community
  depends on a collective awareness of the social causes of ill health,
  and positive health
— that the monopoly of information about health and ill health by
  professionals must be challenged both individually and collectively.

Probably the most important common feature of all the community
health projects is the work with small groups of local people. The groups
may be specially set up, or may already be in existence in the form of
mother-and-toddler groups, pensioners' groups, etc. Group-work
emphasises mutual support, and the building up of confidence in
individuals to discuss their private experiences, difficulties and opinions
on health issues. People can learn together how to seek out and use
specialist information from health professionals and from medical literature, which is often impossible for an individual on his or her own. The
information gathered collectively may be useful to the individual, but
can also be shared by producing a pamphlet, leaflet or a video. The
acquisition of technical skills necessary to do this is a further boost to
individual and group confidence, and the skills can be used in new
situations. This kind of group activity is important in combating apathy,
mystification and acceptance of poor health and poor treatment.

Interpersonal relationships – a crucial factor

Even establishing easy working relationships with individual health
workers can be difficult. Attempts by people in the community to
address health issues in anything but a voluntary and private way will
often be greeted with suspicion by medical professionals, or occasionally
by attempts to colonise the initiative, and bring it into the safe confines
of the Health Service. The 1978–9 report of the Waterloo Health Project
describes a meeting for pensioners organised by the project on rheumatism, where a health visitor and a GP were involved.
    'A lively discussion started fairly easily, as everyone relaxed after the
film and a cup of tea. However, the health workers had a traditional
attitude to rheumatism. It was difficult to emphasise alternative
methods of coping with rheumatism such as massage, relaxation, exercise, osteopathy etc., although they all agreed that diet was particularly
important to those overweight.'
    The difficulty of collaboration also works the other way. A GP who
has been centrally involved with one of the other projects described how

it took about a year for him to be accepted as an ordinary person by the local people involved in the project, rather than some kind of superior being!

Ease of working together between professionals and the community takes time to develop and may at times be impossible to achieve if different interests are involved. The medical and health professions frequently develop their own needs which may be at odds with those of the community. A community-based health initiative threatens the traditional monopoly of health and illness held by the medical profession. The threat to the status and value system of the medical profession may provoke hostility which in turn will become a hurdle to the progress of a community project. It is therefore important for the project to become rooted in the community and confident before it attempts to meet the health services themselves more directly. Perhaps this explains the separation that existed in the early days between community-based health initiatives and the health services and professions.

Identifying expectations and goals

Another difficulty for workers in community projects in relating to health professionals is the divergence of expectations about what the project should be aiming to achieve. General agreement usually exists that it is a good thing to improve health, but how exactly you show that you are doing that is the starting point of a seemingly endless debate. For the health professional, this may mean demonstrating that the uptake of immunisation has increased, or that the occurrence of a particular illness has decreased as a result of a campaign or particular intervention. It may seem that an estate or neighbourhood where community development work on other health issues is taking place is ripe for an experiment of this kind. But for that community this way may not be a priority. Co-operation with a campaign or intervention initiated from within the health service may threaten the autonomy of the project, and inhibit the development of other activities which demand a different style and pace of work and a more flexible approach.

Nor have the community health projects emphasised environmental and industrial health issues, although lead pollution and health and safety at work are mentioned in several project reports and planning documents as possible areas of future work. Perhaps these issues have not taken priority because they are not experienced in the same immediate way as the health problem encountered by the individual. Community workers work where people are, and the people who spend most of their time at home on the estate are women with small children and old people. As women have traditionally had little choice about their primary role in caring for the family, it is not surprising that it is easier for many women to relate to the private, domestic world of women's health, children's health and old people's health, rather than the 'masculine' public worlds of the environment and industrial work. As unemployment increases and technological change gives rise to enforced 'leisure time' there may be more involvement by men in community health work. It is also possible that the growth of the popular movements around environmental issues such as nuclear power and lead pollution may stimulate the work of the projects in these directions. But to someone living in damp, overcrowded accommodation on a decaying old council estate, or a badly constructed new council estate, dampness and condensation at home is still likely to take priority over the future threat of handicap through lead absorption or a nuclear accident.

The future

A major issue for the Community Health Movement in the next few years is going to be its position in relation to the NHS. The recession and the evergrowing competition for resources in the voluntary sector leads many projects to consider seeking funding from the NHS itself. While the funding of such initiatives by the NHS can indicate an important political victory (that community-based health initiatives are a necessary and valid part of primary health care in its broad definition), it would also pose some considerable problems about autonomy and control. Nevertheless, the NHS needs to acknowledge and make room for these activities even if not to fund them, and this will involve major shifts in the attitudes of many health workers. There needs to be more input about the community in the training of all health workers. It also must be realised by health professionals and community activists that no single formula for community involvement in health will suffice, since needs differ greatly from place to place, and needs also change. The Community Health Movement will not solve the major political problems which currently face the NHS, but it must be encouraged as a vital force for the health of all.

3

Caribbean Home Remedies and their Importance for Black Women's Health Care in Britain*

NICKI THOROGOOD

Introduction

This article looks at the use of bush and other home remedies amongst Afro-Caribbean women in Britain.

The findings in this article are based on in-depth interviews with thirty-two Afro-Caribbean women living in Hackney. The sample was drawn equally from two age groups (16–30 years and 40–60 years) and two locations (a local Health Centre and by 'word of mouth' in the local community). The research methodology aimed to make visible aspects of the subjects' lives as they saw them. In this manner it was hoped to distance this research from assumptions made by other work based on notions of ethnicity and culture. This neglects any consideration of racism – that is, the structural manifestation of power inequalities – and reduces everything to the short-comings of individuals and their cultures (Pearson, 1986).

---

*This is an abridged version of a chapter in Abbott, P. and Payne, G. (eds), *New Directions in the Sociology of Health*, The Falmer Press, pp. 140–52, 1990.

The research on which this article is based (Thorogood, 1988) suggests that this is an area worth considering. For although most of the interviewees felt that 'bush' was very much a thing of their past, certain attitudes and practices remained nevertheless. Further it is a fascinating and comprehensive system which by its very existence in their past necessarily informs this group's experience of and response to the present. Indeed, I would suggest it plays a considerable part in helping to understand the actions of these people in relation to the medical establishment, whether state or private. This paper aims to conceptualize 'bush' not as an exotic or totally independent system but like other lay systems, as part of a multi-faceted strategy for managing health. It is suggested that the use of 'bush' is rooted in historical experience but can also illustrate contemporary relationships in health care.

Caribbean 'folk medicine': bush and other home remedies

Perhaps the best way of understanding how the remedies were (and are) used, and what they are used for is to 'catalogue' those mentioned by the women (Table 3.1). There were three main groups: (a) bush (herbs), (b) proprietary remedies bought from a chemist or shop and (c) home remedies – concoctions made at home that were neither bush nor bought. Several remedies were used for more than one 'complaint', and most 'complaints' had more than one remedy (see also Littlewood, 1988). Several were often mentioned by the same woman. Most of these remedies were those they had used in the West Indies although some were still used in Great Britain. Many women remarked on how their children or grandchildren in this country would not drink the bitter herbs. (Indeed, in general, the women used their GP more and their own remedies less in this country (Thorogood, 1988).)

The remedies listed have been grouped according to the 'complaint' they were used for. There is of necessity some overlap and some areas which are less clear. One of the largest groups by far were 'washouts' and they were taken as diversely as daily or once a year. This inventory shows the wide range of remedies in use as well as the categories of illness which were considered suitable for home treatment. This is not to suggest that they did not use doctors and hospitals – they did; but to suggest that there were constraints upon this use and that these constraints were (and are) structured by race, class and gender.

The list of complaints and remedies often covers three generations and spans two places. The list includes all those self-administered remedies mentioned, whether they referred to children, mothers or grandmothers and whether they were used here or 'home'. However, whilst there were some remedies that belonged specifically to the

Caribbean or to Britain, there was a great deal of overlap and many differences were a consequence of the differing times and circumstances rather than a change of attitude. To uncover more about these women's attitudes to, and experience of, bush and home remedies both as children and adults, here and in the West Indies, I shall turn to what they said.

Bush is exactly what is sounds like. The leaves, stalk and sometimes the root of bush is boiled in water with the resulting liquid used as a 'tea' or to bathe with.

Along with the easily available bush were the proprietary tonics and washouts and some foods mentioned specifically as being used to maintain and promote health. I have grouped them together because they are used in similar ways. All were at least perceived as traditional (either to the family or the Caribbean), were self-administered and were controlled by the interviewee or her mother. No men were mentioned in relation to the decision-making about or administering of appropriate treatment, although Littlewood (1988) notes; 'Men are believed to know more about bush than women, and they treat themselves when working in the bush. 'Similarly, Morgan and Watkins (1988) in their study of hypertension note the use of bush remedies amongst their West Indian (*sic*) respondents with no apparent distinction between genders.

It was often suggested that there was a 'proper' (i.e. in accordance with the Western 'scientific' medical model) medicinal or health-giving content of these herbal remedies and that they were in some way the 'raw material' of 'much modern medicine'; that is, tablets and 'medicine' (liquid in bottles) (see also Littlewood, 1988). As one older woman said:

> I think that most of those things, because if you get the medicines from the . . . you go to the chemist and buy something sometimes and if you read the contents you will find that a lot of those things are what we used to have. And these health foods and health shops, a lot of these things that they sell are the same things that we used to have to take. (*Dorothy*)

Washouts

'Washouts' constituted the most frequently used (and mentioned) remedies as well as the longest list of both herbs and proprietary brands and most of the women (twenty-six) had, at some point during their lives, used a washout regularly.

It seems that for the most part life in Britain has changed these habits. Some of the women (five, all older) continue to use washouts, though apparently not very often. Many women said they had stopped as soon as they grew up and their parents stopped forcing them – although this did not always prevent them from forcing their own children! Those that

TABLE 3.1   Bush and other home remedies

Washouts
Cerasee (also called Miraculous
    Bush)
Camomile tea
Benjamin herb
Bush tea (herb unspecified)
Senna and Sennakot
Castor oil
Syrup of figs
Exlax
Epsom Salts
Fynnon Salts
Glauber Salts
Shark oil
Physic
Scotts Emulsion
Liquid of Life (proprietary tonic)

Headaches
Turpentine bark (cooling
    poultice)
Cudgil or bat root (tea and a rub)
Ice poultice
Limeacol
Laite
Bay rum
'Whizz' (a brand of analgesic)
Aspirin
Panadol

Rashes
Meths

Eczema
Calamine lotion

Skin care
Cocoa butter
Shark liver oil (drunk as tonic)
Soft candle (for babies)
Olive oil (rubbed in to prevent
    stretch marks during pregnancy)

Tonics
Tree and bush roots (collected,
    dried, mashed and boiled, then
    bottled)
Liquid of Life (proprietary tonic)
Cerasee
Wincarnis or Halls 'tonic wine'

Sarsparilla
Stout and condensed milk and nutmeg
Brandy, milk and water
Guinness
Malt
Vitamins – multivits, Vit. C,
    Seven Seas cod liver oil
Metatone (proprietary brand)
Complan (proprietary brand)
Nutriment (proprietary brand)
Nu-nu Balsam (spelling uncertain)

Stomach aches
Cerasee
Camomile
Peppermint
Angostura bitters
Cod liver oil
Andrews Liver Salts
Blue bush root (to prevent
    biliousness from mangoes)
Boiled orange peel tea

Asthma and bad chests
Ganja (as tea)
Warm Vaseline and menthol rub
Camphor
'Steam trap' from chemist
Vick
Mucron

Faintness
Limeacol
Smelling salts

Toothache
Vinegar in saltwater
Brandy
Teething powder (babies)

Mumps
Warm ash on flannel and tied
    round cheek
Scarf tied round cheek
Corn meal poultice
Tobacco leaf poultice

Colds (with no temperature)
Cerasee
Peppermint

TABLE 3.1 *(Continued)*

Red bark
Leaf of life
English plantain
Aniseed
Indian root pills
Honey, lemon and sugar
Lime juice
Coconut oil and garlic (for chest
  colds)
Ganja (for chest colds)
Salt water gargle (sore throats)

Worms
Worm medicine
Yeast food

Calming down
Limeacol
Bay rum
Ganja tea
Laite
Vinegar in warm water
Cerasee

Period pains
Cerasee
Ginger tea
Anadin (sent from WI at first)
Bush (unspecified)

Whooping cough
Bush rat

Chicken-pox
Bush rat soup
Jeyes fluid (diluted in bath)

Nourishment
Soup
Beef, iron and bone broth
Greens
Orange juice
Sunshine (Vit. D)

Cuts and grazes
Antiseptic cream
Iodine

Fevers
Thimble bush with egg whites
  and brandy

Thimble bible steam bath of field
  weeds (made with odd number
  of herbs, e.g. 3, 5, 7)
Quinine (malaria)
Fevergrass
Limeacol (cooling rub)
Laite (cooling rub) (particular to
  St Lucia)
Bay rum

Jaundice
'Biliousness powder'

Muscle pains
Bay rum
Limeacol
Sacron (proprietary 'rub')
Deep Heat
Canadian healing oil
Jamaican healing oil
Caribbean healing oil
Soft candle, nutmeg/rum

Measles
Measle bush (tea and to bathe skin)
Pimento bush
Fever grass root
Tamarind leaf tea (and bath)
Calamine lotion
Parched corn tea (i.e. dried maize)

After birth
Corn meal porridge
Metatone

Coughs
Linctuses (all from chemist)
Syrups (all from chemist)
Ferral compound (all from chemist)
  (UK only)
Benylin (all from chemist)
  (UK only)

For children – UK only
Phensic
Junior Aspirin
Beechams Powders
Lemsip
Benylin
Vick
Antiseptic

continued abandoned bush from necessity and resorted instead to the more readily available proprietary brands such as Sennakot and Epsom salts. Some women felt washouts were no longer necessary as they had a healthy diet (see below), and others felt that there was no time in this country. This is because after taking a washout it is wise not to go too far away from home for a day or two and as Yvonne says, this is a hard condition to fulfil in this country:

> Because she is with a childminder I don't like the idea of her having diarrhoea and that. If I didn't work Saturday, I'd have the whole weekend and then I could give it to her Saturday and then Sunday we are at home I don't mind. I just try to leave her and give her fresh orange juice or something like that will keep her loose.

In general, those children of the older group who were born in the West Indies, were the most likely to have been given washouts.

Suffice to say here that during the interviews the West Indian diet was generally praised as being 'fresh', 'natural', 'healthy', etc. It is something of a contradiction to find this emphasis on good diet in Britain to some extent compensating for washouts. I suppose that 'fashions' in health care change and it is generally the younger women who talk about diet in this way. As they have said, purgatives no longer fit in which their routine. Neither are children in this country disciplined to take nasty medicine.

What these comments and descriptions show is, I believe, the commonly held view that keeping your 'insides clear' is important whether through washouts or diets. There may be a number of reasons for this. Firstly, taking purgatives and laxatives is a widespread practice. It may also be historically related in that it is more fashionable in some periods than in others. Nevertheless, it seems there is a qualitative difference in attitude between keeping 'regular' or responding to constipation and 'washing your insides out' (although the outcome might be much the same). Washouts, I suggest, indicate different theories and beliefs about the body and ways of treating it and this is consistent with the views of diet outlined above. Central to this set of beliefs is the conceptualization of the body as containing a central passage running from top to bottom, which has to be kept free from 'blockages'. Kitzinger (1982) discusses this, and the possible origins of this type of belief, in her article:

> Jamaican concepts of sickness are composed of two in some ways disparate body cosmologies, one derived from the mediaeval European 'humours' and the other from West African concepts of blockage by objects which whether by sorcery or other means, have obstructed passages so that body substances can no longer flow . . . This is related to the bodily concept in which there is one

passage leading between the mouth and the lower orifices, passing through the uterus and the stomach on the way (pp. 198–9).

As the white women in the study to which this research was linked (Gabe and Lipschitz-Phillips, 1982) were regular users of laxatives it would seem likely that their cultural heritage derived from that of mediaeval 'humours'. It is, I suggest, the combination of this and the West African cosmology which leads to the very particular meaning and use of washouts I found amongst Afro-Caribbean women in Britain. Although the women were well aware of the laxative properties of the washouts, there were other elements to it, purifying, cleansing, body maintenance ideas, something like 'Dyno-rod' for humans:

> Arlene: . . .it was more like maintenance, just making sure you had it a certain time every week and that was it. Like you have a wash every day, you have that every week or every month.
> NT: A kind of washing you inside?
> Arlene: Yes, it's not because anything was wrong with you. No it was a regular thing.

Rather more emphasizing the cleaning out aspect was this comment:

> She would give us a regular washout, basically before we went back to school, because she said we ate too much junk at school. I think just once a year. (*Joy*)

and

> Cerasee – that's a form of washout. That cleanses not only your digestive system but it cleanses your womb and everything. (*Pearl*)

This last comment shows a very clear conception of the linking of internal organs by a central passage. It also seems to me that there are two strands running through these comments, not only that of cleaning or clearing out in a practical sense, but also of cleansing and purifying in a ritualistic way, symbolizing a fresh start, renewal or recreation, particularly of the reproductive organs.

Tonics

One further kind of internal treatment frequently mentioned, was that of 'tonics'. Some of these were also washouts (Cerasee, Liquid of Life) and therefore cleansing but most were presented as strengthening, 'body building' and nourishing. Tonics were also presented as being a useful pick-me-up:

> I think she (mother) used to take a tonic. Beef, iron and wine, that was it. They used to take it if they feel a bit run down. (*Thomasina*)

This mixture, therefore, contains 'strength' and 'nourishment' and there were a number of other references to alcohol as tonic.

Littlewood (1988) also suggests that alcohol belongs to the hot/cold system, and notes that stout is used to build women up again after childbirth which is seen as purging (and therefore cooling).

The clearest indication of tonic as nourishment was when it was perceived as a direct substitute for food:

> . . .as I said, I've never really felt that down when I was in the West Indies to say I have to take tonics for sickness, you know, or body building or anything. We just normally have the proper meal from day to day and as I said, everything is fresh you know. In my family we never specially had to have tonic to sort of build us up or anything like that. (*Ann*)

Helman (1981) categorizes tranquillizers according to whether they are perceived as 'tonic', 'fuel' or 'food'. The basis for the distinction is made on (a) the level of control over the drug the user feels they have and (b) whether they perceive the drug effect as acting on themselves or (indirectly) on their relationships. Helman also suggests that: '*all* "chemical comforters" – from coffee, alcohol, tobacco and "vitamins" to more powerful psychotropic drugs – can be fitted into this classification' (1981, p. 521)

The descriptions and explanations of 'tonics' amongst these women do fit Helman's category of 'tonic' (episodic, self-administered, acting on the taker) although they are not necessarily reserved for the treatment of illness. Helman (1986, p. 218) adds that prior to the easy availability of psychotropic drugs the symptoms described by 'tonic' users had frequently been treated by patent 'Nerve Tonics', 'Restoratives' and 'Elixirs of Life'. However, the descriptions of 'tonics' given by the women in my sample do not particularly relate to low spirits, loss of vitality, anxiety or tension. They are, it seems, perceived more as a means of 'restoring balance' to 'the system', of providing nourishment and strength, either as an addition or as a means of 'keeping going' (see also Dunnell and Cartwright, 1972; Blaxter and Paterson, 1982).

This example highlights cultural differences in the experience and perception of illness and therefore the appropriate ways for dealing with it. Whilst it might be possible to fit all 'chemical comforters' into the categories of 'tonic', 'fuel' and 'food', the meanings of these categories is culturally specific. The use of tonics amongst these Afro-Caribbean women was as a source of nourishment, for restoring balance and (occasionally) to keep going and was largely episodic: therefore crossing all three of Helman's categories (see also a discussion of their use of benzodiazapines in Gabe and Thorogood, 1986a). This way of conceptualizing health and illness perhaps has more in common with Chinese and West African systems.

Discussion

How then do bush and other home remedies act as a resource, and what impact do they have on the health behaviour of these women in other domains, e.g. the private and state health services? They act as a resource because they form a body of knowledge about the way the body works and the sources of risks and dangers to it (symbolic and actual) which has grown out of the historical experiences of these women. The way they experience health and illness and the appropriate ways of dealing with this are an expression of their 'culture', their history and their current experience as black women. In this way 'culture' can be reappropriated and seen as art of a dynamic interactive process. Bush and home remedies are completely under the control of the women in my sample (or their mothers) and as such mediate their relationships with both health and illness (structually experienced) and the institutional health care systems.

What is it that defines an illness as sometimes suitable for treatment by common sense and sometimes worthy of a doctor's attention? It may be that doctor's medicine is sometimes 'unavailable' with the doctor acting as gatekeeper either because surgery hours are short and inconvenient or because he or she (but mostly he) is unwilling to prescribe anything (Stimson and Webb, 1975). Graham suggests that: 'These meetings typically occur at the point where the resources of informal caring have been exhausted' (1984, p. 165). This implies that the same 'illnesses' or at least the same set of symptoms that were once suitably treated at home shift into the public sphere at the point where 'normal' life cannot be maintained (Blaxter and Paterson, 1982). There are also categories of illness which demand instant medical attention (e.g. broken limbs) and are thus clearly outside the common sense boundaries and yet others which may never require a doctor (e.g. colds) (Cornwell, 1984, p. 130). The content of these categories, as we have seen, is not fixed but varies with the social, cultural and historical contexts as with the older women, some of whom regarded malaria as an everyday complaint to be dealt with at home. The decision to 'see a doctor' is a complex process involving advice, consultation, help and caring from friends and relatives (Friedson, 1961).

The particularity of these women's relation to home treatment has implications for institutional medicine. Bush and home remedies may be seen as constituting an alternative to 'real medicine' as a way of both treating and thinking about 'illness'. When a decision to consult a doctor is made a number of changes take place: a different status is conferred on the 'illness'; control and responsibility, in theory at least (see Stimson, 1974), shift from the private (women's) to the public (doctor's) sphere; different behavioural rules apply and are legitimated. Consequently a new set of social relations is constructed.

The relationship of these women to medicine is both an expression and a consequence of their class, race and gender positions. Bush constitutes one of a range of alternatives in health care available to this group. Its use is not discrete and we cannot label this practice as a relic of tradition (or 'culture'). Instead its use should be viewed as an active part of managing their contemporary lives and best understood when analysed in terms of the women's structural position.

References

Blaxter, M. and Paterson, E. *et al.* (1982) *Mothers and Daughters: a three generational study of health attitudes and behaviour*, London, HEB.

Cornwell, J. (1984) *Hard earned lives: accounts of health and illness in East London*, London, Tavistock.

Dunnell, K. and Cartwright, A. (1972) *Medicine Takers, Prescribers and Hoarders*, London, Routledge and Kegan Paul.

Friedson, E. (1961) *Patients' Views of Medical Practice*, New York, Russell Sage Foundation.

Gabe, J. and Lipschitz-Phillips, S. (1982) 'Evil necessity? The meaning of benzodiazapine use for women patients from one general practice,' *Sociology of Health and Illness*, Vol. 4, No. 2, pp. 201–9.

Gabe, J. and Thorogood, N. (1986) 'Prescribed drugs and the management of everyday life: experiences of black and white working class women', *Sociological Review*, Vol. 34, No. 4, pp. 737–72.

Graham, H. (1984) *Women, Health and the Family*, Brighton, Wheatsheaf.

Helman, C. (1981) 'Tonic, fuel and food: social and symbolic aspects of the long-term use of psychotropic drugs', *Social Science and Medicine*, Vol. 15B, No. 4, pp. 521–33.

Helman, C. (1986) 'Long term use of psychotropic drugs' in Gabe, J. and William, E.P. (eds), *Tranquillizers: social, psychological and clinical perspectives*, London, Tavistock.

Kitzinger, S. (1982) 'The social context of birth', in MacCormack, C.P. (ed.) *An Ethnography of Fertility and Birth*, London, Academic Press.

Littlewood, R. (1988) 'From vice to mad men: the semantics of naturalistic and personalistic understandings in Trinidadian local medicines', *Social Science and Medicine*, Vol. 27, No. 2, pp. 129–48.

Morgan, M. and Watkins, C.J. (1988) 'Managing hypertension: beliefs and responses to medication among cultural groups', *Sociology of Health and Illness*, Vol. 10, No. 4, pp. 561–78.

Pearson, M. (1986) 'Racist notions of ethnicity and culture in health education', in Rodmell, S. and Watt, A. *The Politics of Health Education*, London, Tavistock.

Stimson, G.V. (1974) 'Obeying doctor's orders: a view from the other side', *Social Science and Medicine*, Vol. 8, No. 2, pp. 97–104.

Stimson, G.V. and Webb, B. (1975) *Going to See the Doctor: the consultation process in general practice*, London, RKP.

Thorogood, N. (1988) *'Health and the management of daily life amongst women of Afro-Caribbean origin living in Hackney'*, University of London, unpublished PhD thesis.

4

From Psychometric Scales to Cultural Perspectives

WENDY STAINTON ROGERS

Introduction

Some years ago I found myself lying in a hospital bed bristling with drips and drain tubes, feeling extremely ill, bemused and fuzzy, but with a vague memory of the night before when I had insisted on talking to the surgeon before signing the consent form for an emergency operation. A nurse was arguing with a woman in the bed next to mine that the television could not be turned on because of a desperately sick patient on the ward who needed absolute 'peace and quiet' if she was to have any chance of surviving. Looking round, the realisation gradually dawned that, as I was the only other person there, this had to be me. It was quite a shock. That I 'lived to tell the tale' is evident in my writing this article. Its contents stem from my puzzlings during my three month recovery, as I tried to make sense of why I became so ill as to need major, life-saving surgery, and to decide whether I should hold myself responsible or should blame somebody else. Like many social theorists, I later drew upon my own experience as a basis for my research, out of which I ultimately gained a doctorate and wrote a book (Stainton Rogers, 1991). This article describes some of the empirical and theoretical work I did as part of those projects into how people explain health and illness.

Approaches to the study of everyday explanations of health

As a psychologist, during my recovery I rapidly got very fed up with most of the material that conventional psychology had to offer to help me make sense of my experiences. In particular I became increasingly critical of the way that the notion of locus of control has been and was being used (in the form of the Health Locus of Control – HLC – Scale) for investigating people's attributions of responsibility for health and illness. I came to the conclusion that this approach is both theoretically and methodologically unsound. Drawing upon a positivistic view of human cognition, it treats people as lacking in insight and understanding of their own thinking, divorced from a 'real world' which constrains their actions, and uninformed by the powerful messages of both the mass media and professional groups (notably the medical establishment and the 'health industry'). This did not appeal to me at all. I will begin this article, then, by describing for you some of its pitfalls as I came to see them.

Health locus of control

Probably the most commonly used technique for exploring how people's beliefs about health and illness affect what they do is based on Rotter's theory of locus of control (Rotter, 1966). This set of ideas, based on social learning theory, assumes that how people explain what happens to them is a product of their learning experiences. The theory argues that those with early experiences of good behaviour being rewarded, and bad behaviour punished, come to see their successes as just rewards for hard work. These people, termed 'internals', are those who have learned to site control within their own behaviour. In contrast, those who were rewarded and punished indiscriminately in childhood were seen as becoming fatalistic, siting control externally in the vicissitudes of 'good' and 'bad luck' and consequently labelled 'externals'.

It was Wallston and Wallston (Wallston, Wallston and De Vellis, 1978) who adopted Rotter's ideas as the basis of a multi-dimensional health locus of control (MHLC) scale. Following earlier work with a two-dimensional scale, they created a new scale which divided people up between three categories – 'internals' (who see their health and illness as the outcome of their own behaviour); 'externals' (who see them as determined by chance); adding a third category, 'powerful others' (for people who attribute their health or illness to the care given by doctors and family). This addition was made after their earlier version proved very disappointing, and drew on the work of Levenson (Levenson and Miller, 1976). However, Wallston and Wallston's use of the 'powerful others' construct was quite different from Levenson's original formulation, which was in terms of the *un*helpful influence of other powerful people, such as the way in which left-wingers blame Government and Capitalists for the oppression of the poor.

It has to be said that Wallston and Wallston's new scale also proved largely ineffective. Virtually all attempts to establish empirical links between the MHLC scale and measures of health preventive or treatment compliance behaviours failed dismally. All the researchers could establish were self-evident differences between groups of people, which had little to do with their health beliefs. A good example is a study by Harkey and King (cited in Wallston and Wallston's 1981 review) which found that contraceptive users and women who had had an abortion scored higher on the 'internality' items in the MHLC scale than umarried mothers, and that more 'externality' was expressed by the women with lower levels of education, and of lower socio-economic class. Such results simply showed that people who score low on 'internality' and high on 'externality' or 'powerful others' on the MHLC scale are people who have every reason to believe that they truly do not have much control over their lives in general and their health status in particular!

When they came to review these studies, Wallston and Wallston were however, faced not just with a whole series of disappointing results, but ones which were (from their theoretical standpoint) highly paradoxical. While in a few studies 'internality' did give some weak positive indications of being linked to 'healthy' actions, externality was (albeit still infrequently) a *better* predictor. It was more often the case that it was the self-motivated 'internals' who were least likely, and the 'fatalistic' externals who were most likely to do what health professionals wanted them to do! Wallston and Wallston were forced to conclude their review of studies using the MHLC scale by saying: 'health locus of control research is still in its adolescence, full of pimples and promises, quivering on the brink of adulthood' (Wallston and Wallston, 1981, p. 235).

Limits of the health locus of control construct

I have to admit that I read all this work with growing amazement. For, despite all these problems, the MHLC scale continued (and continues!) to be extensively used – and this despite profound shortcomings, both theoretical and methodological, with the whole approach itself. As far as theory is concerned, I came to the conclusion that such a simplistic view of how people think inevitably confounds a number of quite different concepts. For instance, the approach subsumes notions of self-blame and self-determination within the 'internal' dimension, yet they are conceptually far from equivalent. Moreover, this kind of approach is ideologically biased, ethnocentric and naïve about how others view the world. The MHLC scale not only treats views about the impact of poverty on health as no more than 'fatalism', it treats 'fate' and 'chance' as equivalent – plausible, perhaps, from a Western viewpoint, but nonsensical from the standpoint of religions like Hinduism and Buddhism.

My current position is that the whole idea of 'locus of control' is at fault. Its problem is that it is grounded within a modernistic, scientistic, methodological approach – psychometrics – in which a limited number of predetermined categories are all that are available for response. Psychometric method thus imposes the researchers' view of 'how the world works' upon participants' responses, and then interprets their responses only within that framework. For example, the MHLC scale assumes that people's attributions are constant for all situations and cannot accommodate the storyline that falling ill is mostly a matter of bad luck, but getting better is mostly about getting proper treatment and looking after yourself. Such 'inconsistent' responses (however plausible and commonsensical and indeed consistent with biomedical orthodoxy) simply cannot be dealt with by the scale. Psychometric scales are, in my view, incapable of measuring anything 'real' at all. At the very best, they can show where there is consistency between one 'story of reality' and another, but nothing more. What they do is reify the understandings of a few, Western, academic psychologists as an 'objective reality', and then establish that other people from the same cultural niche share this view of the world. This is no more profound than observing that all the clocks in a household tell about the same time – agreement is no more than a matter of working by the same operating rules.

Cultural analysis

In searching for an alternative approach to the study of explanations of health and illness, I started to come across an idea that seemed to be gaining currency over a very broad range of disciplines, including art and literature as well as in the social sciences. It was that our understandings and perceptions may be viewed in terms of 'texts' being offered to us in a 'cultural marketplace' of ideas and stories. In this view, social researchers should give up their love-affair with science, stop trying to test hypotheses, and be satisfied with getting some impression of what these different texts are like, and seeing what they can do to decipher the messages they are intended to convey. I found particularly useful Mulkay's (1991) argument that this idea of 'text' is a liberation from the conceptual wild goose chase after validity, and means that you can ask more interesting questions, like what conduct does a particular text prescribe or warrant, or what ideology is it peddling?

In order to make the shift, however, I needed not just a good idea, but a method. Most usually adopted in this field are forms of cultural analysis which examine texts as cultural products (the term 'text' is used for images as well as documents, and includes things like movies and advertisements). Constructed out of a complex weave of contradictory ideas and images intermingled, texts are seen as being able to be read in different ways according to the 'gaze' employed (cf. Foucault, e.g. 1963). For instance, the image of a model in a magazine is read differently, according to whether it is viewed through a male gaze or a feminist gaze. Cultural analysis consists of disentangling author from text, and text from gaze, and seeking to locate them all in their cultural and historical contexts. It includes analysis of archaeologies of knowledge (i.e. how what constitutes knowledge changes and gets sedimented over time) and of 'cultural tectonics' (i.e. how different discursive accretions mould and impact upon each other).

However, I took the view that most forms of cultural analysis suffer from methodological problems, particularly the covert nature of the analysis itself, where little is (or maybe even can be) reported about how the links are made or insights are arrived at. Since all that researchers can draw upon are their own stock of collective cultural knowledge and their own skills of interpretation, it is they (not the participants in the study) who determine what 'stories' are articulated in the text, and are reported in the analysis. Inevitably this means that some 'stories' will be given the limelight while others will remain unidentified or muted. This was the reason I decided against using discourse analysis (cf. Potter and Wetherell, 1987) despite its obvious allure as a well-established means of exploring how people act as 'competent negotiators of reality' in the explanations they construct. Instead I chose a form of pattern analysis – Q methodology (devised by Stephenson in 1935).

What I liked about the Q-method was that it sets out not to 'measure' anything objectively (although some people have misused it in that way) but to enable the process of cultural analysis to be shared between the researcher and the people who participate in the research. Participants express particular viewpoints by sorting statements (written on cards) chosen, via an initial cultural analysis, to reflect the range of ideas and arguments about the topic in question. Participants sort them in a predetermined triangular pattern along a dimension (e.g. from 'strongly agree' to 'strongly disagree') with two or three at each extreme and more in the middle. The responses are coded, and then factor analysed by-person, using rotation, to generate independent factors, each one repre-senting an alternative sorting pattern. Thus, although at first sight Q looks like a psychometric method, it is not, since the categories of response are not preordained against an assumed 'objective' set of criteria. Furthermore, what matters is not what any individual does, but the patterns that have been created by participants, since it is these (rather than the researcher's own insights) which determine the classi-fication of accounts. By examining which items have been placed in what positions in each pattern, it is possible to get a fair sense of the constituents of each account. When you start out on a Q study you may have some hunches about what you will find, but I have never done one yet which has not brought its surprises, which is half of the fun of doing them.

Studies of explanatory diversity

Between 1985 and 1987 I used the Q-method in a series of studies to look for some of the different explanatory accounts of health and illness operating in British culture. I began by carrying out a number of interviews, and conducting a detailed cultural analysis of various texts – ranging from television programmes, through popular magazines and academic journals, to conversations at the hairdressers and in the local village shop. From this and detailed pilot-testing I devised two Q-sets of items, one broadly concerned with how people explain health and illness, and the other focusing in on issues of blame and responsibility. Obviously this initial stage of designing a set of items is critical, since people (like artists) can only use the 'raw materials' you give them. You cannot determine what they portray, but you can (if you do not select items well enough) constrain them to a monochrome. In my studies I typically had item sets of eighty statements, with about seventy people doing the sorting. Participants included 'ordinary folk', medical professionals, practitioners of 'alternative medicine' and people I thought might have unusual ideas (e.g. members of religious sects and people suffering from congenital disease), and I included my own sorting in the data. From these studies I identified eight well-articulated, and very different accounts. I will summarise these very briefly here although obviously the accounts I obtained were a great deal more subtle and complex than I have room to describe in this article.

1 A *'Body as Machine'* account, expressed mainly in the sorting of some medical professionals. This supported the conventional medical view of health and illness, seeing modern therapeutic achievements as having made major contributions to health care and fighting disease. It saw us as fortunate to live in a world of medical excellence, and medicine as a science, based on technological expertise rather than 'bedside manner'. It portrayed the body as a machine that can either run smoothly (if properly fed, serviced and maintained) or break down (if neglected, or if there is a breakdown) with medicine a technical 'fix' for mending it.

2 A *'Body under Siege'* account was expressed in the sorting patterns of 'ordinary people' (e.g. a fire-fighter and an English teacher). In it the individual is seen to be constantly under threat and attack from germs and diseases, interpersonal conflicts and the stress of modern life, acting

upon the body through the agency of 'mind'. Unlike other accounts, this one stressed feelings of guilt and blame. The overall image is of a helpless individual trying to cope in a hostile and dangerous world, constantly liable to attack, having few resources of his or her own to fight off disease and having to rely on outside aid, particularly expert medical treatment.

3   A *'Health Promotion'* account was, not surprisingly, articulated in the sorting of people actively engaged in health education. The account itself focused very specifically on health rather than illness, saw it as a fundamental human right, and 'one of the most important things in life'. Good health was seen as a matter not of luck but of lifestyle. There was guarded approval of modern medicine, and an acknowledgement that some people cannot help but live unhealthy lives (e.g. if poor or lacking in education). However, what matters most in this account is individual health-promoting behaviour.

4   An *'Inequality of Access'* account was provided in the sorting patterns of people who described their political views as 'left-wing'. Convinced of the benefits of modern medicine, concern was expressed about the unfair allocation of those benefits and their lack of availability to those who need them most. To blame for bad health were the Government with its privatisation policies and Capitalist exploitation of the workers. This kind of analysis is described by Ehrenreich (1978) as an old-style Marxist critique.

5   A *'Cultural Critique'* account. This label is also taken from Ehrenreich's writing, and is well articulated in his book. My own sorting patterns fitted this account, along with those of a number of other middle-class academics and professionals well versed in this field. This account was concerned with power, both over knowledge and resources, particularly critical of the dominance of biomedicine and the power of the medical profession. This account in fact contained a number of variants, including an expressly feminist version (which placed the major blame for ill-health in the hands of male oppression and patriarchal power). I resisted attempts by participants expressing this variant to include more feminist-informed items, demonstrating the power of the researcher to constrain what gets reported as data! My justification was a desire not to limit the stories that could be told, by overemphasis on those stressing ideology.

6   A *'God's Power'* account was provided by a number of people who described themselves as religious including a Hindu and a Christian Spiritualist Healer. Its distinguishing feature was its strong focus on the

power of spirital forces, God and prayer being regarded as the major sources of healing. It strongly rejected luck as an influence and viewed health as a product of 'right living', spiritual well-being and God's care.

7   A 'Willpower' account was articulated in the sorting of several practitioners in 'alternative medicine', and also a number of entrepreneurial business people. It saw the body's functioning as a resource, biological (in terms of its self-healing properties) and psychological (in terms of state of mind aiding recovery) upon which the individual can draw to promote health and fight off disease. Health, in this view, is something we need to work for, not so much in our actions as in our state of mind. This account is well described in a chapter by Crawford (1984).

8   A 'Robust Individualism' account was expressed by a variety of people who were far less concerned with explaining health and illness than with the importance of the individual's freedom to choose how to live his or her life. Health was portrayed in some versions as an 'investment' – a commodity that can be bought, sold, insured and squandered. In other versions, the account was a resistance against health promotion – the idea expressed was that "It's my body, my risk to die young, my lungs, and I reserve the absolute right to decide, and not be dictated to by a doctor or so-called expert from the Health Education Council' (a comment written by one of the participants).

Alternative accounts of health

Whereas psychometric studies focus on two or three alternative systems of belief, in my studies I was able to identify eight accounts which differ widely in the kinds of explanation they offered and what they regarded as salient. Some were forms of self-presentation, others provided models of how society operates, or how the role of medicine should be understood. Although expressed by the sorting patterns of a number of individuals, I see most people as having access to them all. These are just some of the texts, available to us in our culture, out of which we are able to 'make sense of' health and illness. I think this is a more plausible understanding of what they do than claiming that there are specific, enduring personality traits, psychological mechanisms or social forces that constrain people to think in particular ways. It is a situation in which diverse accounts dynamically coexist in an 'ecological domain' of cultural tectonics, within which they evolve and jostle in competition with one another.

The accounts described above do convey a certain library-like quality. Having read them all, one is left with a sense of different 'texts' that a person could, at different moments and in different circumstances, pull off the shelf, digest, use where they are helpful to push the story along, thrust back when they seem irrelevant or look nonsensical – 'texts' one would cite, use, manipulate, reject, as different needs arise. A theory of explanation based upon such a notion portrays people as storymakers who weave a narrative in and out of different 'texts'. Storymaking selects from one 'text' and then another, gradually weaving a narrative that 'makes sense' of the topic or issue in question.

I think accounts are likely to be selected at least in part in terms of their explicatory power. When people ask questions like 'What do I do now?', which account to use would depend upon the situation. If bitten by a rabid dog neither the 'cultural critique' nor the 'Willpower' accounts would be much help. I suspect most of us would chose from two – the 'body as a machine' model (find a doctor, fast) or the 'God's Power' account (pray, hard), and many people would draw on both. Other accounts would be better for answering 'Why me?' questions; others for 'Why now?'. The accounts each of us use will also be influenced by other, broader, aspects of our strivings to explain the world, such as our political ideology, or our religious beliefs (or lack of them). These in their turn would be mediated by our experiences, upbringing, stage in the life-cycle, access to media and so on, and shorter-term factors, such as moods, frames of mind, and things like attempts to 'pull ourselves together'. The use of accounts interpersonally will relate, for example, to the way in which individuals seek to construct reality for others, for either their own purposes (e.g. to persuade them to act in certain ways, like visit a doctor, or 'take it easy') or to meet other people's needs (e.g. to comfort, or reassure them).

Conclusions

I enjoyed the research enormously, and learned a lot. It told me I could in fact explain my illness in several different ways, according to what I want to achieve. I also think it has some lessons for health professionals, for it says we need to be aware that people are neither consistent, nor are their understandings easy to understand. But unless we try to discover what texts an individual is using, we are unlikely to get our messages over to him or her. What I like most about this approach is that it respects and celebrates human inventiveness. It suggests that people can change the way they see the world, and, by doing that, they can change the world. But then, I always was an optimist, even lying there scared stiff in my hospital bed.

References

Crawford, R. (1984) 'A cultural account of health: Control, release and the social body', in McKinlay, J.B. (ed.), *Issues in the Political Economy of Health*, London, Tavistock.

Ehrenreich, J. (ed.) (1978) *The Cultural Crisis of Medicine*, New York, Monthly Review Press.

Foucault, M. (1963) *Naissance de la Clinque*, Paris, Presses Universitaires de France.

Levenson, H. and Miller, J. (1976) 'Multi-dimensional Locus of Control in sociopolitical activists of conservative and liberal ideologies', *Journal of Personality and Social Psychology*, **33**(2), pp. 199–208.

Mulkay, M. (1991) *Sociology of Science: a sociological pilgrimage*, Buckingham, Open University Press.

Potter, J. and Wetherell, M. (1987) *Discourse and Social Psychology: beyond attitudes and behaviour*, London, Sage.

Rotter, J.B. (1966) 'Generalised expectancies for internal versus external control reinforcement', *Psychological Monographs*, **80**(1).

Stainton Rogers, W. (1991) *Explaining Health and Illness: an exploration of diversity*, Hemel Hempstead, Harvester.

Stephenson, W. (1935) 'Technique of factor analysis', *Nature*, **136**, p. 297.

Wallston, K.A. and Wallston, B.S. (1981) 'Health Locus of Control Scales', in Lefcourt, H.M. (ed.), *Research with the Locus of Control Construct, Vol. 1: Assessment Methods*, New York, Academic Press.

Wallston, K.A., Wallston, B.S. and De Vellis, R. (1978) 'Development of the multidimensional health locus of control (MHLC) scales', *Health Education Monographs*, **6**, 161–70.

5

The Disappearance of the Sick Man from Medical Cosmology 1770–1870*

N.D. JEWSON

The concept of medical cosmology

Medical cosmologies are basically metaphysical attempts to circumscribe and define systematically the essential nature of the universe of medical discourse as a whole.[1] They are conceptual structures which constitute the frame of reference within which all questions are posed and all answers are offered. They set out the first principles of problem orientation, explanatory strategy, methodology, and acceptable results which are not so much tested as celebrated in the intellectual activity of their adherents. Medical cosmologies are an indispensable first order of relevance and relation which enable their adherents to make sense of and to act within the world. They provide an overall definition of the field and a preliminary affirmation of its form. Hence cosmologies are not only ways of seeing, but also ways of not seeing. Cosmologies prescribe the visible and the invisible, the imaginable and the inconceivable. They exclude in the same moment as they include.

Cosmologies should not however be conceptualized as static normative frameworks – rather they are ongoing sets of possibilities, not so much states of knowledge (and ignorance) as ways of knowing (and ignoring).

*This is an abridged version of an article that was first published in *Sociology*, Vol. 10, pp. 225–244, 1976.

Three types of cosmology

Bedside Medicine was the mode of production dominant in Western Europe at the beginning of the period covered by this paper.[2]

The vision of the sick-man institutionalized within the tenets of Bedside Medicine was that of a conscious human totality – a viewpoint that transcended, not merely united, the distinctions of psyche and soma found in modern medicine.[3] The two major growth points of Bedside Medicine were phenomenological nosology and speculative pathology. Both activities generated a large number of often mutually contradictory theories, and as a result medical knowledge consisted of a chaotic diversity of schools of thought. The definition of the field was diffuse and problematic, disciplinary boundaries weak and amorphous. The fundamental premisses of the subject were a matter of dispute and debate. Rivalry between the proponents of the various theories was commonly conducted at the level of personal abuse and dogmatic polemic.

Within this disarray, however, a common set of cosmological principles may be discerned. Controversy centred around differing interpretations of the same open ended model of bodily processes. Thus, for example, despite differences in the specific contents of their theories, nosologists constructed their pathological entities according to the same general principle, i.e., by grouping together experientially related symptoms. Hence disease was defined in terms of its external and subjective manifestations rather than its internal and hidden causes. In accordance with this principle diagnosis was founded upon extrapolation from the patient's self report of the course of his illness.

Pathology was speculative, systemic and monistic. Medical investigators sought to discover a single basic cure for all the ailments known to man. This was achieved by invoking some universal first cause of illness. The study of proximate and precipitating causes was neglected in favour of the elucidation of the general underlying predisposition to ill health. These morbid forces were located within the context of the total body system rather than within any particular organ or tissue. Furthermore, in addition to physical disposition, all aspects of emotional and spiritual life were deemed relevant to the understanding of the functions of the constitution. It was also believed that each individual had his own unique pattern of bodily events which the practitioner had to discern in each case. The practitioner was expected to adopt an active therapeutic role, intervening in the pathological processes afflicting his clients through the heavy application of heroic remedies.

In the era of Bedside Medicine cosmological analogies emphasized an image of the body as a microcosm, a reality *sui generis* subject to its own peculiar laws of growth and decay, comparable to the macrocosm of the physical universe.

A dramatic transformation in the form of medical cosmology occurred at the Parisian hospital schools during the first three or four decades of the 19th century with the introduction of a new mode of production of medical knowledge, here termed Hospital Medicine.[4] The raw materials of medical theorizing now became the innumerable morbid events, occurring within the gross anatomical structures, which presented themselves to the clinical gaze on the crowded wards. Medical investigators concentrated upon the accurate diagnosis and classification of cases rather than upon the prognosis and therapy of symptom complexes.[5] The sick-man became a collection of synchronized organs, each with a specialized function.

The four great innovations of Hospital Medicine were structural nosology, localized pathology, physical examination and statistical analysis. The major achievement of the Parisian School was the delineation of objective disease entities by means of correlating external symptoms with internal lesions. Pathology took the form of a local solidarism, focusing upon specific morbid events within the tissues rather than upon general disturbances of the constitutional system as a whole. Symptoms were demoted from the status of defining characteristics to that of secondary indicators of disease. The surface appearances were made subservient to the hidden underlying causes. Diagnoses were founded upon physical examination of observable organic structures rather than verbal analysis of subjectively defined sensations and feelings. This was achieved during life by means of a number of specially invented 'scopes and after death by means of autopsy. Pathological anatomy, indeed, became the all pervading research technique of Hospital Medicine. A novel degree of certainty was introduced into both pathology and diagnosis by the use of quantitative methods. Statistics quickly devasted the claims of the traditional materia medica, and ushered in an era of therapeutic scepticism. The new conceptions of disease were accompanied by radical innovations in medical analogies and metaphors.

Laboratory Medicine was first established within the German university system in the middle decades of the 19th century. The transformation in cosmology precipitated by this innovation was founded upon the application of the concepts and methods of natural science to the solution of medical problems.[6] The two major areas of development were histology and physiology. Numerous discoveries concerning the properties of tissues were organized into a coherent synthesis by the cell theory. The latter proposed that the ultimate structural and developmental units of all living animals and plants are the cells. Following the announcement of this theory intensive studies were made of the

TABLE 5.1 Three modes of production of medical knowledge

	Patron	Occupational role of medical investigator	Source of patronage	Perception of sick man	Occupational task of medical investigator	Conceptualization of illness
Bedside medicine	Patient	Practitioner	Private fees	Person	Prognosis and therapy	Total psychosomatic disturbance
Hospital medicine	State; hospital	Clinician	Professional career structure	Case	Diagnosis and classification	Organic lesion
Laboratory medicine	State; academy	Scientist	Scientific career structure	Cell complex	Analysis and explanation	Biochemical process

TABLE 5.2 Medical cosmologies, 1770–1870

	Bedside medicine	Hospital medicine	Laboratory medicine
Subject matter of Nosology	Total symptom complex	Internal organic events	Cellular function
Focus of Pathology	Systemic – dyacrasis	Local lesion	Physico-chemical processes
Research Methods	Speculation and inference	Statistically oriented clinical observation	Laboratory experiment according to scientific method
Diagnostic Technique	Qualitative judgement	Physical examination before and after death	Microscopic examination and chemical tests
Therapy	Heroic and extensive	Sceptical (with the exception of surgery)	Nihilistic
Mind/Body Relation	Integrated: psyche and soma seen as part of same system of pathology	Differentiated: Psychiatry a specialized area of clinical studies	Differentiated: Psychology a separate scientific discipline

processes of cellular function and reproduction. Progress in physiology was largely the result of the deliberate introduction of the theories and techniques of physics into the study of living organisms, pioneered by a small group of young scientists at the University of Berlin.

Pathology also was totally reconstituted. It was asserted that observational anatomy would never explain the causes of disease. Hence the new pathology was built upon the findings of experimental physiology. Since the cell was the fundamental unit of life, then it must also be the locus of disease. Life thus became the process of interaction within and between the cells, disease a particular form of these physical and chemical processes. Clinical diagnosis was reorganized around the application of a series of chemical tests of body substances designed to identify morbid physiological processes. Medical practice became an appendage to the laboratory.

From person to object-orientated cosmology

The eclipse of Bedside Medicine by first Hospital and then Laboratory Medicine represented a shift away from a person orientated toward an object orientated cosmology (see Tables 5.1 and 5.2).

In the era of Bedside Medicine the patron consisted of a small coterie of patients drawn from the ruling class. The role of medical investigator was not differentiated from that of practitioner to any significant extent. Hence the relations of production were formed in private practice and centred around the collection of fees by medical personnel from the sick. In this situation the political and economic power of patrons insured that they retained ultimate control over medical investigators and the process of production of medical knowledge.[7] It was the sick person who decided upon the efficacy of his cure and the suitability of his practitioner. Hence practitioners, and thus medical investigators, formulated their definitions and explications of illness so as to accord with the expectations of their clients.

The social structure of Bedside Medicine consisted of a network of segmental, unregulated patient–practitioner relationships. Medical investigators were fragmented into numerous local groups, each dedicated to the service of one part of this small but multifaceted medical market and each ranked according to the social standing of their patrons. The various shades and grades of practitioners offered a wide selection of theories and therapies to the sick. The sick-man sought to penetrate behind the practitioner's public performance in order to assess the veracity of the latter's claim to occupational competence and integrity. The medical practitioner, on the other hand, won the favours of his patron by individually proving his personal and professional suitability in the context of a primary face-to-face relationship. He sought to discover the particularistic requirements of his patient in order to satisfy them to the exclusion of his ubiquitous professional rivals.

The person of the patient in all his aspects remained the focal point of medical knowledge. The sick-man's subjective experience of his symptoms were the raw materials from which the pathological entities of medical theory were constructed. His perception of himself as a unique individual with specific personal problems of physical and mental health were reflected in the enormous variety of pathological conditions generated by the phenomenological nosology. His lack of demarcation between physical and emotional disturbance was mirrored by the integration of physiological and psychological forces in contemporary theory and therapy. His obsessive search for relief from his pains and hope of a recovery were matched by the sweeping claims of the array of heroic remedies accompanying each system of pathology.

Occupational success was dependent upon the ability to attract the interest and approval of a client or patron. Medical men sought to advertise their services by means of the allure of their own personal collection of speculations and concoctions. Hence the social organization of Bedside Medicine stimulated the production of innumerable superficial novelties each derived from a common set of assumptions – a characteristic blend of individual display and popular conservatism. The apparent confusion, ambiguity, and the interminable controversy of Bedside Medicine were not a function of crisis within medical cosmology but rather a key feature of its normal operation.

Hospital Medicine represented the first major step towards the institutionalization of an object orientated medical cosmology. Two aspects of this transformation will be identified and discussed. Firstly, at the same time as the sick-man found himself unequivocally subordinated to the medical investigator, the focus of medical knowledge moved away from the person of the former towards esoteric entities defined in accordance with the perceptions of the latter. Secondly, as control over the occupational group of medical investigators was centralized in the hands of its senior members the profusion of speculative systems characteristic of Bedside Medicine was replaced by an ongoing consensus upon matters of theory and therapy.

A two tier system of medical practice was devised in which hospital clinicians became the new elite of the profession. The thousands of poor and destitute sick housed within the hospitals had little opportunity to exercise control over the activities of the medical staff. The powerlessness of the patients, combined with an enormous size of the hospital system, provided the clinicians with an inexhaustible fund of acquiescent research material. Clinicians thus gained control over and autonomy within the technical process of production of medical knowledge. A 'collegiate' system of occupational control had emerged within the community of medical investigators.[8]

Hospital Medicine was thus based upon a new type of relation between the sick-man and the medical investigator. Henceforth the medical investigator was accorded respect on the basis of the authority inherent in his occupational role rather than on the basis of his individually proven worth. The new occupational standing of the clinician was matched by the emergence of a new role for the sick-man, that of patient. As such he was designated a passive and uncritical role in the consultative relationship, his main function being to endure and to wait.

These social realignments were reflected within the cosmological system of Hospital Medicine. At the centre of the new medical problematic was the concept of disease. Interest in the unique qualities of the whole person evaporated to be replaced by studies of specific organic lesions and malfunctions. Diseases became a precise and objectively identifiable event occurring within the tissues, of which the patient might be unaware. The fundamental realities of pathological analysis shifted from the total body system to the specialized anatomical structures. The experiential manifestations of disease, which had previously been the very stuff of illness, now were demoted to the role of secondary signs. The patient's interest in prognosis and therapy was eclipsed by the clinician's concern with diagnosis and pathology.

As medical investigators gained power over the conditions of their own recruitment, education and practice they became a much more homogeneous occupational group. A unified system of intellectual conduct could now be enforced throughout the system of production and distribution of medical knowledge by medical investigators themselves. Medical investigators obtained their posts through a system of selection which was under the direct control of senior members of the occupational group. Henceforth, therefore, the distribution of resources and rewards depended less upon the satisfaction of the patient than upon recognition among professional peers.

The centralization of power within the occupational community heralded the imposition of a cosmological form which made the controversies of Bedside Medicine redundant. Ambiguity and confusion were replaced by certainty and order.

Furthermore, relieved of the necessity of laying claim to the understanding of each and every ailment clinicians were free to introduce a new division of labour into the process of medical investigation. Occupational subgroups began to concentrate their gaze exclusively upon specific anatomical structures, each applying the same general cosmologically prescribed rules of theory and method.[9] As a result the integrated conception of body functions characteristic of Bedside Medicine was superceded by the fragmented and partial images of a host of specialisms.

A new phase in the emergence of an object orientated cosmology opened with the development of Laboratory Medicine. Whereas under Hospital Medicine the direction of the power differential between the sick and medical personnel had been reversed, under Laboratory Medicine the patient was removed from the medical investigator's field of saliency altogether. This increase in the social distance between the sick and medical investigators was accompanied by a relocation of the fundamental realities of pathology in microscopical events beyond the tangible detection of patients and practitioners alike.

The study of illness became part of a much wider investigation into the organization and functions of organic matter. Morbid events were no longer regarded as a discrete area of enquiry but were studied in the context of a general analysis of both normal and abnormal physiological processes. Indeed the scientific revolution in medical knowledge may be said to have undermined the very existence of medicine as a distinct discipline in its own right. Medicine ceased to be a subject defined by its explicit and exclusive contents, and became instead an applied science, consisting of a pragmatically derived range of disciplines and techniques, distinguished by its specific purpose.

The realignment of the boundaries of the medical investigator's quest were but one part of a general metamorphosis of work tasks characteristic of the shift from Hospital to Laboratory Medicine. The occupational activity of medical investigators henceforth took the form of the extension of certified knowledge rather than the servicing of clients. The authority of the research-worker was a function of his capacity to manipulate abstract symbols and concepts. A study of the emergence of occupations based on scientific knowledge must take cognisance of this transformation which is rooted in the nature of the activity itself. This development represented a significant gain in the social detachment of the medical investigator from the sick. It enabled him to conceptualize the sick-man as a material thing to be analysed, and disease as a physico-chemical process to be explained according to the blind inexorable laws of natural science. Thus whilst Hospital Medicine had dissolved the integrated vision of the whole man into a network of anatomical structures, Laboratory Medicine, by focusing attention on the fundamental particles of organic matter, went still further in eradicating the person of the patient from medical discourse.

The career struggle among medical investigators was fought out through the manipulation and appropriation of scientific knowledge, the patterns of intellectual property rights playing a key part in determining the patterns of deference shown in interaction among occupational peers. The formal organization of the medical cosmology of Laboratory Medicine provided a vehicle for the institutionalization and reinforcement of a range of status obligations and role identities within the scientific community. Thus the process of innovation in medical knowledge was inspired by a belief in and a search for a single rational order in both the physiological processes of organic matter and the social inequalities among medical investigators.

Conclusion

This paper has attempted to formulate an albeit brief and incomplete sketch of one or two of the concepts which, it is hoped, may prove fruitful in the sociological explanation of changes in the perception and conceptualization of the human body by medical personnel during the course of the industrialization of western societies. Many important aspects of such a study have been neglected or glossed over here of course. Thus, for example, no analysis has been made of the processes of change within and between modes of production of medical knowledge; no reference has been made to the interaction between the production of medical knowledge and other types of cultural endeavour; no examination has been made of the relationship between intellectual production and other 'practices' within the social formation, such as the economy and polity; and so on. Attention has been drawn, however, to the changing appearance of the sick-man within pathological theory and to the changing relationship between the sick-man and medical investigators. In the era of Bedside Medicine the sick themselves determined the course of medical knowledge. The student was under the control of the object of study. The triumph of blind physico-chemical law over the idiosyncratic personal experience of the sick-man within the worldview of the medical investigator did not occur until the latter had achieved a degree of detachment from the demands of the sick. This increase in social distance may be discussed in the context of transformations in the relations of production of medical knowledge.

Notes

1. The notion of medical cosmology bears a close resemblance to Althusser's 'problematic', see L. Althusser and E. Bailbar, *Reading Capital* (trans. Ben Brewster, New Left Books, London, 1970) esp. pp. 25–8, and also L. Althusser, *For Marx*, (trans. Ben Brewster, Allen Lane, The Penguin Press, 1971). In recent years a number of authors have formulated comparable concepts. None of these terms have been adopted here, however, in order to avoid responsibility for and discussion of the wider theoretical contexts within which they are located.

2. On the tradition of bedside medicine in Edinburgh medicine see A.C. Chitnis, 'Medical Education in Edinburgh 1790–1820 and Some Victorian Consequences', *Med. Hist.*, Vol. XVII, April 1973, No. 2; V.B. Bullough, 'The Causes of the Scottish Medical Renaissance of the Eighteenth Century', *Bull. Hist. Med.*, 1971, Vol. LXV, No. 1. On the significance of the 18th century clinical facilities at Edinburgh see M. Foucault, *The Birth of the Clinic* (trans. A.M. Sheridan Smith, Tavistock Publications, London, 1973), Chapter 4.

3. Cf. Merleau-Ponty's notion of the 'body-subject', M. Merleau-Ponty, *The Phenomenology of Perception*, (Routledge and Kegan Paul, London, 1962).

4. On the rise of Hospital Medicine in France see; M. Foucault, op. cit. E.W. Ackerknecht, *Medicine at the Paris Hospital 1774–1848* (John Hopkins Press, Baltimore, 1967); I. Waddington, 'The Role of the Hospital in the Development of Modern Medicine: A Sociological Analysis', *Sociology*, Vol. 7, No. 2, May 1973, pp. 211–24; G. Rosen, 'Hospitals, Medical Care and Social Policy in the French Revolution', *Bull. Hist. Med.*, Vol. XXX, 1956, pp. 124–49.

5. Cf. Foucault's point that Bedside Medicine related to 'health' whereas Hospital Medicine related to 'normality'. M. Foucault, op. cit., p. 35.

6. On the development of medical knowledge in mid-19th century Germany see E. Mendelsohn, 'Physical Orders and Physiological Concepts: Explanation in 19th Century Biology', *B.J. Hist. Sci.*, Vol. 2, No. 7, 1965; D.H. Galaty, 'The Philosophical Basis of mid-19th Century German Reductionism', *J. Hist. Med.*, Vol. XXIX, No. 3, July 1974, pp. 295–316.

7. In terms of the very useful typology of systems of occupational control proposed by T.J. Johnson, *Professions and Power* (London, Macmillan, 1972), this situation may be described as one of 'oligarchic patronage' (see Chapter 5).

8. See T.J. Johnson, op. cit. Chapter 4.

9. See E.W. Ackerknecht, op. cit. (1967), Chapter XIV.

6

From Clinical Gaze to Regime of Total Health

DAVID ARMSTRONG

Introduction

In histories of medicine the late eighteenth century stands out as a particularly fertile period in that it gave birth to the modern system of clinical pathological medicine. This remarkable achievement is usually presented in terms of discovery: certainly there were political and social struggles surrounding the emergence of this new medicine, but in the end we are left with the clear image of the triumph of truth as medical scientists uncovered the diseases previously hidden within the human body.

At the heart of this new framework for understanding the nature of illness lay the notion of the pathological lesion. Prior to the end of the eighteenth century illness was perceived as moving between bodies and environments (as in humoral medicine) without ever stopping to become analysable. However, with the dissection of the corpse and concomitant developments in clinical technique, specific anatomical lesions were identified inside the body: these seemed to account for the outward appearances of illness – the so-called clinico-pathological correlation. Thus, for example, pain and tenderness on the 'outside' were seen to signify the existence of inflammation in internal tissues beyond immediate vision. These discoveries ushered in the hospital as a place in which bodies could be examined with proper rigour, the post-mortem as the event in which the true nature of disease was finally revealed, and the many facets of clinical method which still underpin medical practice today.

The clinical gaze

Although conventional histories of medicine acclaim the late eighteenth century discoveries of clinical pathology, it is still possible to pursue a less arrogant and self-centred analysis of Western medical history. Instead of seeing the period until the end of the eighteenth century as essentially one of darkness to be illuminated by the new truths of the dissecting room and post-mortem, we can view the latter developments as simply one more construction or perception about the nature of illness. Central to this new perception, as Michel Foucault argued in 'The Birth of the Clinic',[1] was the fabrication of the body by means of the 'anatomical atlas': the anatomical atlas directs attention to certain structures, certain similarities, certain systems, and not others, and in so doing forms a set of rules for reading the body and for making it intelligible. In this sense the reality of the body is only established by the observing eye that reads it. The atlas enables the anatomy student, when faced with the undifferentiated amorphous mass of the body, to see certain things and ignore others. In effect, what the student sees is not the atlas as a representation of the body but the body as a representation of the atlas.

The atlas is therefore a means of interpreting the body, of seeing its form and nature and establishing its reality. The modern body of the patient, which has become the unquestioned object of clinical practice, is a product of the exercise of those same clinical techniques. The clinical gaze, encompassing all the techniques, languages and assumptions of modern medicine, establishes by its authority and penetration an observable and analysable space in which is crystallised that apparently solid figure of the discrete human body.

Mechanisms of power

The analysis of the way the body is seen, described and constructed, Foucault suggests, might be called 'political anatomy'.[2] It is political because the changes in the way the body is described are not the consequences of some random effects or progressive enlightenment but are based on certain mechanisms of power which, since the eighteenth century, have pervaded the body and continue to hold it in their grasp. From that time the body has been the point on which and from which power has been exercised.

In eighteenth century European society the body became treated 'as something docile that could be subject, used, transformed and improved'. The body became surrounded and invested with various techniques of detail which analysed, monitored and fabricated it. These various techniques all involved surveillance: bodies had to be inspected to judge their status, they had to be analysed to identify their deficits and they had to be monitored to evaluate their functioning. The importance of surveillance is illustrated in particular in the various techniques of examination that emerged to prominence in the eighteenth century such as the clinical examination in the hospital, the inspection in the prison, the test in the school and the military inspection in the barracks. Why is it, asks Foucault, that the school, the hospital, the prison, the barracks and the workshop have so much in common?

The clinical gaze of medicine was one of the new techniques through which bodies were analysed. It is apparent, as Foucault observed, that late eighteenth century medicine began to perceive a body which had a new anatomy. Every time medicine had cause to deploy its new techniques and treat an illness, it drew the anatomical outline of a docile body. At first the procedure was unsure and the outline hazy but with time and with refinement the shape became more clear. As the nineteenth century progressed each and every consultation of the new pathological medicine functioned to imprint, by its sheer repetition, the reality of a specific anatomy.

An extended medical gaze

During the twentieth century the diagram of power has been rearranged.[3] The clinical gaze, which for over a century had analysed the microscopic detail of the individual body, began to move to the undifferentiated space between bodies. Indeed, it is possible to discern in the early years of the century the beginning of a new framework for understanding illness. This emergence can be traced through various extensions to the dominant clinical gaze. First, the locus of illness can be seen to have begun to shift from within the body to a space which might be described as between bodies. Second, it is possible to map a series of new techniques which have developed to interrogate this new space of illness. And third, the actual impact of these new approaches on the shape and character of the body can be identified as a new political anatomy emerges.

The main change in the nature of the clinical gaze during the twentieth century can be summarised as the extension of surveillance from the interior of the body to its exterior points of contact: disease has become increasingly located in the spaces between people, in the interstices of relationships, in the social body itself. In this new conceptualisation pathology is not seen as an essentially static phenomenon to be localised to a specific point – as construed by the great historic breakthrough of the eighteenth century clinic – but as a movement through the social body, appearing only intermittently. This new model of illness can be seen in the 'reconstruction' of certain established diseases such as tuberculosis and venereal diseases, and in the invention of several new forms of pathology.

Tuberculosis, which had, until the closing decades of the nineteenth century, been primarily a disease of individual bodies and of environmental neglect, became a disease of contact and social space. Equally the early twentieth century concern with venereal disease and contact tracing illustrated the mapping of a social domain for the locus of illness. So too the increasing concern with contagion of more minor illnesses. Around the end of the first decade of the century it was recognised that schoolchildren might spread infection between themselves through contact. Schools therefore deployed a regime of surveillance which stressed less the significance of sanitation and more the importance of personal hygiene. Children with infectious diseases, from measles to the common cold, were required to remain at home for specified periods to prevent the spread of illness throughout the school and thereafter the community.

Under the nineteenth century system of public health the natural environment was the potential source of ill health. Under the new hygiene the natural environment was not of itself dangerous, but merely acted as a reservoir. The danger now arose from people and their point of contact. In one form venereal disease existed within the body as a specific identifiable infection: but from the early twentieth century it was also construed as existing in the space mapped by intimate relationships. As the traditional techniques of clinical method could not interrogate this new space of illness new procedures had to be developed. The epidemiological gaze therefore began to shift from the environment to the mode of transmission between people and to the ramifications of social relationships. Preventive medicine was therefore no longer restricted to environmental questions and sanitation but became concerned with the minutiae of social life. Might not health, Newman argued, be promoted 'by maintaining a clean mouth and clear breathing, and by abstinence from spitting, sneezing, coughing and shouting at each other?' [4]

Together, these various measures outlined an organizational structure which could both survey and constantly monitor the whole community. Hence, also, the emphasis on close scrutiny of details of patients' contacts and relationships, and the creation of a thorough record of family networks, friends and acquaintances through which to co-ordinate home-visits, checks and follow-ups. In addition, this social surveillance raised the consciousness of health matters in the community thus observed and, on the one hand, enabled the intrusion of surveillance to be more easily justified, and, on the other hand, made the potential patient a part of the surveillance machinery.

A psychosocial space

The space between bodies that emerged early in the twentieth century was a physical space which micro-organisms could cross; but, more important, it was also a 'social-psychological' space in which could crystallise those attributes of bodies which are now referred to as identity. A powerful illustration of the emergence of this new space was the 'discovery' of the neuroses less than a century ago.[5] Whereas nineteenth century psychiatry had only been concerned with separating the mad from the sane, twentieth century mental health has sought to monitor everyone's ability to cope with interactions and feelings.

The fabrication of this psychosocial space surrounding all bodies can also be discerned in the techniques which doctors have deployed to 'interrogate' the patient.[6] Nineteenth century manuals on clinical method only described how to examine the body and made only perfunctory reference to the patient's 'history'. However, in the early years of the twentieth century there was a growing interest in what the patient might say. At first it was a question of provoking the pathological lesion to speech – achieved through the patient's history. Then it was recognised that the patient's words might not exactly speak for the pathological lesion as had previously been assumed: doctors were therefore advised on the use of certain techniques, such as avoidance of leading questions, to prevent the patient speaking of symptoms which could mislead the search for the lesion. By the late inter-war years these strange words which patients often spoke were no longer construed as the background 'noise' which might prevent the clinical truth from emerging clearly; instead the words represented the patient's affective state, and accordingly doctors were advised to seek out the patient's fears, feelings and anxieties as a legitimate part of medical 'case-taking'.

The increasing emphasis on monitoring the patient's mental functioning as part of the normal medical interview has continued. Nowadays doctors are taught the importance of affect and cognitions in the patient's story and the possible interrelationship of organic lesion to mental state. For example, it is now reported that most appendicitis is preceded by significant negative life events and that the psychological effect of these often lasts beyond the surgical operation to remove the offending appendix.[7] Thus even surgery, the great bastion of the clinical gaze, is coming to extend its gaze from the body's interior to the psychological states and social relationships of that body. Why else have psychology and sociology, which both emerged as distinct and autonomous disciplines in the twentieth century, become essential components of the medical curriculum?

Sociology made its principal contribution to post-war medicine when its mastery of survey techniques made it of value to an extended medical gaze intent on exploring the surveillance possibilities of this newly discovered technology. Sociologists, in close alliance with medicine, opened up areas of the health experiences of 'ordinary' people through surveys of health attitudes, of illness behaviour, of drug taking and of symptom prevalence.

More recently, as the medical gaze has focused on individual idiosyncrasies, personal meanings and subjectivity, sociology too has turned its attention to fresh possibilities. On the one hand, various survey techniques have been made more sophisticated so that they might take into consideration, bring out or measure, individual meanings; on the other hand, some sociologists have explicitly rejected survey techniques on the grounds that they objectify respondents and have turned instead to methodologies which, they hold, more clearly respect or enhance patient subjectivity. Within the last two decades proponents of interaction analysis, participant observations, ethnomethodology, and other more naturalistic methods have been critical of the dehumanising aspects of medicine and of sociology itself; and yet the effect of their stance is to have strengthened the power of gaze of the new medicine to the essentially subjective.

Thus, at the same moment as patients entered medical discourse as subjects, they appeared in a parallel discourse in the human sciences; indeed, the changes in medical discourse often took precedence. This is not to argue that the human sciences have simply been the handmaidens of medicine: their frequent alliances, points of contact and shared concerns do not reflect a relationship of domination but of a common object, namely, the body and its relationships, and a common effect, the subjectivity of that same body. The human sciences have thus produced an often independent but parallel gaze to the body and within this independence have forged a new 'regime of truth'. This knowledge has increasingly been concerned with the subjectivity of experience and has often sought to conceal its recent invention through the notion of alienation which presents subjectivity as the imminent human condition that the human sciences have succeeded in 'liberating'.

Over the last two decades there has been an historical project in the human sciences and parts of medicine[8] which has concerned itself with the identification of a distant disappearance of 'a sense of wholeness, inviolability and ethical judgement' through forces of repression and domination – which then enables claim to be made for the parallel rediscovery and reappearance of the sick-man.[9] In effect, the recent social origins of the sick-man are blurred as a historical discourse on alienation provides him with a political credo, a universal status and a plausible history; an invention is translated into a language of liberation, a positive power which creates is concealed in the identification of a repressive power which is lifted. As Foucault points out, we continue to 'describe the effects of power in negative terms: it "excludes", it "represses", it "censors", it "abstracts", it "masks", it "conceals". In fact, power produces; it produces reality; it produces domains of objects and rituals of truth. The individual and the knowledge that may be gained of him belong to this production'.[10]

It is all too easy to see the changes accompanying the extended medical gaze in terms of a pernicious movement to constrain the lives of free citizens, indeed it cannot be coincidence that *Brave New World* and *Nineteen Eighty-Four* were written as these surveillance opportunities were deployed throughout the population. Yet this is to see surveillance as the instrument of a sovereign power, of a calculating centre which is intent on dominating and controlling others. In this model the extended gaze would be a dangerous force to be resisted, as several critics of medicine have advocated.[11] However, according to Foucault's notion of disciplinary power surveillance is a productive rather than repressive force.

The extended medical gaze does not repress the liberty of the individual, but rather creates it. It is only through the extended gaze – within medicine and other agencies – that the psychological and social characteristics of wholeness and identity come to exist for those inert corporal masses which the clinical gaze had fashioned throughout the nineteenth century. It is ironic that having had their subjectivity fabricated those same subjects insist that subjectivity is an invariate and universal component of human life; but it is also a subtle device through which the operation of this productive power is concealed.

Disciplining bodies

Although the major changes in medical surveillance during the twentieth century would seem to embrace the psychosocial space between bodies, this does not mean that the physical body itself has continued as a passive recipient of observation, as in the nineteenth century. In part through developments in the educational field, but increasingly through our preoccupation with the notion of 'health behaviour', the movement of bodies has become a major focus for twentieth century disciplinary techniques.[12]

Early in the twentieth century it would have been impossible to conceptualise the notion of health behaviour. Indeed while the problem of behaviour was to achieve some limited recognition in 'behaviourism', most of the new discipline of psychology was concerned with the subject of human 'conduct' which was held to be the 'highest type of behaviour'. The term behaviour itself was reserved to describe 'certain peculiarities which are only found in the movement of living things'.[13]

The shift from a world of instincts, conduct and habits to one of attitudes and behaviour can be traced through the attempts to discipline and manipulate the body of the child in the elementary schools earlier this century, a strategy which produced the great alliance between physical education and hygiene. Universal primary education had the task of managing and transforming the body of the child and to accomplish this goal the new schools at first simply borrowed the same techniques which had evolved in the army to transform raw recruits into disciplined soldiers. Drill routines, 'marching, counter-marching, diagonal marching, changing ranks and so on', were initially popular, later being replaced by more 'carefully graduated and scientifically calculated' movements.[14]

The disciplining of bodily movement in both army and school was gradually widened from the rigidity of drill to the more generalised techniques of physical training and physical education. The individual body could be trained, particularly through repetitive actions – so inculcating 'habits' – to achieve some goal such as fitness and efficiency. Training took control over the general physical development of the child ensuring that full physical capacity was achieved and it also had a 'corrective effect' remedying or adjusting 'any obvious defects or incorrect attitude or action of the body, or any of its parts'.[15]

But it was not only the drill sergeant and the teacher who trained the child's body but also the child itself; training could equally well, and undoubtedly more efficiently and permanently, be achieved through education. Pure training only worked at the level of habit forming: 'the child unconsciously acquires habits of discipline and order, and learns to respond cheerfully and promptly to the word of command'.[16] Yet the more valuable aim was to instill the word of command into the child so it could function as its own drill master. Posture, fitness and efficiency were the initial objectives but with the gradual extension of the techniques through which the body was manipulated – physical culture, sports, gymnastics, dance, exercise and athletics – the goal widened towards a regime of total health.

Movement of the body had its effects on the mind: exercises could inculcate habits and, moreover, it seemed that the discipline of movement could focus the mind on the task in hand, eliminating stray thoughts – perhaps of a sexual nature – and build up 'character'. But equally, movement in some way reflected mental functioning. For example, it was claimed that there was a very close relationship between intelligence and success in athletics, and mental problems might be expressed in poor movement co-ordination just as true character could be read from the sports field, the gymnasium, the athletics ground and the dance school.[17] Such strategies were, of course, largely limited to development of the child; but where education left off, medicine had techniques to pick up the management of behaviour throughout adult life.

The active patient

Clinical medicine from the late eighteenth century involved an interaction between clinician and pathological lesion. The patient, as a person, had only existed within this dyad as a repository or, at most, as a rather unreliable translator for the lesion. In effect, the patient was no more than a passive physical object.

In the new public health of the twentieth century, however, which stressed the importance of both the physical and the social relationship between bodies, the individual was constituted as a more active physical and social being. Personal hygiene addressed this individual because it required commitment to certain activities, particularly those involving the sanitisation of body interfaces such as skin, mouth, ears, teeth, bowels, etc., to prevent the transmission of disease from one person to another. In effect the object of the new personal hygiene was not the organic lesion but some activities of its potential host.

The reconstruction of patient identity through the new public health towards a more active and acting object was however only one part of this transformation in medicine. The other component of the new personal hygiene was the recruitment of the patient to the medical enterprise. In the nineteenth century the public health official alone could monitor and control the dangers of natural environment. The new hygiene however could not rely on these officials as its agents of surveillance, instead it demanded involvement of 'patients' themselves. If human bodies were to be monitored and sanitised medicine required the active co-operation of those same bodies; patients therefore had to be enlisted to practice their own hygienic regime; patients had to become agents of medicine, their own self-practitioners.

Thus the two related features of the new public health were forged early in the twentieth century. On the one hand the patient as a person became the object of medical attention, particularly in his or her own actions. On the other hand patients were also the subjects of medicine in the sense that they were recruited to monitor their own bodies. Since then, these two (and often confused) facets of patient identity have been explored, developed and reinforced. The active body of the patient required study, guidance and control if illness was to be avoided and health achieved. The malleable subjective mind of the patient in its turn demanded education and training if it was successfully to monitor and bring under some control its otherwise capricious body.

Early in the twentieth century the patient as actor was recognised in regimes of personal hygiene and in concerns for patient 'defaulters' from treatment, particularly from that of venereal disease. And by the middle of the century health education was firmly established as an essential part of the public health programme. 'Health authorities', wrote Derryberry in 1945, 'are becoming increasingly aware that many diseases are uncontrollable without the active participation of the people themselves'.[18] Whereas a few decades earlier the community was only involved in public health in so far as their electoral or political support was required, now people had to be involved from the very beginning of any programme because they themselves were the agents of health practice.

Opportunities for applying these new strategies emerged with the preventive health programmes of the immediate post-war years, particularly those relating to polio vaccination, community X-ray programmes for TB, and the new multi-phasic screening programmes. What were the public's attitudes towards vaccination? What factors precluded their involvement? How was participation and non-participation to be explained? Whereas during the early part of the century human behaviour had been seen as governed by instinct, that is from a fixed biological point, during the late 1950s public health discovered beliefs as the mainspring of human action. The theories of Rosenstock *et al.* of 1959 of why people failed to seek polio vaccination had become, by 1965, the basis for a more generalised model of health beliefs and focus on patient activity.[19]

One of the effects of the recruitment of the patient as an integral component of health management was the change in the status and nature of 'patient' identity. The boundary between healthy person and patient became problematic. In the past the transition from person-status to patient-status had been marked by 'coming under the doctor'. In the new regime, which made the patient both an object of medicine and a lay health practitioner, patienthood began to lose its old meaning. This shift was marked by the extension of patient status (or at least potential status) as everyone came under medical/health surveillance through the gradual recruitment of everyone to the medical enterprise. Post-war surveys of population morbidity and symptom prevalence confirmed that a rigid distinction between health and illness was meaningless: everyone had health problems, everyone was 'at risk', health care merely touched the tip of the morbidity iceberg.[20] In addition the now problematic boundary between person and patient was subjected to a close analysis in the new subject of 'illness behaviour' which attempted to explain how and why patients chose to consult with a doctor.

Illness behaviour, a term invented by Mechanic in 1960,[21] has often been challenged as being too restricted, as failing to encapsulate the wider concerns of health behaviour. Yet illness behaviour was not only an explanation of certain health-related activities but also part of the post-war fascination with the weakening person–patient boundary. The concept of illness behaviour showed that the transition between health and illness, between person and patient, was not predicated on an absolute and biological difference, but was underpinned by the notion of a person as his or her own health practitioner making judgements and decisions on the nature and limits of health and illness.

The patient was inseparable from the person because all persons had become patients, and with it changed their identity. Until the post-war years behaviour had been relatively unchangeable, set by heredity and repetitive patterning. In the post-war years behaviour became contingent: social psychologists, for example, discovered attitudes with which to replace instincts as one of the prime determinants of behaviour, the patient thus becoming a more unpredictable and variable being.

Promoting total health

In 1990 medicine was represented by the physician armed with tools for the exploration of individual physical bodies; the patient was that body, essentially passive, involved only to the extent that it must respond to and report the outward manifestation of the organic disease. Health was the state which was gained or lost by the disappearance or appearance of the lesion.

In the new regime of public health, medicine is no longer represented by the solitary figure of the physician but by a vast network ranging from the post-war integrated and comprehensive health care system to community and 'informal' care. The patient is a member of this network of surveillance, a 'producer' of health through health-protective behaviour. The patient is also a consumer, an object of this medical enterprise; but whereas in the nineteenth century the patient only existed as a passive body, the patient is now constituted as a psychosocial being whose every movement and gesture is monitored, evaluated and reordered by a medical machine based on a new ideology of health. The patient has become an object within biographical and social space rather than within strictly anatomical boundaries and these extended features of patienthood have received increasing attention.

The dream of the new medicine has reformed the relationship between health and illness. No longer polar opposites within a binary classification, they have become inextricably linked within a great continuum of health. One the one hand health is contained in illness; the disabled, the chronically sick, the dying and the diseased can promote their health by appropriate health behaviour, enabling reactions and successful coping. Equally the germ of illness is now contained in health. Health has become a temporal trajectory containing the seeds of illness which, nevertheless, can be countered by preventive action, health promotion, healthy living, and healthy lifestyles.

A health behaviour approach helps reconstitute the objects towards which it is directed: the patient, the nature of health and medical knowledge itself. The active participating individual proceeds from behaving to acting – better to capture the voluntaristic element in human activity; illness moves further from the body of the patient to social spaces, to problems of coping and adjustment; and medical strategies shift from the pronouncements of experts towards 'informed choice', non-directive counselling and a non-judgemental health behaviour as the old referents finally disappear. Influencing, manipulating, transforming, the new medicine of continuous surveillance is a dream of enlightenment in which the population achieves liberation under a totalitarian regime of health.

Acknowledgements

This article is based on themes from a number of previously published papers. I am grateful to the editors for suggesting how these themes might usefully be integrated.

Notes

1. Foucault, M., *Birth of the Clinic: an archaeology of medical perception*, London, Tavistock, 1973.
2. Foucault, M., *Discipline and Punish: the birth of the prison*, London, Allen Lane, 1977; see especially Part III on discipline.
3. This section draws on Armstrong, D., *Political Anatomy of the Body: medical knowledge in Britain in the twentieth century*, Cambridge University Press, 1983.
4. Newman, G., quoted in 'Editorial', *British Medical Journal*, **1**, p. 646, 1920.
5. Armstrong, D., 'Madness and coping', *Sociology of Health and Illness*, **2**, pp. 293–316, 1980.
6. Armstrong, D., 'The patient's view', *Social Science and Medicine*, **18**, pp. 737–44, 1984; see also Armstrong, D., 'The doctor–patient relationship: 1930–80', in Wright, P. and Treacher, A., *The Problem of Medical Knowledge*, Edinburgh University Press, 1983.
7. Creed, F.H., 'Life events and appendectomy', *The Lancet*, **1**, pp. 1381–5, 1981.
8. Armstrong, D., 'The problem of the whole person in holistic medicine', *Holistic Medicine*, **1**, pp. 27–36.
9. Jewson, N., 'Disappearance of the sick-man from medical cosmology, 1770–1870', *Sociology*, **10**, p. 225, 1976.
10. Foucault, M., *Discipline and Punish*.
11. Ivan Illich expresses this view particularly cogently but under the guise of a right-wing libertarianism. Illich, I., *Medical Nemesis: the expropriation of health*, London, Caldar Boyars, 1974; see also the revised version, *Limits to Medicine*, London, Caldar Boyars, 1978.

12. This section draws on Armstrong, D., 'Historical origins of health behaviour', in Anderson, R. *et al.* (eds), *Health Behaviour: research and health promotion*, Oxford University Press, 1988.
13. McDougall, W., *An Introduction to Social Psychology*, London, Methuen, 1908.
14. Atkins J.B., *National Physical Training: an open debate*, London, Ibister, 1904, p. 151.
15. Board of Education, *Suggestions for the Consideration of Teachers*, London, HMSO, 1909.
16. Ibid.
17. Campbell, R.B., 'The psychological aspect of physical education', *Edinburgh Medical Journal*, **47**, p. 351, 1940.
18. Derryberry, M., 'Health education in the public health program', *Public Health Reports*, **60**, p. 1401, 1945.
19. Rosenstock, I.M., 'Why people use health services', *Millbank Memorial Fund Quarterly*, **44**, p. 94, 1965.
20. Last, J.M., 'The clinical iceberg', *The Lancet*, **2**, pp. 28–30, 1963.
21. Mechanic, D. and Volkart, E.H., 'Illness behaviour and medical diagnoses', *Journal of Health and Human Behaviour*, **1**, p. 86, 1960.

7

Mental Health for All*

SUMAN FERNANDO

Concepts about mental health developed in one culture may be very different from those in another. Moreover, in aiming to develop a way of understanding mental health that is globally applicable, questions of race and culture must be confronted; racist views of cultures and people must be avoided and 'health' must be seen in the context of culture. And deviations from 'health' must be evaluated by procedures that incorporate culture and race, and not in a manner that excludes culture from 'illness' and denies or ignores the effects of racism – as is the case, for example, in the research into 'mental illness' conducted by the World Health Organisation (WHO).[1]

Three key imperatives should be followed concurrently – not consecutively – if mental health care is to have relevance to people everywhere. First and foremost, racist conceptions of cultural forms and habits must be challenged. This entails an honest approach towards developing a non-racist view of cultural, religious and medical practices all over the world that are to do with the maintenance of mental health – from family systems to idioms of distress, from beliefs in deities to religious ceremonies, from definitions of illness to exorcism rituals. An anti-racist stance is required in all mental health work, in anthropology, in sociology and, most of all, in psychiatry. Secondly, all aspects of mental health must be seen as cultural matters to be considered in relation to other aspects of culture. Clearly, a medical viewpoint has a part to play, for in all cultures the world over, some forms of human distress and 'madness' are seen as illness. But it is necessary to recognise that medicine, too, is a part of culture and not a system with a life of its own outside the culture in which it lives – as it seems to be considered in Western thinking. Admittedly, the development of a secular medical science that attempts to be objective and purely biological has promoted the progress of medical knowledge, but such an approach has been, and

---

*This is an abridged extract from Fernando, S. (1991), *Mental Health, Race and Culture*, London, MIND, Chapter 8.

will be even more so, a drawback in the case of understanding mental health. Finally, close attention must be paid to the spiritual needs of people, their social experiences and their economic situations seen in their cultural and political contexts since the mental health of human beings the world over is fashioned – sometimes in very different ways – by these factors as much as by their biological and genetic make-up.

The whole field of mental health requires realignment in terms of race and culture. But the cards are stacked against a remodelling of thinking on mental health designed to take an anti-racist stance and incorporate the wisdom and experience of Asia and Africa. A revision of current thinking would challenge the cultural arrogance and racist ideology incorporated in many of the assumptions of the West, reflected (for example) in that of Western psychiatry in propagating its 'scientific knowledge' about mental health. The question of power is crucial. A new approach to mental health must stand apart from the power structure in the world today: it must accept the fact that most of the world is neither culturally Western nor racially white; it must take on the validity of the black experience in a white-dominated world; it should acknowledge the importance of concepts about human life from Asia and Africa and the relativity of all 'knowledge' in a subject that encompasses human feelings, beliefs and behaviour. The situation in multicultural and multiracial societies is of special concern: the white domination of black people promotes and often imposes, a cultural domination so that ways of thinking, family life, and patterns of mental health and mental health care that are identified as 'European' in tradition, or 'white' by racial origin, are seen as superior to others. This must be overcome if mental health is to have a real meaning in all cultures and to people of all races.

Redefining mental illness

Western thinking about mental health is dominated by psychiatry and propagated throughout the world as a 'scientific' approach. And mental illness and mental health are generally seen as two sides of the same coin. Further, the province of psychiatry is much wider than situations defined in terms of 'mental illness' *per se*; sexual and marital difficulties, family conflicts and many other forms of human distress or misbehaviour in general seem to fall within the purview of psychiatric expertise. And inevitably, the medical aura carried by psychiatry means that problems in all these fields are implicitly, if not explicitly, medicalised into being conceptualised and acted upon in terms of illness, even if problems are not actually designated as such. Many forms of human distress and misbehaviour, seen through Western eyes as 'illness', are not medicalised in other cultures – at least not unless Western models have been imposed. But in every culture, there appear to be certain problems that are accepted as illness, presumably because it is through an illness model that they are traditionally handled within the culture. However, an illness model in one culture may not be the same as that in another. Similarly, all cultures appear to recognise 'madness', roughly – but only roughly – translated into the Western idea of 'psychosis', although here, too, the definitions may not be identical across cultures.

The fact that both 'illness' and 'madness' are concepts that are cross-culturally valid means that some agreement may be possible on what is, and is not, essentially illness or madness. But when attempts are made to develop a common language for defining mental illness that cuts across culture – as the World Health Organisation has tried to do in its International Pilot Study of Schizophrenia (IPSS) – what actually happens is that real cultural differences are ignored and, even more importantly, Western ideas are imposed across the world with racist perceptions dominating the process. In any case, illness in non-Western cultures is not always dealt with by treatment as understood in the West nor is madness always considered as an illness. An explanatory model for the genesis of illness is not necessarily bound up with the concept of illness; and a condition can be an illness or madness and be dealt with by (seemingly) religious manoeuvres or medical treatment – or a mixture of the two. For all these reasons, a search for a common language for defining mental illness across cultures must be abandoned.

In Western thinking, an illness is generated by one or more causes arising from biological or psychological change, i.e. a cause–effect model is generally adhered to. In older cultures, all changes are seen as relative – as in the thinking of modern physics – and illnesses are seen as resulting from imbalances of various types. It is possible that Western ideas in psychiatry, which at present emphasise biological 'causes', can be incorporated into a relativity model, for this clearly is the model for the future. It would mean the reinterpreting of much of the information about mental illness that is available – not an impossible task. Thus, if a genetic predisposition is postulated for psychosis, it is a genetic balance/imbalance that should be looked for rather than a genetic determinant or cause. It is not biochemical causes but the balances of biochemical influences that are significant. But more than that, biochemical, genetic and other influences must be seen as being in dynamic balance/imbalance with other influences – social, spiritual and cosmological. The importance and significance of the various influences would depend on the society, the culture and the person concerned, as well as the knowledge available.

A relativistic approach to (Western) conceptions about 'mental' illness would be the first step towards opening it up and improving communication with other ways of thinking. This would lead to a fluidity of thought (about illness) that is culture-sensitive and flexible – and free of racist ideology. In practice, it is a way forward that is being proposed, not a comprehensive theory. The final vision is that a concept of illness will remain but it will be very different from the present one, and one that will not be fixed in firm categories that are supposed to be universally applicable. Different societies will develop variations on what may be, eventually, one or more universal themes; and culture will be an integral part of the way that 'illness' will be defined and recognised. The explanatory models will vary with the culture, again each and every model incorporating culture into its fabric. Any one type of explanation will not be seen as superior to another because they will *all* be embedded within their cultures but understandable on the basis of universal themes – and hence, not 'culture-bound'. There will be diversity within unity; a culturally relativistic view integrated into a universalist approach.

Restructuring mental health

Strategies for changing attitudes and practices in order to bring about a universal understanding of mental health must be directed at the international – global – scene and the national scene, as well as being concerned with personal (individual or family) matters. And such strategies must face and overcome racism at all these levels.

The first strategy at an international level is to influence the WHO to change its ways of working so that the alliance between the WHO and Western economic interests may be broken.

Clearly, the WHO has to be cautious but must reorientate its projects, including its research, in the mental health field. It can set the scene for a change of direction by, for example, controlling the indiscriminate sale of powerful psychotropic drugs, which are presented by commercial interests as the 'scientific' approach to establishing mental health, and by introducing proper standards for assessing their usefulness in countries of the Third World. The practical projects undertaken by the WHO in the mental health field should be aimed primarily at identifying and alleviating stress, rather than diagnosing and 'treating' mental illness based on Western concepts. Research promoted by the WHO should be directed at evaluating ways of helping people that are culturally consonant and tuned to the real needs of the people in the countries concerned. WHO projects should concentrate on developing indigenous methods of mental health promotion using local experts in the field, supported where necessary by Western expertise in organisation. And, most importantly, the WHO must eliminate racial bias at all levels with careful regulation of its research projects, selection of 'experts' who provide consultative advice and organise the delivery of services, and staffing of the organisation itself. Obviously, if there is a change of direction and the WHO takes on both anti-racism and cultural sensitivity, many ways of promoting universal mental health would emerge. It is essentially a political shift that is needed to begin with.

Changes at a national level must take place in both the rich Western countries – the developed world – and the poor, developing 'Third World'. In general, the former provide 'aid' in various forms to the latter. Over the past forty years, Western technology has built dams, factories, irrigation works etc. in the Third World, but vast numbers of people in those countries still cannot earn a living. Schumacher (1973)[2] has pointed out that Western 'high technology' is actually exacerbating the plight of the world's poor by distorting their economies and misusing their resources. Applying this view to the mental health field, current Western intervention in the Third World may, on the one hand, be creating mental ill health through its economic and political pressures, and, on the other hand, be failing to promote mental health with its 'high tech' psychiatry that uses inappropriate methods of diagnosis and treatment. Further, the imposition of Western psychiatry may actually cause cultural damage by medicalising human suffering and tying 'remedies' to the purchase of expensive drugs from Western countries. Thus, Western 'aid' in the mental health field must change gear in order to address the needs of the people it is supposed to help. The following principles enunciated by Schumacher for an 'intermediate technology' to replace 'high technology' in aid programmes may be usefully applied in the mental health field. First, aid programmes must be located in villages and towns, where most of the poor live; secondly, the programmes should not require much financial capital investment; thirdly, new training should be minimal; and finally, maximum use should be made of local talent and resources.

A change in the policies of aid-giving countries must be matched by changes in the attitudes of governments and mental health professionals in the Third World. The assumption of Western superiority in *everything* – an attitude that is rife in many parts of Asia and Africa – must be seriously confronted and changed in a realistic fashion. The limitations of Western expertise in the field of mental health care and in particular the ethnocentricity of Western psychiatric practice must be faced. The sort of change in the ethos and structure of 'aid' indicated here must lead to Western psychiatry becoming involved in the Third World on the basis of mutual benefit with a give and take of knowledge about mental health. And so a sense of mutual respect may emerge between rich and poor, Western and non-Western, Black and White. An exchange of technology on an equal basis must be underpinned by an acceptance of cultural relativity of ideas about mental health and methods of dealing with mental ill health – and the concept of illness itself.

The restructuring of mental health at a personal level must be concerned with developing a universal psychology that is sufficiently flexible and free of racism to understand mental health and ill health cross-culturally. But if such a psychology is to be devised, the aim is not to build bridges between culturally distinct psychological–philosophical systems that are forever separate but to evolve strategies to promote interaction (between cultures) that result in a better understanding *on both sides*, so that culture will be a part of that understanding and not something that divides people.

At the practical level of working together, it could be envisaged, as Welwood (1979)[3] believes, that a combination of 'the experiential, holistic, and enlightenment-oriented traditions of the East with the precision, clarity, skepticism, and independence of Western methods could lead to a new kind of psychology that transcends cultural limitations'. But Welwood (ibid.) warns: 'Many Westerners seem to assume that they understand Eastern ideas if they can use the correct jargon and key phrases, while underestimating the radical changes in one's life orientation that the Eastern paths are pointing to'. He quotes Harvey Cox (1977)[4] as seeing the danger of Eastern ideas falling prey to Western 'consumer mentality' and greed for new experience: 'It could pervert them into Western mental-health grimmicks and thereby prevent them from introducing the sharply alternative vision of life they are capable of bringing to us'. Eastern psychotherapies are essentially ways of contemplative awareness but much of Western psychotherapy is directed towards problem solving or decision-making, reflecting the value given in Western thinking to personal self-sufficiency and control of events. What is called neurosis – an illness – can be a path to enlightenment for a Buddhist. An amalgamation seems unthinkable but Welwood (1979)[3] outlines the basis for one:

> In short, such a new approach in psychology, based on self-knowledge disciplines, would include the whole range of human consciousness in the study of human behaviour; from the automatic responses that behaviourism has studied, to the unconscious patterns that psychoanalysis brought to light, to the farthest reaches of human possibility that Maslow called self-transcendence. Such an encompassing approach might provide a meaningful context and framework for interpreting and guiding research in experimental and clinical psychology. It might also provide a secular framework in which people might begin to glimpse the possibility for a meaningful life beyond the confines of the isolated ego, and to realize a more ecological relationship with the world around them. This approach would not be a substitute for traditional spiritual paths, but might serve as a bridge to them, as well as a neutral meeting ground where practitioners of different self-knowledge disciplines

could come together and work out common understandings of human development as a conscious process.

Welwood's approach to the amalgamation of systems of psychology might be applied to the field of psychiatric research and theory. Self-knowledge may replace objective understanding as the basis of research and psychiatry may take on the study of consciousness, including altered states of consciousness, without identifying some states as pathological. Thus, for example, people who hear 'voices' or have intensely meaningful experiences will no longer be seen as pathologically 'hallucinated' or 'suffering' from symptoms of 'passivity feelings'; illness will relate to disturbances of balance – within individuals, families and societies in a context of their relationship with the universe. Religion and psychiatry will not be considered in separate compartments, but as one system that deals with all aspects of human existence.

In applying fundamental principles from theory to practical psychiatry in a world context, racist connotations and value judgements must be abolished: all cultures must be seen as equally valid and important; and communication between cultures must be freed from the barriers arising from racism and the power structure in the world. A generally open system of defining individual mental health in terms of balance must be accepted; a much 'loosened' psychiatric diagnostic system can be a special ethnocentric variant of this but other systems too must be accepted as equally valid. Once this is done, the need for ethnocentric practices should be faced because, in practical terms, cultures must continue to remain separate though equal in value. As communication is opened up and the interchange of ideas and methods of help-giving and help-seeking is promoted, the pragmatism of people the world over will make itself evident; people will give and take to evolve, eventually, a psychiatry that is culturally flexible and racially neutral. All this, of course, is an ideal. Its realisation depends not on the goodwill of practitioners alone, since psychiatry in Western countries, being tied to political systems, holds the power and the purse-strings. Until these shift or are shifted – and international organisations, such as the World Health Organisation, become truly globally sensitive, there is little likelihood of much change towards a world psychiatry.

Notes

1. World Health Organisation (1975) *Schizophrenia: A Multinational Study. A summary of the initial evaluation phase of the international pilot study of schizophrenia*, Geneva, WHO.
2. Schumacher, E.F. (1973) *Small is Beautiful: a study of economics as if people mattered*, London, Blond and Briggs.

3. Welwood, J. (ed.) (1979) *The Meeting of the Ways: explorations in east/west psychology*, New York, Schocken Books.
4. Cox, H. (1977) *Turning East: the promise and the peril of the new orientalism*, New York, Simon and Schuster.

8

Genetics – A Philosophy of Perfection?

ELIZABETH N. ANIONWU

Introduction

'With the introduction of population-based genetic screening programmes, many people will learn for the first time that everyone carries some abnormal genes, only some of which may harm either their own health or that of their actual or potential children. As details become known of the genetic basis of the more common diseases, such as cancer or heart disease, so genetic screening will expand to cover the detection of genes that influence the risk of developing these diseases.'[1] This paper examines some of the choices, risks and tensions that such expansion poses for lay people and professionals in the field of genetic health.

As the mortality associated with traditional childhood infectious diseases is lessened so the impact of individuals with genetic disorders becomes more apparent. This is highlighted in a recent report by the Royal College of Physicians[2] which notes that two to three per cent of couples are at high and recurrent risk of having children with an inherited disorder. It goes on to describe the need to develop community genetic services, involving population screening, counselling before, during or after pregnancy, and the management of abortion for fetal abnormality.

Table 8.1 focuses on four conditions that are relevant within multi-ethnic Britain, viz.: sickle-cell anaemia, thalassaemia, cystic fibrosis and Tay-Sachs disease. It shows that a significant number of people in virtually every ethnic group could be silent healthy carriers for one or more of these conditions. If their partner is also a carrier their children could then inherit the illness.

For these and many other conditions genetic technology has resulted in the possibility of:

(a) identifying those who are at risk of having children with certain genetic conditions and

(b) prenatal diagnosis – screening unborn babies to detect whether or not they have inherited a genetic disorder. The couple then have the choice of terminating affected pregnancies.

The resources allocated to the international Human Genome project demonstrates the considerable enthusiasm there is to speed up the discovery of the location of genes for conditions that have so far eluded the scientists. Major ethical dilemmas are posed by the different objectives that exist concerning the use of genetic technology in the field of screening and counselling.

Case study – sickle-cell anaemia

The following is an extract of a taped interview in 1981 with a mother of an affected child when she visited the Brent Sickle Cell Counselling Centre, the only such service in existence in Britain at this time.

'It started just over a year ago, when Julie was about two years of age. She had a temperature and I took her to the doctor. He said, "It's natural for a child of her age to have a temperature." But I insisted that she should have a blood or urine test. So he sent me down (for the blood test) and he diagnosed sickle-cell anaemia. He said, "It's sickle cell, which the majority of coloured people, black people have; and there is no cure." He just told me that. He said, "They can't do anything about it, but if she gets any funny symptoms I should try giving her Junior Disprin or aspirin and try to keep her warm; and that's about it." But she keeps on going in (to hospital) very often, with swollen legs and hands and pain in her tummy, which I couldn't understand, which they didn't really explain.

Sickle-cell anaemia can cause great pains and it's all different ways. She's off her food, she has pains in her joints and she gets urine infection pretty regular, or sometimes she passes blood with her urine. These are her symptoms. When she is getting the attack she goes very quiet, doesn't play with her sister; she just lies and wants to go to sleep and sometimes she wants water. Just water all the time. She doesn't want to eat or anything. Then the temperature begins and I know she's going funny.

(Before that) I had never heard anything about sickle-cell anaemia. It was only after the diagnosis that I was reading in the West Indian World paper about your Sickle Cell Centre in London. So my sister here in London advised me to come and get more advice about it and I put it off. I said, I can't do anything because here is Dr G telling me one thing and different people tell me another. Finally they persuaded me: if I didn't come to London my child would probably die on me and I would probably be blamed by the Welfare for not taking care of her. They should explain better how you can deal with it and where you can get advice. The doctor says there is nothing to worry about, but you do worry. You could scream. You could feel like hitting them over the head, if you know what I mean, but when you have the child 24 hours and they "Oh, Mummy, I'm this and that," it really gets you down.

I have had to come 60 miles to hear more about it (from the Sickle Cell Centre), which I don't think is right. I think it should be the GP that you turn to really.

No I'm going to go and see my doctor and have a word with him. I know you don't really think about these things until your child is ill but it's really terrible. You say "It couldn't be me because I'm never ill and my husband says it couldn't be him: and we're blaming each other, but there is none of us to blame really, it's just traits; we can't help it'.[3]

One in 10 of the African-Caribbean community is at risk of having children born with the illness, and this case history illustrates the lack of knowledge of the family and health professionals about the condition. The lack of information, tests and counselling add to the burden and guilt of the parents. This is despite the vast amount of knowledge about the condition contained within the scientific literature. As a result couples have been denied the opportunity to even discuss the implications in relation to their family's health and well-being.

It is ironic that a family affected by one of the most well-understood genetic conditions was not referred to a genetic counselling service. The failure of Regional Clinical Genetic Departments to encourage general practitioners, paediatricians and obstetricians to refer such families may be explained by the following quotation from a textbook on genetic counselling published in 1976: 'Sickle-cell anaemia is not of great consequence to us in the context of genetic counselling in the United Kingdom. The sickling trait and sickle-cell anaemia appear to be confined to people of African and Eastern origin'[4] (see Table 8.1)

Details gathered about this case history revealed gaps in health service provision that exacerbated the stress to the family and left their daughter vulnerable to severe and possible fatal complications in early childhood before the diagnosis was made. In addition various choices open to the couple were denied due to a failure to provide information at particular periods. The background to this complex decision-making process is described by parents of children with sickle-cell disorders resident in Newham, East London.[5]

'I had to make up my mind on what I really wanted. I had to have a lot of discussion with my husband... we had to agree, disagree, ... it's not something I would like someone to go through. At that point I knew there was no way I could face two sickle-cell sufferers... You have to wait about 2 weeks... then they just ring you up over the phone and tell you... and then even when you get the result, you don't know what to do, do you go ahead and have the termination? I had a lot of fighting to do with my conscience.'

TABLE 8.1   Frequency of various recessively inherited conditions

Condition	Ethnic group	Carrier frequency
Cystic fibrosis	White British	1 in 25
	Pakistanis	1 in 50*
Tay-Sachs disease	Ashkenazy Jews	1 in 25
	Non-Jewish	1 in 250
Haemoglobinopathies		
Thalassaemia	Cypriots	1 in 7
	Asians	1 in 10 to 30
	Chinese	1 in 30
	Afro-Caribbeans	1 in 50
	White British	1 in 1,000
Sickle-cell trait	Afro-Caribbeans	1 in 10
	West Africans	up to 1 in 4
C trait	Afro-Caribbeans	1 in 30
	Ghanaians	up to 1 in 6
D trait	Punjabi Sikhs	1 in 100

Note: Certain genes for haemoglobinopathies are also found in ethnic groups not listed above, e.g.:
Sickle-cell trait: in those originating from Asia, the Mediterranean and the Middle East.
D trait: found in various other ethnic groups including White British.
*Personal communication from Dr Bernadette Modell.

'I felt, we'd coped with (my daughter) so I could cope with another. I wanted the baby anyway. (After the child was tested) I was very worried waiting for the letter (with the result) to come.'

He did not have the disease.

The variable severity and unpredictable nature of sickle-cell anaemia add to the difficulties of couples contemplating the dilemma of whether they would wish to consider terminating an affected pregnancy. The Brent experience is that approximately 50 per cent of couples at risk of a child with sickle-cell anaemia offered the test during pregnancy accept and 50 per cent refuse.

Objectives of genetic screening and counselling

On the one hand there is the view that the objective must be to prevent the births of children with genetic disorders.

'This philosophy of perfection opens up all sorts of dangerous avenues and we will have to be extremely careful about the choice and education of genetic counsellors in the future'.[6] According to Katz-Rothman[7] the history of pre-natal diagnosis has roots in the eugenics movement in that 'it has been an attempt to control the gates of life: to decide who is, and who is not, fit to make a contribution to the "gene pool", whose seed is worth passing on. Thus began eugenics.' In reviewing the eugenics movement Weatherall notes that 'ever since the birth of the science of human genetics the idea of improving the human race in one way or another has never been far below the surface'.[6]

The most extreme example of eugenics occurred in Nazi Germany with Mengele's experiments, sterilisations and slaughter in the pursuit of the pure Aryan race. Harper[8] has recently reminded the medical profession that many presently working in the field of medical genetics 'are ignorant of the past abuse of our subject. It is easy to regard the excesses of the eugenics movement or the abuses in Nazi Germany, as disconnected from present day medical genetics, but a closer look at these chapters show that their key feature was the subordination of individual decisions to the broader based population goals.'

The other view concerning the objectives of genetic information is that individuals must be allowed to decide for themselves whether to accept the offer of information, screening and termination of affected pregnancies. Lappe *et al.*[9] established the following goals for screening:

— to contribute to improving the health of persons who suffer from genetic disorders
— to allow those that are carriers for a given variant gene to make informed choices regarding reproduction
— to move towards alleviating the anxieties of families and communities faced with the prospect of serious genetic disease.

Harper[10] has defined genetic counselling as 'the process by which patients or relatives at risk of a disorder that may be hereditary are advised of the probability of developing and transmitting it and of the ways in which this may be prevented or ameliorated.' He goes on to stress that 'it is also important that those giving genetic counselling do not judge "success" or "failure" in terms of a particular outcome, and that they give support to families whatever their decisions may be.'

Clarke[11] appears to have touched a raw nerve in asking 'Is non-directive genetic counselling possible?' The very offer of pre-natal diagnosis, he claims, implies a recommendation to accept that offer, which in turn 'entails a tacit recommendation to terminate a pregnancy if it is found to show any abnormality. I believe that this sequence is present irrespective of the counsellor's wishes, thought, or feelings, because it arises from the social context rather than from the person-alities involved – although naturally the counsellor may reinforce these factors.'

He questions how clinical geneticists decide which disorders justify pre-natal diagnosis and termination of pregnancy and suggests the adoption of criteria based on broad social considerations, e.g. profound retardation, very severe physical handicap or the prospect of prolonged physical suffering. The subsequent correspondence from five pro-fessionals in the field of clinical genetics eloquently highlighted the complex dilemmas and disagreements that exist in this area.

Pembrey[12] argues that the 'transfer of information inevitably transfers responsibility, and this additional responsibility can be a great burden, but I do not agree that medical geneticists should draw an agreed line between the acceptable and the unacceptable. They are not up to it. The ideal is for the decision makers to be well informed on the genetic and medical facts, to know all the social circumstances and the strengths and weaknesses of those being called on to cope, to be able to assess the impact on other family members, and to be so concerned as to ponder their decision day and night, free at all times to call on the help of friends and professionals. Only the couple themselves, properly supported, can begin to meet those criteria.' In view of all these complex issues it is not surprising that some individuals prefer not to make use of screening opportunities. Kaback[13] supports them: 'While this may appear "anti-intellectual", it is clear that one must protect against subtle or even overt coercion forcing people to submit to a carrier screening test.'

The experience of those at risk of the inherited red blood cell disorder sickle-cell anaemia highlights some of the complex issues involved in developing sensitive genetic screening and counselling services. It is a useful example for the following reasons:

— The molecular basis of sickle-cell anaemia was recognised as far back as 1956.[14]
— A relatively simple blood test will detect those healthy carriers who are at risk of producing children with the disorder.
— It is possible to test the unborn baby from as early as nine weeks in the pregnancy. However there are considerable dilemmas for a couple trying to decide what to do as the condition is extremely variable. Whilst the majority of affected individuals now survive well into adulthood there are still deaths in younger people.[15] In addition the quality of life can be affected by episodes of excruciat-ing pains, serious infections and complications that can occasionally occur such as strokes, loss of vision and problems in the lungs, hips and shoulders.[16]

— It mainly affects people whose ancestors originated from parts of the world where malaria was endemic, e.g. Africa, the Eastern Mediterranean, Asia and the Middle East. Thus, in this country, the majority of the population who are at risk of having children with this condition are black and minority ethnic groups. It is therefore possible to consider the impact of ethnocentrism and racism in relation to the priority given to developing sensitive services.

Conclusion

The burden of genetic knowledge requires that families have access to information and support. Sickle-cell anaemia is but one example and has been used to illustrate some of the difficult issues faced by families at the receiving end of genetic screening. 'They should do the screening, it's a good idea. . . but you can't explain it to somebody just like that – and it's no good giving them leaflets, because people take leaflets and put them down, get on with their housework, kids throw away the leaflet. So they should give them another appointment for them, specifically to give them half an hour and explain it in *simple* terms. . . . They'll have to put more people into it and pay them'.[5]

My own experience, spanning more than a decade, of identifying needs and developing counselling services for sickle-cell disorders has demonstrated the complex issues involved. The idea that people may still decide to have affected children in the face of known genetic risk is seen as irresponsible in certain quarters. On the other hand, others are unhappy that couples should choose to terminate an affected pregnancy for an illness that is unpredictable and variable in severity. I would endorse Harper's view that 'Any applications of genetics in public health need to retain the respect for the autonomy of individuals and for the inevitable variation in decisions that people make'.[8]

Notes

1. Marteau, T.M. (1992) 'Psychological implications of genetic screening', pp. 263–73 in Evers-Kiebooms, *et al.* (eds) *Psychosocial Aspects of Genetic Counselling*, New York, Wiley.
2. Royal College of Physicians (1989) *Prenatal Diagnosis and Genetic Screening: community and service implications*. London, RCP.
3. Anionwu, E.N. (1989) 'Running a sickle cell centre: community counselling', Chapter 14, pp. 123–30 in Anionwu, E.N., *Ethnic Factors in Health & Disease*, London, Wright.
4. Stevenson, A.C. and Davison, B.C.C. (1976) *Genetic Counselling*, p. 274, London, Heinemann.

5. Black, J. and Laws, S. (1986) p. 365, p. 180, *Living with Sickle Cell Disease*, London, Sickle Cell Society.
6. Weatherall, D.J. (1991) p. 353, *The New Genetics and Clinical Practice*, Oxford University Press.
7. Katz-Rothman, B. (1988) p. 33, *The Tentative Pregnancy. Prenatal Diagnosis and the Future of Motherhood*, London, Pandora.
8. Harper, P. (1992) 'Genetics and public health', *British Medical Journal*, Vol. 304, p. 721.
9. Lappe, M., Gustafson, J.M. and Robin, R. (1972) 'Ethical and social issues in screening for genetic disease', *New England Journal of Medicine*, **286**(21), pp. 1129–31.
10. Harper, P.S. (1988) *Practical Genetic Counselling*, 3rd edn, London, Wright.
11. Clarke, A. (1991) 'Is non-directive counselling possible?' *The Lancet*, **338**, p. 998.
12. Pembrey, M.E. (1991) 'Letters to the Editor', *The Lancet*, **338**, pp. 1266–7.
13. Kaback, M.M. (1982) p. 249, 'The control of genetic disease by carrier screening and antenatal diagnosis: social, ethical and medicolegal issues', *Birth Defects: Original Article Series*, pp. 243–54.
14. Ingram, V.M. (1956) 'A specific chemical difference between the globins of normal human and sickle-cell anaemia haemoglobin' *Nature*, **178**, pp. 792–4.
15. Gray, A., Anionwu, E.N., Davies, S.C. and Brozovic, M. (1991) 'Patterns of mortality in sickle cell disease in the United Kingdom', *Journal of Clinical Pathology*, **44**, pp. 459–63.
16. Serjeant, G.R. (1985) *Sickle Cell Disease*, Oxford University Press.

9

Concepts in Alternative Medicine*

C.W. AAKSTER

Introduction

Medical sociologists are gradually becoming aware that at least two realities exist within Western health practice: the official and the unofficial, the legal and the illegal, the bright, scientific and heroic hospital doctor vs the unscientific therapist or quack. This article intends to explore the scientific and societal position of the latter.

Main alternative approaches

In this section we discuss the main alternative approaches, at least in The Netherlands, in two respects. A short outline of the technical aspects is followed by consideration of its – assumed – theoretical and philosophical backgrounds.

Acupuncture

In acupuncture it is assumed that the human body possesses 12 meridians whose main function is to transport energy. Upon them we find about 950 points which are connected with internal organs. The notion is that by inserting small silver needles into these points and manipulating them, the energy-balance may be influenced and, by so doing, the disease may be cured. As the acupuncture points are specific, it is essential that the needles are inserted into the right (combination of)

---

*This is an abridged version of an article that was first published in *Social Science and Medicine*, Vol. 22, No. 2, pp. 265–273, 1986.

points. The stimulation may be done manually, by electric means, by moxa burning or by pressure techniques. Diagnosis is arrived at by means of the acupuncture points and the sophisticated art of pulse-reading.

A most interesting aspect of its underlying philosophy is the principle of Yin and Yang. Both are distinctive but unseparable poles of the life energy Tsji (= pneuma, prana or spiritus vitalis). They are involved in an ongoing dance, they presuppose the existence of each other, together they maintain a dynamic balance, neither of them being better or more valuable than the other. The life energy Tsji is acquired at birth and supplemented by breathing and food-intake. The principle of a dynamic balance between two poles of the same underlying phenomenon has been described as a characteristic feature of the (old?) Chinese way of thinking, and contains a fundamental difference compared to Western thinking. The latter usually holds one of the poles to be the better one: masculinity is better than feminity, quantity is better than quality, material is better than immaterial, objective is better than subjective, body is better than mind (e.g. Jung[1] and Van Dijk and Aakster[2]).

In acupuncture, illness is seen as a dysbalance of Yin and Yang which may be restored by adding or distracting energy from the diseased organs. In its classical interpretation, this is done in combination with dietary advices, physical exercise, massage, etc.

Homeopathy

Hahnemann's 'Similia Similibus Curentur' became a world famous adage. It points to the principle, already acknowledged by Hippocrates, that the disease may be cured by means that cause similar symptoms in healthy persons. Thus, therapeutic drugs are developed, mostly on a herbal base, by observing their main features when administered to healthy persons. A second characteristic of homeotherapy is that it tries to restore the self-healing potential of the organism. To this end it works with the lowest possible dose that is able to provoke a reaction in the organism, expressed in terms of D_1, D_2, D_3, ... Dn, which relates to first, second, third to n-order dilutions. These dilutions are prepared by a special way of shaking, the 'potentializing process'. Homeopathy tries to arrive at a total-diagnosis of the person, in which the limited symptomatology of official medicine is extended into the realms of constitution, mental functioning, the body's reactions to food, to sudden changes in temperature and so on.

Though amazing effects have been observed by the application of homeopathy, its theoretical base remains largely hidden and is the object of bitter polemics, even within the bosom of homeopathy itself.

Naturopathy

The naturopathic physician dedicates himself to restoring or stimulating the ability of the person to heal himself. The person is approached as a whole, living in continuous interaction and exchange with his environment, whose integrity may be challenged by unhealthy ways of eating, breathing, relaxing and so on. Disease is essentially the consequence of a disbalance of vitalizing and disruptive forces, which cause the organism to form auto-toxic or otherwise useless residues in the body, the so-called homotoxines hypothesis. At first the physician will try to clear the body of these homotoxines (by means of fasting or – even more drastically – provoked vomiting or the application of lavements). As a second step the vitalizing forces are strengthened by a strictly natural diet (whole foods only, no smoking, no alcohol, no meat, preferably raw vegetables and juices, etc.) and physical exercises. These measures may be supported by hydrotherapy, massage, herbal medicines, blood letting, etc.

In its diagnosis, naturopathy interprets symptoms as signs of the regulation and restoration process the organism is engaged in. The driving force behind all this is 'nature', the principle that lends unity to everything that exists. It is the natural forces in the diseased person that should be strengthened, it is the natural means and life habits that should cure him.

Manual therapies

Under this heading we include osteopathy, chiropractics and certain types of other manual therapies. Generally speaking, these therapies concentrate on the spinal column and the stature of the person. Many, if not all diseases are believed to be caused by, at least related to deformations of or jammed nerves/arteries within the area of the spinal column. The therapeutic approach is mainly mechanical. Diagnosis is based upon information about the movement-pattern; diseases are interpreted as the result of a complex of factors, which drive the internal system out of balance.

Anthroposophical medicine

This type of medicine is based upon the ideas of the German philosopher Rudolph Steiner. It considers itself as an addition to regular medicine, rather than as an alternative. Anthroposophical medicine distinguishes between body, mind and soul, and tries to influence the three of them simultaneously in case of illness. Illnesses are interpreted as attempts of the person to re-establish harmony between the self and its (cosmic) surroundings. In therapy, regular and anthroposophical remedies are combined with expressive therapy, massages and other natural therapies.

Other characteristic features of this approach are: the assumption that the individual human being and cosmic factors are related, the belief that the soul reincarnates, the conviction that mental forces are superior to physical ones, the idea that illness is the result of a disturbance of the balance between vitalizing and disruptive forces.

Paranormal medicine

This type of medicine is also known as Mesmerism or magnetism, or (slightly different) spiritual healing. The typical treatment exists in striking movements with the hands, by the therapist, close to but not on the body surface, especially at the sides where the disease has been located. The therapist may get information from the patient by clairvoyance. The mechanism is unexplained. Some therapists believe that they are the instrument by which cosmic energies are transmitted to the person, and to the diseased organs in particular. Healing at a distance (e.g. by concentrating on a picture of the patient) is said to occur regularly. One approaches the patient as a whole person, who is closely interconnected with his material and immaterial surroundings.

Mental therapies

Some of the better known of these are bioenergetics, Gestalt therapy, bio-release, re-birthing, unitive psychology, alfa-training, autogenic training.

According to Capra,[3] academic psychology still functions within the Cartesian schism of body and mind. The newer, alternative approaches transcend this age-long schism, they approach the world as a whole, and the person as a whole person, in whom physical and mental forces are almost inseparable. In doing so these approaches transcend determinism. Self-renewance and self-transcendance are important phenomena (Capra). They often work with methods of deep relaxation, in order that hidden and repressed tensions will be released and the person will become aware of his real self (however, see Schur[4] for a critical evaluation). Deep breathing is essential in many of these approaches to arrive at a relaxed state, suggesting a relationship to the concept of vital energy in yoga and acupuncture.

This short presentation of some of the more important fascinating new (= old) approaches in health care give an impression of the various thoughts and practices in this field (also see *The Alternative Health Guide*).[5]

Concepts in alternative medicine

Concepts are more than just words or building blocks of theories; they represent the observer's image of reality. This becomes very clear if we compare some of the concepts that are in use in regular, official or orthodox medicine, with their use in alternative medicine, as will be done below.

Health

Conventional medicine has considerable trouble in defining health. The development of a theory of health and of its determining forces, lagged behind that of the development of theories of diseases and their management. Apparently, this has been due to a preoccupation with disease in regular medicine; health is taken to be a deviance from disease.[6]

Conversely, alternative approaches are much more directed toward maintaining health, with illness regarded as a deviation from health. In these approaches, health is a balance of opposing forces: the life-building, constructive, vitalizing, positive forces or energies on the one hand, and the destructive, negative, disruptive and ill forces on the other hand. A constant and dynamic interplay between the two exists. Capra[3] speaks of an 'eternal dance'. This dynamic balance is maintained in a continuous interaction between man and his environment. If a person wants to be healthy, he should take care of his daily food intake, his physical movement pattern, a right balance between tension and relaxation, the right way of breathing, his mental attitude and so on (and influencing the environmental conditions). This is clearly expressed in ayurvedic medicine from ancient India, whose principles became known in the West via yoga and (other) meditation practices.

Disease

Conventional medicine has no general theory of disease and its development/management. It has theories on the development of mental illness, of infectious diseases, of coronary heart disease, but none of disease in general. A general state of illness does not officially exist, notwithstanding the fact that on two occasions I have found empirical evidence for such a general state;[7] also Moss' concept of general susceptibility seems to point to such a general state. It is interesting to compare this view with the approach of the German naturopathic physician Reckeweg.[8] Reckeweg's ideas (the homotoxine hypothesis) were developed on the basis of general system theory.[9] Illness is a biologically appropriate reaction of the organism, in order to get rid of the homotoxines (auto-toxic substances or residues). According to Reckeweg, the organism uses six defence-levels with increasing severity and threat for the integrity of the whole body. In cases of threat or an imbalance or overload, the organism's first reaction will be to employ the normal excretion channels to get rid of the homotoxines: kidneys, lungs, menstrual blood, catarrh. The second and third phases' are termed reaction and deposition phases. The fourth to sixth phases lead to irreversible tissue changes: penetration, degeneration and neoplasmic. Always, Reckeweg argues, the organism first uses the lowest levels of defence before it falls back upon higher, more complex and radical defences. One can recognize from the type of defences that the organism employs which phase of progression the disease process has reached, and which therapeutic strategies are indicated. The alternative cancer-approaches of Moerman, Gerson and Issels[10] seem to support these views of Reckeweg. In these theories the appearance of tumours is interpreted as the last phase in a long process of increasing dysbalance in the human organism especially of its metabolic system.

Diagnosis

Diagnosis is a holy matter in conventional medicine. The emphasis on identifiable signs and symptoms of a local character, can be explained historically as follows: when in 1560 Vesalius for the first time – at least in public – broke the taboo on opening a human corpse, he made it possible to investigate the deformations in organs that correspond to certain illnesses. It was discovered that different diseases correspond to different deviations in organs, and the need arose to classify these different diseases and to develop the art of diagnosis.

The type of diagnosis that regular medicine produces may be termed 'morphological', while the type of diagnosis in alternative medicine is more functional. In several alternative approaches we notice a lesser preoccupation with diagnosis (in the morphological sense); the diagnostic procedures rest more upon 'body language', frequently used techniques are those of iris-diagnosis, acupuncture points, stature, tenseness of musculature, dietary habits, pulse reading, mental blocks, constitution-type, though regular diagnostic measures are also relied upon. But the predominance of computerized output as in regular clinical medicine, is quite uncommon in alternative medicine. The total person's evaluation comes in the place of matching symptom complexes with diagnostic categories on the basis of 'objective' data.

Therapy

Two different though not mutually exclusive therapeutic strategies are the following, assuming that disease may be interpreted as the result of an imbalance between vitalizing and destructive forces. Strategy one is: destroy, or at least suppress, the demolishing or sickening forces. Strategy two is: strengthen the vitalizing forces. In both cases the result is the same (theoretically speaking): restoration of the (dynamic) balance. It is easy to see that most chemical drugs, surgical measures, and radiation, attempt to destroy the sickening forces, while several of the alternative approaches explicitly aim at strengthening the vitalizing, health-promoting forces.

This, together with the morphological organ-based definition of disease as – often implicitly – applied by conventional medicine, has important consequences.

For if a disease is something with a non-understandable Latin name, which can only be measured by experts and which can only be cured by doctors, who know the solutions, the doctor is by definition someone who should have had at least 7 years of university training, a man (rather than a woman) with great authority (expertness), who takes the lead in the patient's problem-solving. If, however, diagnosis is of the functional type, and the therapeutic measures are of a rather simple nature and require the full and active co-operation of the patient (a profound change of dietary habits, regular exercise, etc.) then medicine becomes more manageable. It reverts to the patient and may lead to deprofessionalization, by merely emphasizing basic rules for healthy living, the responsibility of the patient, explaining things in common language, seeing the person as in integrated whole, as the patient sees himself. In many cases (homeopathy, naturopathy) curing aims at strengthening the healing forces of the organism. In other words: alternative therapies often work indirectly, they seek to defeat disease by strengthening the whole person's resistance/defence/immunity.

The patient

Talcott Parsons described the ideal patient of conventional medicine, the one who does not ask questions and follows orders. When it became clear that not all patients followed this pattern, medical sociologists used the term 'compliance'. In mental health and general practice more subtle forms of persuasion came into use ('patient participation') but, in alternative medicine, the position of the patient really is different. In traditional China, as in traditional India, the doctor served the patient, not the other way around. In naturopathy the same principle is advocated. The patient is expected to cure himself, the doctor is his adviser. And this is the only way it can be, in naturopathy, because no one other than the patient himself, can change his dietary habits, his distorted movement pattern, or attitude toward life and illness. Granted, there are exceptions on both sides, but what we want to emphasize is that it follows from a functional definition of illness and a reliance upon health-promoting forces in therapy, that the position of the patient is basically of a more mature type than when disease (treatment) is mainly a matter of experts versus lay people who know nothing.

Why alternative is alternative

Considering the fact that conventional medicine imposes its method of scientific proof (which itself has methodological, theoretical, practical and ethical shortcomings) on alternative medicine – even without a willingness to seriously discuss alternative methods – the question arises: why? Why does conventional medicine require that the alternative and more holistic approaches have to be tested by its own analytical methods?

According to Feyerabend[11] a natural tendency exists to believe and support theories that have once proved to be successful. Each finding that supports the theory reinforces the strength of the belief and a disregard for alternatives. Therefore, one invests energy and resources in the existing theory at the expense of serious alternatives.[12] In so doing, the theory becomes more of a religion or ideology. In order to gain respect for any alternative therapy or theory, the evidence must be excellent, better than for established theory. For this reason Feyerabend defends a climate of intellectual freedom without prescribing strict rules, for only in such a liberal climate can new intellectual developments fully profit. One example of an unexpected outcome from the free confrontation of old and new ideas/experience quoted by Feyerabend, is the rediscovery of acupuncture in China. Interestingly, he sees a clear association between politics and science. On the one hand the political establishment may support the medical establishment and vice versa: on the other hand, government may take the lead in creating a climate of open competition of official and non-official ideas.

Also of special interest, however, are the insights of Capra.[13] He argues that in Western culture, and thus in the history of science, a certain undulation can be recognized in the dominant way of thinking: rationalism or mysticism. Mysticism prevailed until, let us say, Hippocrates, then we saw about six ages of rationalism (Greek and Roman), thereafter came the middle ages with their strong mystical features. Until the Englightenment (Descartes, Locke, Hume) started off present-day rationalism. Capra compares this to the Chinese way of thinking in which rational and mystical, quantitative and qualitative, masculine and feminine aspects are recognized as two essential aspects or components, neither of them being 'better' than the other. In other words, the Chinese would never let male values dominate female values. This, however, is what happened in the Western world. Therefore, we have a strong, dominating, 'aggressive' medical technology, nuclear power, environmental pollution, alienation. Capra's plea points to the need for a deep change in our values, ways of thinking and dominant institutions, in order that a new equilibrium may be attained among male and female values, rational and intuitive ways of interpreting reality, culture and nature.

Alternative medicine's contributions to future health care

What can alternative medicine contribute to the fulfilment of current and future health (care) needs?

First, it is important that we wish to *learn*. If we are not critical, if we do not constantly ask what is the benefit to people of our splendid societal institutions, we shall never be able to help solve these problems.

Secondly, alternative approaches bring us back to the existential base of human suffering. No longer should illness be approached as a technical problem for which technical means are fitted, but as a human problem to be solved by human means, both at the individual level (awareness, lifestyle) and on the societal level (health conditions for life: income, housing, food, air, peace).

Thirdly, alternative approaches bring back into our care system simplicity, safety, individual responsibility and autonomy.

Fourthly, it may be expected that the application of alternative approaches, with their emphasis on health-strenghening forces and life-style, means that our expensive, highly complex and almost unmanageable health systems might be replaced by a more horizontally organized, smaller professional care-system, of lower complexity on a reduced scale.

Finally, we need to redefine concepts like health, disease, diagnosis, cure, in order to build up a new health system. This requires that we redefine reality.

Notes

1. Jung, C.G. 'Introduction' *I Tjing* Ankh-Hermes, Deventer, 1977. (English title: *The I Ching or Book of Changes*. Routledge & Kegan Paul, London.)
2. Dijk, P.A. van and Aakster, C.W. *Literatuuronderzoek alternatieve geneeswijzen*. VAR-reeks 1980, No. 3, Ministerium of Welfare, Health Care and Culture, Kleidschendam, Netherlands.
3. Capra, F. *The Turning Point – Science, Society and the Rising Culture*. Wildwood House, London, 1982.
4. Schur, E. *The Awareness Trap – Self-Absorption Instead of Social Change*. Quadrangle/The New York Times Book Co., 1976.

5. Inglis, B. and West, R. *The Alternative Health Guide*. Michael Joseph, London, 1983.
6. Exemplified in Caplan, A.L., Engelhardt, H.T. and McCartney, J.J. *Concepts of Health and Disease – Interdisciplinary Perspectives*. Addison-Wesley, London, 1981.
7. Aakster, C.W. Sociocultural variables in the etiology of health disturbances – a sociological approach. Thesis, Univeristy of Groningen, 1972; Moss, G.E. *Illness, Immunity and Social Interaction – The Dynamics of Biosocial Resonation*. Wiley, New York, 1973. The general factor may be better identified by the centroid method than by the principal components analysis, according to Harman, H.H. *Modern Factor Analysis*. The University of Chicago Press, 1960.
8. As discussed by Stiekema in Haan, H. de and Dijk, P.A. van. *Niet-universitaire geneeswijzen*. Ankh-Hermes, Deventer and Intermediair, Amsterdam, 1978.
9. The same starting point is defended in Aakster 1972 and 1974, and in Capra, 1982, see Notes 3 and 7.
10. Issels, J. *Ganzheitstherapie der Malignome*. Gesellschaft der Arzte für Erfahrungsheilkunde e.v., Heidelberg 1973 (?); Haught, S.J. *Has Dr Max Gerson a True Cancer Cure?* Major Books, Calif., 1978; Moerman, C. *Kanker als gevolg van onvolwaardige voeding kan genezen dor dieet en therapie* Ankh-Hermes, Deventer, 1978.
11. Feyerabend, P. *In strijd met de methode – aanzet tot een anarchistische kennis-theorie*. Boom, Meppel, 1977. (Original title: *Against Method*, New Left Books, London, 1975.)
12. Lally, for example, highlights the mechanisms that underlie the differential allocation of research money in case of crib death and juvenile cancer. Lally, J.J. Social determinants of differential allocation of resources to disease research, *J. Hlth soc. Behav.* **18**, pp. 125–138, 1977.
13. Capra, F. *The Tao of Physics*, Fontana Collins, London, 1978; also Note 3.

10

The Myth of Alternative Health*

ROSALIND COWARD

The widespread acceptance of alternative therapies marks profound changes in attitudes towards health and the body. Alternative therapies are based on a new philosophy of the body, health, and nature, a new philosophy which has somehow managed to capture or echo popular consciousness. Its central tenets are the beneficial healing powers of nature, natural energies, the possibility and desirability of the whole person, and the importance of attending to the inner 'ecology' of the body, primarily through the medium of food. Interest in alternative therapies rarely stops at using one particular therapy to deal with an ailment when allopathic medicine has failed. The interest invariably extends into a wholehearted adoption of these philosophical concepts.

Within alternative therapies true well-being is linked to views of liberating natural health, and finding a balance of energies. Its rewards will be the possibility of healing in a sick society, either in the form of fighting off illness or in a more mystical sense of a transformed and well person. A healthy equilibrium is thought to involve emotional and mental levels, the involvement of the whole personality. Increasingly, even for those not directly involved with alternative therapies, these are the meanings which are coming to dominate contemporary notions and expectations of health. Health is 'well-being', a state to be won back or achieved. It will involve the whole of ourselves and be our salvation but its success will be our personal responsibility.

People's expectations of health, and their sense of personal involvement in it have changed. So too have beliefs about how much they can exercise conscious 'choice' over health and disease. Even the conception of disease has changed: disease is no longer seen as either the curse of mankind or as a completely arbitrary phenomenon. Instead disease and

---

*This is an abridged extract from Coward, R. (1990) *The Whole Truth*, Faber and Faber.

well-being are both seen as having direct personal 'meanings'. And through the notion of holism, with its implicit privileging of the mind over the body, the 'meaning' of disease is more often than not in the individual's state of mind.

'Holism' is the great strength of the alternative health movement. The claim is that, unlike conventional medicine, holistic approaches see health as the well-being of the whole person, and therefore not just a fit body, but a well mind or spirit. Holism has wondrous associations. It conjures up visions of a medicine which is preventive, gentle, and natural. This is an approach to the body that will not assault, attack or maim. Holism suggests that possibility of integration, of feeling that all parts of ourselves belong to the same essential person and have meaning in relation to one another. Holism has almost religious connotations, suggesting that the whole person can be found and that, when it is, the individual will be healed. Yet this profound conviction that lying within each and every one of us is the kernel of a whole person is not without its own problems. Quite apart from the fact that the idea of a whole person might be a fantasy, there is a way in which the attempt at integrating all parts of a person to one central core has eased the way for a potentially highly moralistic approach to health. In the idea of the whole person, the possibility that an individual has control over health and the possibility that an individual is to be blamed for disease often shade into one another.

Why exactly have beliefs about the body and health changed and what is it that these new philosophies appear to satisfy? Why are they so popular? To answer these questions involves pulling out the recurrent themes of this philosophy and trying to understand their appeal.

One simple answer is that alternative therapies make explicit – and give a theory to – the absolute centrality which the body and health have acquired in our consciousness. Attending to health and well-being has become a major cultural obsession and alternative therapies satisfy something of the sense that we should be 'committed' to our bodies and our health; they cater for the sense that even 'the worried well' should be doing something definite for their health. This new commitment to the body's well-being is far from nebulous; it involves a new sense of the body. Our knowledge of the body has been infinitely extended. We now have before us a whole inner geography, an inner ecology to which we must attend by changing our diets, our posture, and even our attitudes. To some extent commentators are right when they attribute this new and detailed concern with the body's health to the 'privileges' of a society which has high standards of living and hygiene so that it can both permit such introspection and contemplate a society without disease. But the concern is also something far more.

This new concern with the body is a place where people can express dissatisfaction with contemporary society *and* feel they are doing something personally to resist the encroachments of that society. Indeed, so strong is the sense of social criticism in this health movement that many adherents proclaim they are the avant-garde of a quiet social revolution. Yet the journey to this social revolution is rarely a journey towards social rebellion but more often an inner journey, a journey of personal transformation. The quest for natural health has come to be the focus of a new morality where the individual is encouraged to exercise personal control over disease. And the principal route to this control is the route to a 'changed consciousness' and changed life style. With this emphasis on changing consciousness have come all the fantasies and projections associated with religious morality, fantasies of wholeness, of integration and of the individual as origin of everything good or bad in their life. And with these fantasies there has mushroomed the industry of 'humanistic psychotherapies' emphasizing the role of the individual will-power in making changes.

There is nothing particularly new about the body being the focus of a personal morality in Western societies. But previously it was through sexuality that individuals were required to look into themselves, make decisions about how to use their body and find their true worth. It was around sexual behaviour that erstwhile religious concepts like guilt, sin, self-denial and joy continued to live on in the person. And it was in sexuality and sexual behaviour that the individual was called upon to exercise the greatest degree of self-determination, to make choices about behaviour.

It is clearly difficult for a society like ours to abandon the moral categories of Christianity and especially to abandon the requirement that an individual should 'prove' his or her worth through exercising some control over their body. Even though the contemporary health movement emphasizes the integration of body and mind there can be little doubt that these new attitudes conceal a morality where the individual is meant to 'choose' between positive and negative states, right and wrong. The morality may not be very obvious. It is not after all a case of prescriptions as to what we should or should not do. Even so, the contemporary health movement is riddled with the dualism which so typifies Christian views of morality. Instead of good and evil we now have the oppositions between modern society and nature, between disease and health. These two forces carry all the attributes previously located in the terms 'good' and 'evil'. To pursue a natural life style and diet is to find yourself on the side of the 'whole', the integrated, balanced and healing forces of nature. Above all, it is to be on the side of the 'healthy'. To ignore natural laws is to side with the fragmented, the inharmonious, with modern 'mass' society, with junk, technology and destruction. Ultimately it is an alliance with disease. The individual must choose between these forces, between the life-giving forces of nature and the destructive forces of the modern world. And the sign of the choice we make is 'health'. The opposition between health and disease is a profound oppostion between wholeness and fragmentation, between conflict and peace.

But why should individuals, recently freed from the sense of damnation which surrounded them in religion or in sexuality, immediately succumb to a new philosophy in which the body is seen to express their personal will? The answer lies precisely in the term which I have just used. Personal will. We live in a society which believes that the individual is responsible for his or her actions and indeed that the individual is ultimately responsible for whatever happens to her in society, whether she succeeds or fails. This is the legacy of Protestant Christianity with its belief that the salvation of the individual depends on his or her own actions. And these views are still deeply held by our society even though organized religion does not appear to dominate our consciousness. Conservative politicians may try and convince us that society has been weakened by socialist theories which let individuals off the hook by 'blaming' the structure of society for social ills. But the fact is that 'moralistic' views of the individual have never really been shaken. The revival of political Conservatism in Britain merely gave new life to these views which remain the dominant personal ethics in Western societies.

There had been a moment in the early 1970s when, intellectually at least, there was a serious challenge to this ethic of the free individual responsible for his or her own fate. In the wake of Freud many people were prepared to consider that the individual was riven by unconscious contradictions, and that the possibility of changing our life by an effort of will was an illusion. What is more, Marxist-influenced ideas which located the ills of society firmly in the social structure were enjoying a temporary prevalence. These argue that whole classes of people are structurally disadvantaged in a society based on competition for resources and the control of resources in the hands of a few. Although these ideas never gained ascendancy there was nevertheless a growth in state services – education, health, and services for the elderly and the disabled – where society seemed to acknowledge a sense of *social* responsibility, a sense that it was not simply up to individuals to secure their fate. But by the end of the 1970s those new departures were well under attack. Conservative politics were able to take up and articulate all the social problems of the day and blame them on the 'nanny state' and the breakdown of the sense of individual responsibility for their actions. Political Conservatism gave new wind to the idea of individuals as entirely in control of their actions and responsible for their good or bad fortune.

What happened to medicine and attitudes towards health seems symptomatic of what happened at a more general political level. Several criticisms of conventional medicine converged, criticisms which were then hegemonized by a new philosophy of the body and personal responsibility. Conventional medicine in the post-war period was ripe for criticism. There was a growing awareness of the 'inhumanity' of conventional health care. Increasingly people realized that some of the major events of life – birth, illness and death – have been horrendously mismanaged in a society where status and profit predominated. People have found themselves caring for sick and dying relatives and friends without support from the medical profession. Perhaps medical institutions actively contributed to the horrors of illness and loss. Increasingly the attitudes of male professionalism have seemed outrageously at odds with a supposedly caring profession. At the same time, conventional medicine carried a message that disease and illness were arbitrary, having no meaning in terms of the quality of an individual's life. For the first time in Western history disease was firmly separated from any moral or religious discourse. It seems likely that this separation of disease from the 'will of God' or the 'sins of humanity' created a distinct unease for a society steeped in religious beliefs of disease.

What happened with alternative medicine was symptomatic of what happened in many areas of society at the same moment. People blamed everything that was wrong on 'materialism', on philosophies which argued that individuals were not responsible for the good and evil that befell them. Thus, instead of criticizing the structures of work, or the failures and neglects of conventional medicine, there evolved a full-scale attack on the way personal responsibility for health has been downplayed. Alternative therapies came to be viewed as something more than complementing or supplementing the failures of allopathic medicine. They became a place for a new philosophy of personal responsibility. As with other social developments, lack of personal responsibility became an easy way of describing all the complicated reasons why institutions and practices have evolved in certain ways. Rather than a historical or political analysis of why things had gone wrong, it was easy to blame 'materialism'. And when alternative therapies did look for a history or a theory, they sometimes found it in a simplistic feminism, which divided the world into feminine and masculine principles with conventional medicine 'explained' by the dominance of male, materialist, technological values.

Many practitioners of alternative medicine will doubtless be angered to find themselves linked to conservative views of society. For them the movement is giving voice to a discontent with the social status quo.

Yet their criticisms almost invariably slide towards a polarization between the generalizations of 'the modern' on one hand and 'nature' on the other. It is rare for these criticisms to join up with a more thoroughgoing challenge to the structures of a capitalist society. A sense of social powerlessness is expressed as hatred of the machine.

Frequently the criticism of society expressed in alternative therapies turns into a nostalgia for an imagined wholeness and health, for what has been destroyed by modern society. This opposition between nature and modern society is hardly a new one. In past periods nature has similarly featured as a term permitting a nostalgia for something lost and a critique of existing society – perhaps a lost innocence as with the Romantic poets, or a lost sense of sexual spontaneity as in the 1960s. Now it signifies a lost wholeness and health. And the criticisms of society can be deduced from all those attributes which are set up as the opposite of nature. In the alternative health movement, nature is none of the following things: it is not technological, scientific, rationalist; not industrial; it is not fragmented, arbitrary and without meaning; it knows nothing of bad posture, bad parenting, bad diet; above all, it knows nothing of disease. Clearly the critique of modern society is a very limited one. It focuses on the corruptions of the modern world and their effect of causing the body to degenerate. Indeed the fear of degenerative diseases seems of overwhelming significance as if the worst thing to be said about modern society is that we are ill, and that this can be blamed on the lack of control individuals have over their bodies.

The health of the body is presented as the vital front line by which the individual can counter the excesses of 'modernity', of 'industrialization' and impersonality. Becoming healthy has become synonymous with finding 'nature' and 'a natural life style' and this is to be the route by which advanced industrial society will be resisted. The resistance does not rest on an analysis of social structures, of social divisions, of unequal control of resources. Instead it is a vision of personal resistance, of making oneself 'immune' to modern life. The alternative health movement has become a place where the individual can play out, in a highly personal way, a sense of the corruptions of modernity and the struggle against these corruptions. Now the corruptions are no longer the religious sins of greed, sex, and envy, nor the economic sins of capitalism but rather bad parenting, bad diet, bad posture, the abuse of food and nature. The solutions to these are rarely political. They are individual. It is up to individuals to transform themselves, to deal with the pain and suffering imposed by modern life.

Some would want to argue that these views of the corruptions of the world derive from very real political fears: fears of the impersonality of bureaucracy, and fears of the obliteration of ourselves and the planet earth by technological developments which appear out of our control. From this perspective, the reinstatement of individual responsibility is both a symptom (of that general sense of powerlessness) and a necessity, a new stage of personal politics. Until individuals assume responsibility for their bodies and counter the forces making them ill, then there is no hope for wider transformations. But this explanation is by no means sufficient. The sense of the corruptions of the world is too symbolic and personalized to derive exclusively from internalized political fears. These ideas of the corruptions of the world are the direct inheritors of religious dualities between the corruption of the material world, and the perfectibility of the individual, even if this perfectibility is now played out in relation to the body rather than the soul, and in relation to the here and now rather than the afterlife. Even the fears of the destruction of our planet sometimes have a millenerian inflection – if we can save ourselves, we can save the planet.

It is clear, too, that the emphasis on personal responsibility rarely generates political empowerment. It may generate a sense of being able to accomplish things within the existing status quo, but it rarely promises the ability to transform social structures. The crucial aim in all this work is that the individual should feel better, less in conflict and less dragged down by the horrors of modern life. The rewards of this are very often rather paradoxical. The individual will be able to do better, achieve more, and live in greater ease in this society. Very often the aims are almost explicitly conservative. They are aims of harmony, order, balance, the end of struggle, strife, and 'unproductive' conflict. The possibility that there are very real objective interests governing the form of society in which we live is erased in these aims. The healed individual is one who can have and be everything in the existing society. Small wonder then that the 'type' I met most often while researching my book was the wholesome entrepreneur, the perfect resolution of a personal politics of the body with a peaceful co-existence within the existing economic structure.

It is a potential misrepresentation of alternative therapies to concentrate on the philosophies of personal resolution. Many people within the alternative therapies movement are concerned in active ways with anti-nuclear and ecological politics. And it would also be extremely foolish to challenge some of the hopes of this health movement. Who wants to be miserable and in conflict, and possibly even ill, if you can feel well and contented? And what's wrong with starting with the individual and then looking for wider social changes based on a community of changed individuals? The problem is that the aspirations of self-transformation are rarely limited just to feeling in optimum good health or empowered. To achieve this state of well-being the individual will have to transform his or her personality. And this transformation has very definite goals, the individual without conflict, the individual who is no longer up in arms about society, the individual who has expressed and got rid of anger and envy, the emotions which might lead her or him into conflict with society. You will only be well if you can achieve this emotional state. This is truly the route of being 'alternative', for alternative implies co-existing with existing structures not challenging them. And action simply becomes a matter of personal choice between two routes, rather than a matter of creating a different society with different values.

11

The Setting for a New Public Health*

JOHN ASHTON and HOWARD SEYMOUR

In Europe and North America three distinct phases of activity in relation to public health can be identified in the last 150 years.[1] The first phase began in the industrialized cities of Northern Europe in response to the appalling toll of death and disease among the working classes living in abject poverty. The displacement of large numbers of people from the land by their landlords in order to take advantage of the agricultural revolution had combined with the attraction of the growing cities as the result of the industrial revolution to produce a massive change in population patterns and in the physical environments in which people live.[2-6] The predominantly rural ecology of human habitation was ruptured and replaced by one in which a seething mass of humanity was living in squalor.

In Liverpool, in the 1830s one-third of the population was living in the cellars of back-to-back houses with earth floors, no ventilation or sanitation and as many as 16 people to a room. It was not surprising, that epidemics such as tuberculosis, pneumonia, whooping cough, measles and smallpox flourished under such conditions. The response to this situation was the gradual development of a public health movement based on the activities of medical officers of health, sanitary inspectors and their staff, supported by legislation such as the National Public Health Acts of 1848 and 1875 in England.[7]

The focus of this movement was improvements in housing and sanitation standards and the provision of bacteriologically safe water and food.

The Public Health Movement with its emphasis on environmental change lasted until the 1870s and was in time eclipsed by a more

---

*This is an abridged extract from Ashton, J. and Seymour, H. (1988), *The New Public Health*, Open University Press, Chapter 2.

individualistic approach ushered in by the development of the germ theory of disease and the possibilities offered by immunization and vaccination. As the most pressing environmental problems were brought under control, action to improve the health of the population moved on first to personal preventive medical services, such as immunization and family planning, and later to a range of other initiatives including the development of community and school nursing and school health services. The second phase also marked the increasing involvement of the State in medical and social welfare through the provision of hospital and clinic services.[8]

The second phase was in its turn superseded by the therapeutic era, dating from the 1930s, with the advent of insulin and the sulphonamide group of drugs. Until that time there was little of proven efficacy in the therapeutic arsenal.[2] The beginning of this era coincided with the apparent demise of infectious diseases on the one hand and the development of ideas about the welfare state in many developed countries on the other. Historically, it marked a weakening of departments of public health and a shift of power and resources to hospital-based services and particularly those based in teaching hospitals.

Despite the outstanding work of many public health practitioners, in this process the imperative of population coverage which underpins public health rather than concern for individuals who are able to pay for a service has not always been to the fore as evidenced by the continuing and widening inequalities in health.[9-11]

By the early 1970s the therapeutic era was increasingly being challenged. Most countries were experiencing a crisis in health care costs irrespective of their structure of health services; the escalation in costs being in part consequent on technological innovation in treatment methods and an apparently limitless demand for medical care, coupled with the dramatic demographic changes which were taking place with very rapid growth of the elderly population. McKeown's analysis, together with root and branch critiques of medical practice, such as that of Ivan Illich, lent support to the growing interest in a reappraisal of priorities.[2,12]

In 1974, the then Canadian Minister of Health, Marc Lalonde, published a government report entitled *A New Perspective on the Health of Canadians*.[13] It set an agenda for a new era of preventive medicine in Canada; it is arguable that it signalled the turning point in efforts to rediscover public health in developed countries and that it ushered in a new, fourth phase of public health.

What is emerging as the New Public Health is an approach which brings together environmental change and personal preventive measures with appropriate therapeutic interventions especially for the elderly and disabled. However, the New Public Health goes beyond an understanding of human biology and recognizes the importance of those social aspects of health problems which are caused by life-styles. In this way it seeks to avoid the trap of blaming the victim. Many contemporary health problems are therefore seen as being social rather than solely individual problems; underlying them are concrete issues of local and national public policy, and what are needed to address these problems are 'Healthy Public Policies' – policies in many fields which support the promotion of health.[14–19] In the New Public Health the environment is social and psychological as well as physical.

Since 1974, many countries have published similar prevention-orientated documents and there has been an explosion of interest in preventive medicine and health promotion.[18,19] In this growing movement an important lead has been provided by the work of the World Health Organization, in its Health for All by the Year 2000 strategy.

Issues raised by health for all: a conflict between prevention and treatment?

The debate which surrounds the renaissance of public health is often couched in adversarial terms between prevention and treatment. A conflict of sorts between the two approaches has a long history. In the mid-nineteenth century Neumann,[20] arguing for an extended role for the State in public health and the provision of medical care, put it as follows:

> The State argues that its responsibility is to protect people's property rights. For most people the only property which they possess is their health; there-fore the State has a responsibility to protect people's health.

In general, this point of view, albeit in what we would now see as a paternalistic form, seems to have triumphed and to this day an inscription above the door of the borough public health department in Southwark, South London proclaims 'the Health of the people is the highest law'. However, in recent years, and coinciding with the revival of public health, there has also been a revival of the argument over the responsibility for health with a modern 'victim-blaming' view attracting considerable support in some quarters. The issue is complicated by a widespread move against paternalistic forms of administration and services, as part of a general move towards participative as opposed to representative democracy. In the ensuing confusion it has been possible for some governments to construe that the public no longer wishes to have public services.

In public health it is customary to divide prevention into three types: primary, secondary and tertiary. Primary prevention together with health promotion has as its aim the prevention of disorders before they occur, either by positive strategies to affect those factors conducive to disorders in an entire, defied population or else in a subgroup of that population who are identified as being at risk.

Such strategies are only possible when causes are known and preventive strategies are feasible. When they are not it is necessary to fall back on secondary prevention, involving early diagnosis and treatment, including screening programmes, with the aim of limiting the course of an illness and reducing the risk of recurrence.

When even that is not possible recourse must be had to tertiary prevention aimed at reducing the burden of disability to the individual and to society and obtaining optimal health under the circumstances. Clearly, with an ageing population and in our current state of knowledge, there is a host of chronic conditions that we do not know how to prevent but where treatment may make all the difference to the quality of life and thus to health. To the extent to which death is itself inevitable sometime, high-quality terminal care is a form of tertiary prevention.

The common theme of all public health strategies of health promotion and prevention is a shift in the direction of health of the entire population, rather than a concern solely with individuals.

The need for comprehensive strategies of health promotion

The need for a broad view which integrates preventive and treatment medicine and acknowledges the wider political and social dimensions of health is not new.

The need was made explicit in the United Kingdom in the Beveridge report of 1942,[21] which makes quite clear the political nature of health problems and particularly of primary prevention. Clearly an interest in health must be a legitimate concern of all members of the community and not solely of doctors and health workers.

Ever since the inception of the British National Health Services (NHS) only a very small proportion of funds has been given over to the promotion of good health and the prevention of disease. In 1976 the Department of Health published *Prevention and Health: Everybody's Business*, which was intended to stimulate discussion about the scope for modern preventive medicine.[19] This was followed up by the DHSS report *Priorities for Health and Personal Social Services in England* (1976) and *The Way Forward* (1977).[22,23] The Royal Commission on the NHS, reporting in 1979, concluded that a 'significant improvement in the health of all people of the U.K. can come through prevention'.[24]

The Black Report (1980) recommended action within the health services and action in other policy areas with a particular emphasis on the need to abolish childhood poverty and to tackle on a multidisciplinary front the toll of death and disability caused by domestic and road traffic accidents.

More recently, the British Government has accepted the need to take active steps to develop primary medical care and has conducted a fundamental review of the Public Health Function in the light of failures of infectious disease control and environmental health monitoring and weakness in the relationship between the medical and other sectors of relevant public policy.[25-27] In Canada, in keeping with its vanguard position, the government has embraced the HFA 2000 Strategy as part of its own commitment to a defined health promotion strategy.[26-28]

Reorientating primary care

The reorientation of medical care towards health promotion, prevention and primary medical care is an essential part of the World Health Organization Strategy.[29,30] This reorientation involves a further shift from primary medical care (a medical concept based on the equitable availability and accessibility of good quality preventive and treatment services from a team of health workers based in the community) to primary health care, which is a social concept going much wider in that it is concerned with populations as well as individuals and that it seeks to involve a range of people other than trained health workers. The implications for training and organization in achieving this paradigm shift are considerable, particularly in respect of the need to achieve real public participation and intersectoral working.

The World Health Organization concept of primary health care incorporates a recognition that health care should be planned to relate to the resources available. It sees primary health care as the most local part of a comprehensive health system and it recognizes that the public should participate both individually and collectively in the planning and implementation of health care.

Primary health care is envisaged by WHO is hard to find. One celebrated example was the Peckham Pioneer Health Centre established in South London in the 1930s.

In planning the new centre it was felt that the population should be essentially healthy and that it should include a cross-section by age. It would be for people to come to the centre rather than for the centre to proselytize, and what happened in the centre would be for the members to decide. It would be continuously available in leisure time and its aim was to provide opportunities whenever an opportunity could be taken up (see Table 11.1).

TABLE 11.1   The facilities at Peckham Health Centre

Welfare and educational
Antenatal clinic; postnatal clinic; birth control clinic; infant welfare clinic, care of the toddler; nursery school; immunization service; schoolchildren's medical examinations; vocational guidance; sex instruction for adolescents; girls' and boys' clubs; youth centres; sports clubs and recreation clubs of all sorts; keep fit and gymnastic classes; adult cultural education; music, debates, drama, any event desired by members; citizens advice bureau; holiday organizations; outings and expeditions; the bar; billiards; dancing; social gatherings.

Therapeutic
Marriage advice bureau; mothers' clinic; child guidance clinic; poor man's lawyer; social worker; hospital follow-up overhaul; rehabilitation clinic.

Support for the centre was not forthcoming from the National Health Service, apparently because the ethic was not compatible with the ascendant values of the therapeutic era.

At the present time, within many countries there is an excitement and energy attached to preventive medicine and primary medical care which was not there 20 years ago. Some countries have passed special legislation to assist the shift in emphasis from hospital–to community-based services; several have produced 'National Health for All Strategies' and, perhaps most encouragingly, there is a great deal of interest and activity in developing health promotion, preventive medicine and primary care at the local level. In some countries medical students now actively opt for careers outside hospitals. Yet in England and Wales, for example, where many of the desirable elements for the development of primary health care exist, considerable problems remain, not least in the inner-city areas of the conurbations and on the peripheral public housing estates.[24] In these areas the gap between the health experience of different social classes has continued to increase.

In particular, there is a general lack of what might be called the epidemiological or population view of primary health care as espoused by Tudor Hart and Kark, and there is a great need for the injection of epidemiological skills into the normal functioning of primary health care teams.[31,32] The development of appropriate information systems based on the age-sex register, probably supplemented by intermittent sample surveys of the practice population to assess risk factors and answer specific questions, will be a necessary step in providing the conceptual framework for a rational and comprehensive approach to preventive medicine and health promotion.

However, in British general practice there is little to indicate that doctors as prime movers are ready for primary health as opposed to primary medical care.

When it comes to the kind of community-development linkage with primary health care which is to be found in non-industrial countries and which should be regarded as just as important in, for example, inner-city areas of the United Kingdom, there is nothing to suggest that general practitioners regard this kind of work as having anything to do with them.

Community participation and intersectoral action

The elements of the WHO Ottawa Charter, which focus on the creation of environments which are supportive to health and on the enabling of communities through the development of personal skills and health advocacy, are in a real sense a challenge to professional practice as it is found throughout the World.[33] Professional power and prestige is contingent upon the acquisition of specific knowledge and skills which are exchanged for money in return for a service; the autonomy of the professional in the market is central as is his or her freedom to refuse a client. There is no commitment either to population coverage or to sharing power and demystifying knowledge. In this sense, there is a real conflict between the clinical model based on individual transactions and the public health model based on a social contract with entire communities. The consequence of this is that there is a great deal of rhetoric about public participation but a marked unwillingness to really engage in the processes which would bring it about. Most professionals and welfare bureaucracies function only on the lower half of Arnstein's ladder of citizen participation:[34]

Citizen control
Delegated power
Partnership
Placation
Consultation
Informing
Therapy
Manipulation

Yet in wishing for people to take increased responsibility for their own health it is necessary to recognise the close relationship between risk-taking behaviour and lack of empowerment.[35]

Notes

1. Kickbusch, I. (1986) 'Health promotion strategies for action'. *Canadian Journal of Public Health* 77(5), 321–6.
2. McKeown, T. (1976) *The Role of Medicine – Dream, Mirage or Nemesis*, Nuffield Provincial Hospitals Trust, London.
3. Kaye, T. (1829) *The Stranger in Liverpool*, T. Kaye, Liverpool.
4. Chave, S.P.W. (1984) 'Duncan of Liverpool – and some lessons for today', *Community Medicine* 6, 61–71.
5. Kearns, G. (1986) 'Private property and public health reform in England 1830–70'. *Social Science and Medicine*. 26(1), 187–99.
6. Cartwright, F.F. (1977) *A Social History of Medicine*, Longman, London.
7. Fraser, W.M. (1947) *Duncan of Liverpool*, Hamish Hamilton, London.
8. Ashton, J.R. (1979) 'Poverty and health in Britain today', *Public Health* 93, 89–94.
9. Gobder, G.E. (1986) 'Medical officers of health and health services', *Community Medicine* 8(1), 1–14.
10. Townsend, P. and Davidson, N. (1980) *Inequalities in Health – The Black Report*, Penguin, Harmondsworth.
11. Whitehead, M. (1987) *The Health Divide – Inequalities in Health*, Health Education Council, London.
12. Illich, I. (1975) *Medical Nemesis – The Expropriation of Health*, Calder and Boyars, London.
13. Lalonde, M. (1974) *A New Perspective on the Health of Canadians*, Ministry of Supply and Services.
14. Doyal, L. (1981) *The Political Economy of Health*, Pluto Press, London.
15. Navarro, V. (1976) *Medicine under Capitalism*, Croom Helm, London.
16. Milio, N. (1986) *Promoting Health through Public Policy*, Canadian Public Health Association. Ottawa, Canada.
17. St George, D. and Draper, P. (1981) 'A health policy for Europe', *The Lancet* ii, 463–5.
18. Department of Health Education and Welfare (1979) *Healthy People*. The Surgeon General's report on Health Promotion and Disease Prevention. DHEW Publications, Washington, D.C.
19. HMSO (1976) *Prevention and Health: everybody's business*. A reassessment of public and personal health. HMSO, London.
20. Neumann, S. (1847) *Die Offentliches Gesundeheitstflege und das Eigenthum*, Berlin. Quoted in H. Sigerist op. cit.
21. Beveridge, Sir W. (1942) *Social Insurance and Allied Services*. Cmd. 6404, 6405. HMSO, London.
22. Department of Health and Social Security (1976) *Priorities for Health and Social Service in England*, HMSO, London.
23. Department of Health and Social Security (1977) *The Way Forward – Priorities in the Health and Social Services*, HMSO, London.
24. Merrison, A. (1979) *Royal Commission on the National Health Service*, HMSO, London.

25. Department of Health and Social Security (1987) *Promoting Better Health – The Government Programme for Improving Primary Health Care*. Cmnd. **249**, HMSO, London.
26. Acheson, E.D. (1988) *On the State of the Public Health*, The Fourth Duncan Lecture.
27. The Acheson Report (1988) *Public Health in England*. The Report of the Committee of Enquiry into the future development of the Public Health Function. Cmnd. **289**, HMSO, London.
28. Epp, J. (1986) 'Achieving health for all: A framework for health promotion', *Canadian Journal of Public Health* **77**(6), 393–424.
29. Vuori, H. (1981) 'Primary health care in industrialized countries'. In *Die Allgemeinpraxix; Das Zentrum der Artzlichen, Grundverorgung Gottleib Duttwierer* – Institut Ruschlikon, Zurich, pp. 83–111.
30. Hellberg, H. (1987) 'Health for all and primary health care in Europe', *Public Health* **101**, 151–7.
31. Tudor Hart, J. (1981) 'A new kind of doctor', *Journal of the Royal Society of Medicine*, **74**, 871–83.
32. Kark, S.L. (1981) *The Practice of Community Orientated Primary Health Care*, Appleton, Century, Crofts, New York.
33. Chambers, R. (1983) *Rural Development – Putting the Last First*, Longman, London.
34. Arnstein, S. (1969) 'A ladder of public participation'. *Journal of the American Institute of Planners*. Quoted in N. Wates and C. Knevitt (1987) *Community Architecture*, Penguin Books, London.
35. Ashton, J. (1983) 'Risk assessment', *British Medical Journal* **286**, 1843.

12

Maternity: Letters from Working Women*

EDITED BY M. LLEWELYN DAVIES
WITH AN INTRODUCTION BY THE CURRENT EDITORS

Introduction

These letters were written in 1914 by members of the Women's Co-operative Guild in response to an appeal by its general secretary, Margaret Llewelyn Davies, for firsthand experiences of the effects of childbirth and parenting on women's health. Although probably not intended for publication – open discussion of childbearing was virtually unknown – 160 of the letters were published in the following year, and had a great impact on public opinion in Britain and America.

The Guild had been campaigning since the 1890s for the provision of ante-natal and infant care services for poorer women, and it was partly as a result of their pressure that the Liberal government in Britain gave the first maternity grant in 1911. The letters were intended to provide evidence of the sufferings and avoidable loss of life and health that resulted from current negligent or non-existent services. Guild members were asked specifically for their views on 'the difficulty of taking care, the ignorance that has prevailed on the conditions of pregnancy, and how those conditions result in lack of health and energy, meaning that a woman cannot do justice to herself or give her best to her husband or children'.[1] They were also asked for details of all pregnancies, births and deaths, their husbands' occupation and actual weekly wages.

The writers of these letters were long-serving members and officials of the Guild, and their standard of education and weekly family income

---

*This is an abridged extract from Llewelyn Davies, M. (ed.) (1978) *Maternity: Letters from Working Women*, London, Virago.

was almost certainly better than average. Nevertheless, two-thirds of the 386 replies, Margaret Davies noted, 'indicate conditions of maternity which are not normal and healthy'.[2] The seven letters reproduced here have been selected to represent the range of responses and types of experiences chronicled in the published letters. They are numbered as in the original edition of 1915.

6. Healthy and strong

During pregnancy I always looked to my diet, and as my husband never got more than 24s. 6d. per week, I had not much to throw away on luxuries. I had plain food, such as oatmeal and bacon, and meat, plenty of bread and good butter. I may say that during pregnancy and during suckling my appetite was always better, and I ate more and enjoyed my food better than at any other time. I always did my own housework and my own washing, and I never had a doctor all the time I was having children. I have had six, one dead.

During my labour I was never bad more than about three or four hours. I felt I could get out of bed the first day, and I never had the doctor, only an old midwife.

And though I say it myself, nobody had bonnier or healthier children than I had, with fair skins and red cheeks.

I must say that I am a staunch teetotaller, and have been all my life. I think that drink has a lot to do with some women's sufferings.

I had one child born without a midwife at all, before we had time to fetch her, and I did as well as at any other time.

We lived under the colliery, and our rent was only 3s. 6d. a week. We got our coal at a lower price, about 1s. a week. During part of the time we had a lodger, who paid up 11s., which helped us a bit. But you must know we had to be very careful. But, taking all into consideration, we were very comfortably off. We had not many doctors' bills, as our children were all very healthy, and I don't think I have spent a pound on doctoring for myself since I was a baby, for which I am very thankful.

Wages 18s. to 24s. 6d.; six children.

11. 'I was awfully poor'

My first girl was born before I attained my twentieth year, and I had a stepmother who had had no children of her own, so I was not able to get any knowledge from her; and even if she had known anything I don't suppose she would have dreamt of telling me about these things which were supposed to exist, but must not be talked about. About a month before the baby was born I remember asking my aunt where the baby would come from. She was astounded, and did not make me much wiser. I don't know whether my ignorance had anything to do with the struggle I had to bring the baby into the world, but the doctor said that my youth had for I was not properly developed. Instruments had to be used, and I heard the doctor say he could not tell whether my life could be saved or not, for he said there is not room here for a bird to pass. All the time I thought that this was the way all babies were born.

At the commencement of all my pregnancies I suffered terribly from toothache, and for this reason I think all married child-bearing women should have their teeth attended to, for days and nights of suffering of this kind must have a bad effect on both the mother and child. I also at times suffered torments from cramp in the legs and vomiting, particularly during the first three months. I hardly think the cramp can be avoided, but if prospective mothers would consult their doctors about the inability to retain food, I fancy that might be remedied. At the commencement of my second pregnancy I was very ill indeed. I could retain no food, not even water, and I was constipated for thirteen days, and I suffered from jaundice. This had its effect on the baby, for he was quite yellow at birth, and the midwife having lodgers to attend to, left him unwashed for an hour after birth. She never troubled to get his lungs inflated, and he was two days without crying. I had no doctor. I was awfully poor, so that I had to wash the baby's clothes in my bedroom at the fortnight's end; but had I had any knowledge like I possess now, I should have insisted at the very least on the woman seeing my child's lungs were properly filled. When we are poor, though, we cannot say what *must* be done; we have to suffer and keep quiet. The boy was always weakly, and could not walk when my third baby was born. He had fits from twelve to fourteen, but except for a rather 'loose' frame, seems otherwise quite healthy now.

My third child, a girl, was born in a two-roomed 'nearly underground' dwelling. We had two beds in the living-room, and the little scullery was very damp. Had it not been for my neighbours, I should have had no attendance after the confinement, and no fire often, for it was during one of the coal strikes. My fourth child, a boy, was born under better housing conditions, but not much better as regards money; and during the carrying of all my children, except the first, I have had insufficient food and too much work. This is just an outline. Did I give it all, it would fill a book, as the saying goes.

In spite of all, I don't really believe that the children (with the exception of the oldest boy) have suffered much, only they might have been so much stronger, bigger, and better if I had been able to have better food and more rest.

Cleanliness has made rapid strides since my confinements; for never once can I remember having anything but face, neck, and hands washed until I could do things myself, and it was thought certain death to change the underclothes under a week.

For a whole week we were obliged to lie on clothes stiff and stained, and the stench under the clothes was abominable, and added to this we were commanded to keep the babies under the clothes.

I often wonder how the poor little mites managed to live, and perhaps they never would have done but for our adoration, because this constant admiration of our treasures did give them whiffs of fresh air very often.

My husband's lowest wage was 10s., the highest about £1 only, which was reached by overtime. His mother and my own parents generally provided me with clothing, most of which was cast-offs.

Wages 10s. to £1; four children.

20. Stead's penny poets

I was married at twenty-eight in utter ignorance of the things that most vitally affect a wife and mother. My mother, a dear, pious soul, thought ignorance was innocence, and the only thing I remember her saying on the subject of childbirth was, 'God never sends a babe without bread to feed it.' Dame Experience long ago knocked the bottom out of that argument for me. My husband was a man earning 32s. a week – a conscientious, good man, but utterly undomesticated. A year after our marriage the first baby was born, naturally and with little pain or trouble. I had every care, and motherhood stirred the depths of my nature. The rapture of a babe in arms drawing nourishment from me crowned me with glory and sanctity and honour. Alas! the doctor who attended me suffered from eczema of a very bad type in his hands. The disease attacked me, and in twenty-four hours I was covered from head to foot . . . finally leaving me partially and sometimes totally crippled in my hands. Fifteen months later a second baby came – a dear little girl, and again I was in a fairly good condition physically and financially, but had incurred heavy doctor's bills and attendance bills, due to my incapacity for work owing to eczema. Both the children were delicate, and dietary expenses ran high. Believing that true thrift is wise expenditure, we spent our all trying to build up for them sound, healthy bodies, and was ill-prepared financially and physically to meet the birth of a third baby sixteen months later. Motherhood ceased to be a crown of glory, and became a fearsome thing to be shunned and feared. The only way to meet our increased expenditure was by dropping an endowment policy, and losing all our little, hard-earned savings. I confess without shame that when well-meaning friends said: 'You cannot afford another baby; take this drug,' I took their strong concoctions to purge me of the little life that might be mine. They failed, as such things generally do, and the third baby came. Many a time I have sat in daddy's big chair, a baby two and a half years old at my back, one sixteen months and one one month on my knees, and cried for very weariness and hopelessness. I fed them all as long as I could, but I was too harassed, domestic duties too heavy, and the income too limited to furnish me with a rich nourishing milk. . . . Nine months later I was again pregnant, and the second child fell ill. 'She cannot live,' the doctors said, but I loved. . . . She is still delicate, but bright and intelligent. I watched by her couch three weeks, snatching her sleeping moments to fulfil the household task. The strain was fearful, and one night I felt I must sleep or die – I didn't much care which; and I lay down by her side, and slept, and slept, and slept, forgetful of temperatures, nourishment or anything else. . . . A miscarriage followed in consequence of the strain, and doctor's bills grew like mushrooms. The physical pain from the eczema, and working with raw and bleeding hands, threatened me with madness. I dare not tell a soul. I dare not even face it for some time, and then I knew I must fight this battle or go under. Care and rest would have cured me, but I was too proud for charity, and no other help was available. You may say mine is an isolated case. It is not. The sympathy born of suffering brings many mothers to me, just that they may find a listening ear. I find this mental state is common, and the root cause is lack of rest and economic strain – economic strain being the greatest factor for ill of the two. I had to fight or go under. I could give no time to mental culture or reading and I bought Stead's penny editions of literary masters, and used to put them on a shelf in front of me washing-day, fastened back their pages with a clothes-peg, and learned pages of Whittier, Lowell, and Longfellow, as I mechanically rubbed the dirty clothes, and thus wrought my education. This served a useful purpose; my children used to be sent off to sleep by reciting what I had learnt during the day. My mental outlook was widened, and once again I stood a comrade and helpmeet by my husband's side, and my children all have a love for good literature.

Three years later a fifth baby came. I was ill and tired, but my husband fell ill a month prior to his birth, and I was up day and night. Our doctor was, and is, one of the kindest men I have ever met. I said: 'Doctor, I cannot afford you for myself, but will you come if I need?' 'I hope you won't need me, but I'll come.' I dare not let my husband in his precarious condition hear a cry of pain from me, and travail pain cannot always be stifled; and here again the doctor helped me by giving me a sleeping draught to administer him as soon as I felt the pangs of childbirth. Hence he slept in one room while I travailed in the other, and brought forth the loveliest boy that ever gladdened a mother's heart. So here I am a woman of forty-one years, blessed with a lovely family of healthy children, faced with a big deficit, varicose veins, and an occasional loss of the use of my hands. I want nice things, but I must pay that debt I owe. I would like nice clothes (I've had three new dresses in fourteen years), but I must not have them yet. I'd like to develop mentally, but I must stifle that part of my nature until I have made good the ills of the past, and I am doing it slowly and surely, and my heart grows lighter, and will grow lighter still when I know that the burden is lifted from the mothers of our race.

Wages 32s. to 40s.; five children, one miscarriage.

21. How a woman may suffer

I cannot tell you all my sufferings during the time of motherhood. I thought, like hundreds of women do to-day, that it was only natural, and you had to bear it. I was left an orphan, and having no mother to tell me anything, I was quite unprepared for marriage and what was expected of me.

My husband being some years my senior, I found he had not a bit of control over his passions, and expected me to do what he had been in the habit of paying women to do.

I had three children and one miscarriage within three years. This left me very weak and suffering from very bad legs. I had to work very hard all the time I was pregnant.

My next child only lived a few hours. After the confinement I was very ill, and under the care of a doctor for some time. I had inflammation in the varicose veins; the doctor told me I should always lay with my legs above my head. He told my husband I must not do any work for some time. I had either to wear a bandage or an elastic stocking to keep my legs so that I might get about at all. I am still suffering from the varicose veins now, although my youngest child is fourteen; at times I am obliged to keep my legs bandaged up. With each child I had they seemed to get worse, and me having them so quickly never allowed my legs to get into their normal condition before I was pregnant again. I do wish there could be some limit to the time when a woman is expected to have a child. I often think women are really worse off then beasts. During the time of pregnancy, the male beast keeps entirely from the female: not so with the woman; she is at the prey of a man just the same as though she was not pregnant. Practically within a few days of the birth, and as soon as the birth is over, she is tortured again. If the woman does not feel well she must not say so, as a man has such a lot of ways of punishing a woman if she does not give in to him. . . .

Wages 30s. average; seven children, two miscarriges.

22. 'Got on splendidly'

I have only had one child and one miscarriage, but I can assure you I had such good nursing that I got on spendidly. Of course, I was not all allowed to get up before the tenth day, and I do not think that anyone ought to do so, even if they can. I think if everyone at those times had great care and good nursing for a month, there is no reason why they should not get on as well as I did.

One child, one miscarriage.

88. 'Did not like to say anything'

I can safely say that had there been a centre to which I could have gone before my first boy was born I should have been saved the terrible torture I suffered both before and after confinement. I was very ignorant before marriage, and went away among strangers; and when I became pregnant I did not like to say anything to a strange doctor, and I had no lady friends whom I felt I could confide in. So I went about with an ulcerated stomach, sick after every attempt to take food; and when my baby came, I nearly lost my life. He was also very delicate for five years after birth, wholly due, I am convinced, to the state I was in whilst pregnant.

With the other two boys, I have always had to get about too soon. The month I have always had to have a woman in the house, during which time I have been absolutely helpless, being a terrific expense.

The doctor has ordered me to lie down for two hours each day, but that is absolutely impossible for a working man's wife when she has two or three children around her, meals to provide, and the washing and cleaning, etc., to do in the home.

I speak from my own experience, and I know that there are thousands of women who are a million times worse off than I am, for I have the best husband in the world; but his nor any other working man's wages won't pay for help in the home at a cost of at least 12s. a week and food. On the very day my first baby was born my husband was thrown out of work. This was kept from my knowledge for five weeks, and I am sure you will guess all the scheming he used to keep me in ignorance. He had his club money for the period he was out of employment, which amounted to 9s. a week.

Wages 25s. to 30s.; three children.

128. 'Often went short of food'

It is so long since I had all these babies, that I almost forget, but I was married young, and was always delicate on the chest, as I am still. I had children very fast, seven one after another, not more than a year and nine months between them, and in one case only one year and two months. Then I lost a sweet little girl, aged four years and eight months. She was ill a fortnight, and I nursed her night and day. I was so done up with attending her and the grief, that I had a dreadful miscarriage which nearly cost me my life. I had to work very hard to do everything for my little family, and after that I never had any more children to live. I either miscarried, or they were still-born. I have had two miscarriages in a year, one in January and one in August. My husband's standing wage was 28s., but he made a little overtime sometimes, which I always tried to put by for doctor and nurse. The doctor's fee was £1 1s., and I had no nurse under 1s. a day – viz. 7s. or 8s. per week, and their food, etc. I looked after my husband and children well, but I often went short of food myself, although my husband did not know it. He used to think my appetite was bad, and that I could not eat. I never worried him. He was steady, and gave me all he could. You may guess I was always scheming and planning to make ends meet, which was not good for me or the unborn baby. But I always tried to keep a bright face, and made the best of things, and all my doctors have called me plucky. I wish I had had the 30s. the mothers have now; it would have taken a load off anyhow. . . .

Wages 28s.; seven children, three still-births, four miscarriages.

Notes

1. M. Llewelyn Davies (ed.) (1915) *Maternity: Letters from Working Women.* 1978 edn, reprinted by Virago, London, p. 191.
2. Ibid., p. 192.

13

The Limits of the Professional Imagination*

ANN OAKLEY

Some of the most powerful images of women and motherhood are those held by the professional disciplines which lay claim to a special expertise in the field of reproduction – namely, medical science, clinical psychiatry and psychology. In order to review the images of women to be found in each of these professional perspectives, I am going to draw on a wide range of data, from my own observations of work in a London maternity hospital in the mid-1970s and interviews with women having babies, to the assumptions made about women as patients in the medical literature. My basic argument can be simply stated; it is that in the contemporary industrialized world, medical science and allied disciplines, in claiming specialist jurisdiction over all aspects of reproduction, have become the predominant source of social constructs of the culture of childbirth. The professional obstetrical view that childbirth is a pathological process and women are passive objects of clinical attention has become an integral part of the way in which the community as a whole sees childbirth. Science is in this sense itself ideology; it is certainly not a matter of objective 'fact'. However, we cannot let the matter rest there, for there is ample evidence that 'professional' images of motherhood conflict with the experiences of mothers themselves. Most women's experiences of becoming a mother are considerably and uncomfortably out of tune with the expectations they have absorbed from professional advisers to mothers (amongst others) about what the process will be like.

*This is an abridged extract from Oakley, A. (1986) *Telling the Truth about Jerusalem*, Part 2, pp. 73–267.

Images of motherhood and women in medical science

The single most important aspect of medical attitudes towards women as mothers is their concealment behind a screen of what are presented an exclusively clinical concerns. The attitude is that there are *no* attitudes: it is purely a question of how medical knowledge determines the 'best' maternity care policy, one that will guarantee the lowest possible mortality rate for mother and child.

There is, in a sense, no answer to this: for what mother does not want to survive childbirth with a healthy child? But the issue is a great more complicated. In the first place, obstetricians and other makers of maternity care policy have rarely possessed the evidence necessary to prove that any particular obstetric practice is really 'better' than another (or the alternative of no practice at all) as judged by the objective of the lowest possible mortality. In the second place, the assessment of the 'success' of childbirth in terms of mortality (and to a lesser extent physical morbidity) rates is itself an attitude of extreme, if benign, paternalism. It hides two assumptions: (1) the usual but disputable medical-scientific claim, challenged convincingly by Ivan Illich,[1] Thomas McKeown,[2] and others, that improvements in health-care are due principally to medical treatment (rather than to changes in social and economic conditions); and (2) that all other indices of successful childbirth are irrelevant, or at least of very minor importance. The way in which obstetrics has developed has ensured a preoccupation with the *physical* model of reproduction. Social and emotional measures of reproductive success do not count, although the evidence is that such measures are extremely important to mothers themselves. Such evidence is hardly ever collected by obstetric researchers investigating the efficacy of particular obstetric practices. Maternal attitudes to obstetric practice and maternal assessments of successful reproductive outcome as research topics have been considered by obstetricians to constitute the 'soft', and by implication inferior, material of social-scientiic surveys – where, that is, they have been considered at all.

In modern obstetrics, the dominant image of women is a mechanical one: women are seen as reproductive machines. 'To put the matter rather crudely, obstetrics treats a body like a complex machine and uses a series of interventionist techniques to repair faults that may develop in the machine'.[3] The mechanical model is 'man-made' and needs regular servicing to function correctly. Thus antenatal care is maintenance- and malfunction-spotting work. There is a most significant premise here, and that is that any machine can go wrong at any time; there is no distinction between those machines that are in good working order – in other words, the 97 per cent[4] of pregnancies and childbirths that are unproblematic – and those machines with some apparent fault – in other words the small minority of pregnancies and births in which medical intervention does literally save lives. Concretely, as well as ideologically, women appear to become machines. The language of obstetrics itself reflects this – consider such terms as 'uterine dysfunction', 'incompetent cervix' and 'bad reproducer'. Obstetric care in countries such as Britain and the USA is increasingly machine-oriented. In many hospitals all pregnancies are monitored with ultrasound; in some the mechanical assessment of gestation is so important that women are no longer asked for the date of their last menstrual period. Other technological assessments are a routine part of antenatal care. Machines are used to initiate and terminate labour. One machine controls the uterine contractions, while another records them; regional (epidural) analgesia removes the woman's awareness of her contractions so that these do, indeed, have to be read off the machine; and keeping all the machines going becomes what 'looking after' a patient in labour means.

This merging of the pregnant female body with the high-powered technology of modern obstetrics has many implications. But one implication it does *not* have is that obstetricians are merely mechanics to be called in when faults develop, much as one takes a faulty car to the garage to have it repaired. It is usually obvious to a car-owner when her or his car goes wrong, but women cannot be trusted to be experts on their own pregnancies. Thus another prime feature of medical images of motherhood is that women lack the capacity to know what is happening to their own bodies. Doctors are the only experts in the entire symptomatology of childbearing.

Pregnancy and childbirth in the medical model are medical events. For it is only by an ideological transformation of the 'natural' or 'normal' to the 'cultural' and 'abnormal' that doctors can legitimate reproduction as a medical speciality. Any individual pregnancy or childbirth may be normal but it is only so, according to medical dictate, in retrospect. The mechanical model of motherhood conspires with the model of reproduction as pathology to characterize women having babies as possessing only one role – that of pregnant patients, patients in the delivery room and postpartum ward. Being a patient is separated off from the rest of life. The impact of social, economic and psychological factors is admitted by obstetricians only in so far as it is liable to predict the physical symptomatology or outcome of pregnancy. Hence unmarried patients may receive special medical attention and be referred routinely to the medical social worker, while married patients who experience genuine medical and social problems are not routinely viewed as a 'high-risk' group. Low social class and being unmarried are frequently combined with obstetric factors in medical scoring systems for high-risk pregnancies.

The organization of much obstetric care is based on the assumption that a pregnant or parturient woman has no other responsibilities or interests which conflict with her function of producing a baby. Reproduction is a full-time role. In the antenatal consultations I observed, as well as the medical literature, doctors rarely consider that pregnant women have homes to run, many have other children to look after, a significant proportion are involved in the care of elderly relatives, the majority are married and carry the domestic responsibilities attached to the role of a wife, while most are engaged in addition in some form of paid employment. One example illustrates this point:

Doctor: 'Mrs Carter? How are you getting on?'
Patient: 'Horrible.'
Doctor: 'Why?'
Patient: 'I don't know . . . I feel it's so difficult to walk.'
Doctor: 'You shouldn't be walking much at this stage of pregnancy.'
Patient: 'I don't. But I have my housework to do and I've got the in-laws staying.'
Doctor: 'They should be doing your housework for you, shouldn't they? Isn't that what they're for?'
Patient: 'They're not females . . . things aren't very good at home at the moment. . .'
Doctor: 'You do seem to have put on a bit of weight.'
Patient: 'What does that mean?'
Doctor: 'It doesn't necessarily mean anything, but you must take things easy.'
Patient: 'That's what my husband says. It's easy for men to say that.'
Doctor: 'It's your set-up at home. You should have organized things better.'
Patient: 'Well, I've got three children to look after.'

Ninety-three per cent of the questions posed or statements made by patients about social matters and social role obligations in the doctor-patient encounters I observed met with the response of irritation or simple avoidance from the doctor.

Because reproduction is a specialist medical subject, because parenthood is isolated from women's life-circumstances, and because women are typified as essentially ignorant about the process of reproduction, the concept of choice as applied to users of the maternity services is nowhere in sight in the medical model of motherhood. Although many surveys of how women feel about their maternity care show that many wish to be consulted about what kind of medical treatment they receive, the obstetrical claim to unique expertise prevents the exercise of choice by those who have the babies. I am not talking here about those cases in which gross problems in pregnancy or labour clearly necessitate medical intervention, but about the majority of cases in which it is 'policy' in general that determines what proportion of women receive such procedures as ultrasonic monitoring in pregnancy, electronic fetal heart monitoring in labour, and elective induction of labour. Women themselves are often aware that the rules determining their treatment are arbitary, in the sense that these rules vary from one hospital to another, or from one practitioner to another. Under such circumstances it seems reasonable to mothers that they should have a say in what happens; but it is not reasonable to a medical profession whose claim to jurisdiction over the label of illness and any human life-event to which it may be attached ensures the right (if not the responsibility) to disregard the wishes of the 'patient'.

Those who provide maternity care may see women as walking wombs, but they cannot discount completely the fact that women have heads as well. Thus we come to the second key model of womanhood in medical science – that of the biologically determined 'feminine' female.

In the medical literature, including the advice literature available in Britain and other countries written by medical 'experts' for mothers, there is a clearly set out paradigm of 'normal' motherhood.[5] What is a normal mother? She is a person especially in need of medical care and protection; a person who is essentially childish; but at the same time fundamentally altruistic; she is married; and, lastly, she ought to be happy but is, instead, constantly beset with anxiety and depression.

These typifications of mothers are interrelated and also internally contradictory. Women's imputed need for medical care and control is demanded by the very premise of obstetric science – that women can only be 'delivered of' their babies: childbirth cannot be allowed to be an autonomous act. In turn, the need for medical care requires the imputation of ignorance, unreliability and plain silliness to mothers as immutably femine characteristics.

In these ways normal mothers in the medical paradigm are not really adults at all. They are like children; and, like children, have to be guided and disciplined into correct modes of behaviour. Yet here we face a profound contradiction: for normal mothers, that is 'good' mothers, do not put their own needs first. They see the world in terms of their children's needs, which they gauge by a mixed and, again, contradictory process of listening to the experts, on the one hand, and intuition – the much-famed myth of the 'maternal instinct' – on the other. The stereotype of normal mothers as married refers to a central contradiction in obstetrical/gynaecological work (which reflects the illogicality of the association between the two disciplines) – and that is the conflict between the promotion and prevention of childbirth. The image of the nuclear family as the only valid context for childbirth is still immensely powerful in our society, and the medical profession is hardly renowned for its liberal moral attitudes. Husbands are important possessions for normal mothers because they constitute the sole orthodox channel for mothers' emotional and sexual satisfaction.

The final characteristic of normal mothers in the medical paradigm – their proneness to anxiety and depression – actually comes first in political importance in the social construction of motherhood and womanhood. It does so for three reasons. In the first place, the recognition that it is normal for mothers to be depressed before birth and afterwards proceeds from the recognition that the normal condition of women in general is depression. Secondly, the construction of women as depressed provides a rationale for them to be oppressed also. Thirdly, the prevalence of depression in mothers and women raises the question as to why it occurs and what can be done about it. The standard medical explanation for female depression is a biological one – that mysterious term 'hormones'. The standard medical treatment is pharmacological, for it is by the widespread administration of psychotropic drugs that women are 'adjusted' to their situation. A Canadian study came to the interesting conclusion that women who use psychotropic drugs like valium are consciously aware of taking them in order to cope with the social strains of their daily lives.[6]

Psychological constructs of women

In an oft-quoted study carried out in the USA in 1970, a group of mental health clinicians was asked to rate the applicability of a range of personal qualities to three different kinds of people: normal adult men, normal adult women and 'healthy, mature, socially competent' individuals. The results of this study revealed that 'healthy, mature and socially competent' individuals were ascribed masculine characteristics. Normal women were seen as more submissive, less aggressive, less competitive, more excitable, more easily hurt, more emotional, more conceited about their appearance and less objective than the normal men.[7]

In this most significant manner, psychiatry and psychology have tended to reinforce the images of women extant in the medical model. They have underscored three particular aspects of the medical model: the failure to consider the *social* context in which childbearing occurs and women live; the assumption that psychological states (including depression as the normal condition of women) are caused by physiological ones; and the refusal to treat women as human beings because women are a sex apart, 'nature herself'.

The term 'postnatal depression' is part of the language in which women discuss and experience childbirth. But it also exists as a technical concept, which is poorly defined in the literature. However, there is general agreement among the relevant 'experts' that postnatal depression is a form of reactive depression, that is, a response to particular environment circumstances, in this case the prior circumstance of childbirth. The two main psychiatric theories describe its aetiology as (1) hormones, and (2) some disturbance of femininity. Now, while there are clearly considerable hormonal shifts during pregnancy and after delivery, to prove a causal association between these and the various forms of postnatal depression (from the 'blues' of the early postpartum days to a fully-blown psychosis developing some time later) requires research of the kind that has simply not been done. Those few studies which have examined selected aspects of puerperal biochemistry have done so in relation to early postpartum mood only (because hospitalized women are captive subjects) and, for the most part, their findings have been inconclusive.[8]

The second major theme in the psychological construction of maternity assumes that psychological problems result from intrapsychic conflict in the individual as she undergoes the stresses of reproduction. Postnatal depression is the outcome of this internal, individualized conflict. Of course this interpretation also means that women are at the mercy of their bodies. It means in addition that a great deal of medical research has been based on the supposition that reproductive problems in general are caused by women's lack of success in achieving a mature femininity. For example, infertility, habitual abortion and premature delivery have all been analysed as psychosomatic defences, as a result of women's hostile identification with their own mothers, as symptomatic of a general rejection of the feminine role, or as evidence of disturbed sexual relationships with men. The same hypotheses have also been applied to other common complications of pregnancy, such as nausea and vomiting and toxaemia: and the literature is studded with attempts to relate the neonatal condition of the baby to its mother's personality.[9]

It seems to me that the question that should have been asked has not been asked. This question is: Why should it have been considered so important in psychological research on reproduction to demonstrate the link between having a baby and having acquired that particular psychodynamic structure which expresses the socially secondary meaning of womanhood in a patriarchial society? One answer is that there exists a special and mistaken 'psychology of women' which 'implies the need for a special set of laws and theories to account for the behaviour and experience of females'.[10] Another answer is the dominance of the psychoanalytic perspective, according to which much of the sophistication of what Freud actually said has been lost in dogmatic connections between reproductive physiology and female psychology.

Sociological surveys

Because their subject matter is the social, surely sociological studies of women and reproduction have been able successfully to remove motherhood from its deterministic biological underpinnings? To some extent this is true. But just as there has not been, until recently, even the beginnings of a 'sociology of women' so there has traditionally been no 'sociology of reproduction'. Why is this?

Like most professions, sociology has been male-dominated, although perhaps it has been so in less obvious ways than some. The truth is that the 'agenda' of sociology – its defined subject areas, issues and models of enquiry – has been grounded in the working worlds and social relations of men. The accepted fields of sociology – political sociology, the sociology of occupations, the sociology of deviance, and so forth – have been defined from the vantage point of the professional, managerial and administrative structures of our society. Women have been assigned a special place. Both as subject-matter and as practitioners of sociology women have been overwhelmingly relegated to the domain of marriage and family relations.

The consequence of this for sociological conceptions of maternity is that the psychodynamic structure of the marital relationship replaces the psychodynamic structure of the individual (in the psychological paradigm) as the locus in which the meaning of reproduction is to be found. This 'marital' bias is evidenced in four main ways:

(1) research on reproductive intentions and practices has been focused on *married* women (much as gynaecologists are concerned to promote childbirth among the married and prevent it among the unmarried);
(2) the reproductive behaviour of single women has been studied almost exclusively from a 'social problem' perspective, although in many countries 'illegitimate' conceptions are relatively common;
(3) maternity has been viewed as of primary importance to the development of the marriage relationship, rather than to the development (or otherwise) of mothers themselves;
(4) the examination of motherhood has been child- and not woman-centred, reflecting a concern with children's needs rather than with those of mothers.

Largely because of the influence of the functionalist school of thought in sociology, its practitioners were for a long time obsessed with the question 'What purpose does the institution of the family (and the category women-wives) serve for society as a whole?' The answer was couched in terms of families being the sole appropriate factories for the production of human personalities – which are, of course, to the sociologist not born but made. Ultimately, biology seeps in within the functionalist model as the fundamental explanation of gender-differentiation within the family. In particular, recourse is had to 'the division of organisms into lactating and nonlactating classes'.[11]

The functionalist paradigm of motherhood has exerted a tremendous influence on marriage and family sociology, and has got in the way of important alternative questions. These include 'what does the family do to women (and men)?' and 'how does the ethic of marriage and the nuclear family constrain the practice of maternity?' In other words, the sociological paradigm of reproduction as the cornerstone of the family has served to distance women from their reproductive experiences, just as medical appeals to biology or psychological constructions of womanhood have done.

The discipline of medical sociology, which has grown enormously in the last five years or so in Britain and the USA, has given more prominence to maternity than sociology in general.

We now possess a sizeable research literature of studies. Most important of all is the fact that the medical paradigm of motherhood has been reconceptualized as a potential influence on the meaning of motherhood to women themselves.

Once the medical paradigm is extracted from its scientific guise it is possible to see it as a cultural project and, as I have already said, it is a cultural product of enormous significance in shaping commonsense understandings of women and motherhood. But we are still left with the problem of the fissure between the actuality of female experience and its dominant ideological expression. Why do professional paradigms of motherhood contain an image of women as, first and foremost, natural maternal creatures devoted to wifehood and housekeeping? Why does the attribution to mothers of the unselfish motive of reproducing the race hide their characterization as childish and incapable of control? Why are mothers seen at the same time as strong and central to the social structure and as weak and essentially marginal to all mainstream public issues? Why are motherhood and childbirth not themselves public political issues akin to, for example, education and the structure of electoral systems?

To answer these questions we have to set the medical care of women within its broader political context. We must consider both medicine as an agency of social control, and the typical forms of social control to which women have historically been subject.

Notes

1. Illich, I. *Medical Nemesis*, London, Calder and Boyars, 1975.
2. McKeown, T. *The Role of Medicine*, Oxford, Basil Blackwell, 1979.
3. Richards, M.P.M. 'Innovation in medical practice: obstetricians and the induction of labour in Britain', *Social Science and Medicine* 9, 1975, p. 598.
4. Figure cited by the Dutch obstetrician G.J. Kloosterman.
5. I have discussed this fully in 'Normal motherhood: an exercise in self control?' in Hutter, B. and Williams, G. (eds) *Controlling Women*, Croom Helm, 1981.
6. Cooperstock, R. and Lennard, H.L. 'Some social meanings of tranquiliser use', *Sociology of Health and Illness* 1(3), 1979, pp. 331–47.
7. Broverman, I.K., Broverman, D.M., Clarkson, F.E., Rosenkrantz, P.S. and Vogel, S.R. 'Sex-role stereotypes and clinical judgements of mental health', *Journal of Consulting and Clinical Psychology*, Vol. 34, Part 1, 1970, pp. 1–7.
8. See the discussion in Oakley, A. and Chamberlain, G. 'Medical and social factors in postpartum depression' *Journal of Obstetrics and Gynaecology* 1, 1981, pp. 182–7.
9. For a fuller discussion of these themes and references to the literature, see Oakley, A. *Women Confined: towards a sociology of childbirth*, Oxford, Martin Robertson 1980, Chapter 2, 'Psychological Constructs'.
10. Parlee, M.B. 'Psychology' *Signs: Journal of Women in Culture and Society* 1, Autumn, 1975, pp. 119–35.
11. Parsons, T. and Bales R.F. *Family: Socialisation and Interaction Process*, London, Routledge & Kegan Paul, 1956.

Part II

DEBATES AND DECISIONS IN EVERYDAY HEALTH

Introduction

In this section of the Reader we explore health and wellbeing from the perspective of lived experience. If we are to hear 'lay' voices for health then we must pay attention to the raw material from which people weave their personal stories of health. Crawford, one of the contributors to this section, sees health as a concept grounded in the experiences and concerns of everyday life. We focus on the body, the home and the workplace but within these domains we aim to highlight what have hitherto been more 'silent' dimensions. In doing so we generate a perspective on health in which the social has as much weight as the medical, physical or psychological.

The section begins with an article by Crawford who describes the body as a cultural object which is the site of a struggle between release and control. Referring to the 'new health consciousness' he identifies within it exhortations both to take control of the body and to gain release through physical enjoyment. This sets up a potential tension between physical health and wellbeing in which our bodies become a metaphor and a battleground for physical and social conflict.

The view of the body as a metaphor is extended by two associated articles. In one, Willis takes the example of a group of motor-bike boys and argues that it is through the body that minority groups can express their dissatisfaction with the majority culture. In the other article Galler illustrates some of the conflicts in the lives of disabled women, whose bodies she claims have become increasingly subject to the proscriptions of others particularly health professionals and policy makers.

Childrearing practices come under scrutiny by Stainton Rogers who challenges the notion that there is a 'right' way to rear children. Viewed from a social constructionist perspective, expert advice on childrearing loses much of its credibility. This raises issues about the rights of 'experts' to intervene in the private arena of the family, the focus of the next article by Dingwall and Robinson. They explore the role of health visitors in 'policing' the family and highlight the delicate issue of control and responsibility in relation to child health.

131

Child and family health are put in jeopardy when the home is threatened. Home and homelessness are the subject of an article by Davies. She claims that a home is a basic human right – a place to rest, relax, care for and raise children – yet homelessness in Britain in increasing. A decline in the amount of public, council housing stock available for rent in the 1980s, rising unemployment and economic recession combined to create severe disruption and distress in the lives of some families with a concomitant threat to health and wellbeing.

On the surface the next two articles seem to have a tenuous relationship to health, but they represent precisely some of the 'silent' dimensions which we are anxious to tease out. The articles by both Dalley and Enloe are concerned with the social and economic relationships that characterise certain family and workplace situations. In particular they discuss the unequal power relationships which impinge on the wellbeing of women. Dalley takes a critical look at one of the most fundamental forms of social organisation, the family, and suggests that this is supported by a particular ideology – familism. This ideology, she argues, operates to determine the social relations between men and women in both the public and the private spheres and supports an unequal power relationship. Enloe picks up this issue of unequal power relationships and extends it to argue that not only women but all low status groups in developing countries are exploited by international economic interests both in their domestic and in their working lives.

The last article in this section acts as a bridge between this section and the next. Antonovsky proposes a theoretical construct – the sense of coherence – which provides us with a way of analysing many life situations including the domestic sphere and the public workplace. This enables us to focus attention on the health end of a 'health-ease-dis-ease' continuum, thus seeking out what makes for health rather than investigating disease. This in turn raises issues which touch on the basic social structures and value systems of Western society and appropriately leads our thoughts on to 'Health on wider agendas'.

14

A Cultural Account of 'Health': Control, Release, and the Social Body*

ROBERT CRAWFORD

Introduction

The body is not only a cultural object in illness or affliction. Bodily experience is also structured through the symbolic category of *health*. Health, like illness, is a concept grounded in the experiences and concerns of everyday life. While there is not the same urgency to explain health as there is to account for serious illness, thoughts about health easily evoke reflections about the quality of physical, emotional, and social existence. Like illness, it is a category of experience that reveals tacit assumptions about individual and social reality. Talking about health is a way people give expression to our culture's notions of well-being or quality of life. Health is a 'key word,' a generative concept, a value attached to or suggestive of other cardinal values. 'Health' provides a means for personal and social evaluation.

The interviews

In the spring and summer of 1981, I interviewed sixty adults in the Chicago metropolitan area. Conversations averaged from one and a half to two hours and were tape recorded. I did not pre-define my interest in

*This is an abridged version of a chapter in McKinlay, J.B. (ed.) (1984) *Issues in the Political Economy of Health Care*, London, Tavistock, pp. 60–103.

health as either physical or emotional, nor did I identify myself with a medical purpose or carry out the interviews in a professional setting. Interviews took place in the homes of those with whom I talked. I introduced myself as a person writing a book on how people think about health. My intention was to talk with people from a spectrum of American urban life. I did not control for specific demographic characteristics since I was not interested in one particular group or in comparing the views of two or more groups. I attempted, with only partial success, to achieve as much social class, race, sex, and age variance as possible. Initial contacts were made through references from friends and acquaintances and then each person interviewed was asked to recommend one or two other names. Several chains of subjects were developed simultaneously and I followed up those chains that widened the demographics. By the end, however, almost two-thirds of those interviewed were white, middle class, under forty and female. Large and important categories of people were obviously not included or were only minimally included.

The object of this kind of ethnographic research is to see things 'from the native's point of view.' I wanted to know how people describe their health; how they define the term and what concepts are employed (each interview began with the questions, Are you healthy? How do you know?) I also wanted people to talk about their explanations for their state of health: what they identify about themselves or their physical or social environments as important; what they perceive as a threat to their health; and what, if anything, they believe they can or should do to protect or enhance their health. I asked people to identify situations, people, or events that have been important for their health, or for how they think about health. I was also interested in people's notions about responsibility for health and their moral judgments of self and others connected with health.

Health as self-control

To be healthy takes a little more discipline.

A consistent and unmistakable theme runs throughout the interviews. Health is discussed in terms of self-control and a set of related concepts that include self-discipline, self-denial, and will power. When people talk about threats to health, explanations for health, or prescriptions for maintaining and improving health, one or more of these related values frame the discussion and set the moral tone.

Discussion about health as a matter requiring self-control, discipline, denial, and will power is most clearly associated with a conception of health as a distinct goal. In this formulation, health is made the object of intentional action. Health is not a given; nor is it simply a result of good luck or heredity, two alternatives frequently mentioned. Neither is it believed to be an outcome of normal life activities, such as one's work, upbringing or current lifestyle. Health must be achieved. It is independent of health-promoting behaviors. As the goal of health acquires a new-found importance, priorities must be reordered, a commitment made. The goal of health competes with other goals and therefore requires an active choice:

> I think generally we have to have a more healthy attitude. Health has to be a bigger part of our lives. . . . I have to go back and take a look and change my lifestyle. I have to find time for it. . . . I think I have to be more concerned or excited about being healthier. My attitude now is passive. I am thinking a lot about it but I'm not really doing anything. I think I have to have more perseverance with the problem, make it a goal. Just like I have this goal for work, I should have this goal for health.

For this woman the ethic of health must be like the ethic of work. The Protestant world view extends to the body; it invades the domain of leisure. To speak of health in this way is to speak of resolve. Health as a goal necessitates the adoption of a more determined regime of restraint and denial – more 'perseverance.' It involves an effort to impose what are often perceived to be difficult changes on personal behavior and lifestyle, an attempt to curb ingrained, unhealthy inclinations and dispositions.

Judgment of others and self-blame are themes that can be found throughout these interviews, reflecting a general moralisation of health under the rubric of self-responsibility (Crawford, 1980).

While the notion of health as self-control was primarily expressed by professional middle-class people, it was by no means confined to that group. Blue collar workers also spoke of health in terms of the virtues of discipline although there was not the same idea of pursuing health as an active goal.

> I always was competitive in life, more or less, and I've always tried to be up there competing, playing games and sports, and in my studies, and at work, and in order to do that you have to keep yourself in good health. You have to more or less train, discipline yourself, let's call it that. . . . The greatest hazard to your health, one of the greatest, is to be lazy. I think that's a detriment, just as much a detriment to man as smoking and drinking, because that just ruins a man. He can't do a thing when he becomes lazy. He's just no good. His body's no good. He can't perform. He's just no good.

And from a steel worker, here is a similar conception of body and health, even more clearly connected with the virtue of hard work:

I believe in working. I believe in it. If I wasn't at a steel mill it would be some place else. And I would probably work just as hard. Got to have it, man. It is another key to health.

Q: Why is that?

A: You got to work. You got to work at something, put a lot of energy into something. You have to. That is what your body was really designed for – to be functional.

In both of these examples the body is seen as the body of a worker. The orientation is *performative*; health as discipline is *functional* – for, or equivalent to, hard work. And unlike the middle-class woman who equated the goal of health with the goal of work, there is less here a notion of purposive self-creation. The value of discipline is the same as the value of work – they both bestow a sense of self-worth.

Health as self-control: an interpretation

How might one account for the prominence of the self-control theme in these interviews? The most straightforward explanation is that there are *practical reasons* why people associate health with self-control. The argument would run something like this:

Our lifestyle has become health-denying. We consume unhealthy products, live a sedentary life, become addicted to harmful substances, and pursue reckless, high-risk activities. If health does not flow from a way of life, then actions must be taken that require individual determination. The individual striving for health in an unhealthy society must refuse to give in to conventional lifestyles. In such a society, health maintenance is a matter of abstentions and renunciations. In other words, self-control, discipline, denial, and will-power are precisely the qualities of character needed to combat 'bad habits' and to negotiate the minefield of health hazards.

There is much to be said for such an explanation. Within this practical account, however, important questions remain unanswered. What, for example, is the implicit definition of health in the conception of health as self-control? The quotations I have drawn upon to illustrate the theme reveal that health is thought of in physical terms (although as I will discuss below, control figured in some psychosomatic conceptions as well), and most often as the absence of disease. The implied theory of disease causation and therefore disease prevention depends on an idea of the body as a biophysical entity that can be threatened and maintained by physical agents and processes.

Self-control as a cultural theme

There is another way to approach the questions posed earlier: why is health conceived in terms of self-control? And why does a new health consciousness in which self-control is a prominent theme emerge at this time? I have argued that the practical activity of health promotion can only be understood in the context of culture. Now I would like to explore the proposition that 'health' is a moral discourse, an opportunity to reaffirm the shared values of a culture, a way to express what it means to be a moral person (Haley, 1978; Whorton, 1982). From this perspective, the question is raised whether the emphasis on self-control and discipline in the way we talk about health can simply be understood as following from the practical necessities of achieving health; or, might such a conception also follow from the importance within our culture of the values of self-control and discipline? Self-control, self-discipline, self-denial, and will-power may be attempted not only *in order to achieve* health; they may constitute the symbolic substance, the implicit meaning of the pursuit of health. It is possible to say that health is thought about in terms of self-control. It is equally possible that the concept of self-control is 'thought' through the medium of health.

It should not be surprising that 'health', a concept that gives expression to our culture's notions of somatic, psychic, and social well-being, would provide the perfect metaphor for values that so fundamentally structure our social and cultural life. Talking about health becomes a means by which we participate in a secular ritual. We affirm ourselves and each other, as well as allocate responsibility for failure or misfortune, through these shared images of well-being. The 'health' of the physical body – at the same time a social body – validates conventional understandings.

But does the revival of a cultural enthusiasm for health promotion under the sign of self-control indicate an increase in the importance of that sign in contemporary culture? Is there a new mandate for self-control, self-discipline, self-denial, and will power? I believe there are signs that in the last few years the mandate for control has, in fact, grown, that our notions of self and social reality are more infused with symbols of control. Does such a change appear in what we say and do about our bodies?

The cultural reaction to hard times can take many forms. I am suggesting here that one of them is a hardening of bodies. I am not proposing that the new health consciousness is simply a response to the economic crisis. As I have stated, several factors converge to give health its present meanings. The interest in health was growing rapidly before our economic misfortune became fully apparent. I am arguing, however, that as we internalise the mandate for control and discipline, 'health' and 'fitness' are readily available means by which we literally embody that mandate. Our bodies, 'the ultimate metaphor', refract the general mood. We cut out the fat, tighten our belts, build resistance, and extend our endurance. Subject to forces that lie beyond individual control, we attempt to control what is within our grasp. Whatever practical reasons and concerns lead us to discipline our bodies in the name of health or fitness, the ritualised response to economic crisis finds in health and fitness a compatible symbolic field.

The body and 'personal responsibility' for health is, I believe, the symbolic terrain upon which both the desire for control and the display of control are enacted.

Health as release

Q: How would you define health?

A: It's being able to do what you want to do when you want to do it. It's nice to be able to do things. It's nice to be able to eat and drink what you want, not worrying about being overweight or sticking to the diet that the doctor told you to stick to.

Logically entailed in any discourse of self-control is its opposite. A disciplinary regime in the name of health is opposed by a belief in the salubrious qualities of release. One discourse does not exist without the other. And as will be discussed, the interplay between them, apparent within individuals as well as within society, reveals an underlying symbolic and structural order, a logic of 'freedom' and constraint which in advanced capitalist societies is inherent in the contradiction between production and consumption.

The releasing motif suggests pleasure-seeking rather than ascetic self-denials, the satisfaction of desire instead of the repression of desire. Release is the antithesis of discipline, a disengagement of extrication from imposed and internalised controls. Instead of a language of will power and regulation, there exists a language of well-being, contentment, and enjoyment. Whereas in the dominant, control orientation, releases – such as food, drink, or various 'excesses' – are viewed as antithetical to health, the source of bodily decline against which controls must be mounted, those who emphasise release celebrate these pleasures on the altar of health. 'If it feels good it can't be all bad.'

Health is enjoying life without worry and without a self-denying load of constraints. Health is pursuing a free 'lifestyle,' individually chosen and externally obstructed by no one: 'Ideal health is – being able to do my own thing'. Or again, 'Health is being able to do what you want to do when you want to do it.' Health in this conception cannot derive from controls, denials, and disciplines; they only interfere with the positive experience of enjoyment. Perhaps overwhelmed by the endless proliferation of threats, these individuals refuse to get on what they see as a health hazard merry-go-round. Worrying about health will undermine one's sense of well-being, may induce illness 'I have a whole slew of relatives to prove that', and at the very least will interfere with the pleasures that make life worthwhile. The attitude is best summarised in the following comment from a salesman:

Q: Are men healthier than women or are women healthier than men?

A: I think men are on the whole healthier than women due to the fact that I think they feel better. I think they feel healthier. They may have the same aches and pains, but if a man doesn't notice it, or doesn't want to notice it, I would tend to think that that's healthier. The woman may live longer because she does notice it and maybe takes care of it, but if he feels better, who is healthier? It gets back to what my interpretation of being healthy is: if you feel healthy, you are healthy. You may kick the bucket next week but you're healthy. Now a doctor may have a different interpretation than that. You have a foreign body invading your system, he would say you are not healthy. And from his reality he is right. But not from my reality. Because I don't go to a doctor every day and ask him, do I have a foreign body invading my system? From day to day it is how do I feel? And if I feel healthy, I'm healthy. If I feel sick, I'm sick.

This remarkable statement also reveals one dimension of an anti-medical discourse found throughout the interviews. The cosmology of instrumental, future-oriented control is rejected in favor of an immediate, experiential ethic. Here the contrast between a reified, objectifying concept of health and a definition of health grounded in everyday, social-emotional experience is clearest. The physical body (the reality of the doctor) is opposed to the social body ('day-to-day') reality. The comment highlights the distance of the release conception of health from the language of control and its underlying ethos of inner-directedness, goal-seeking, and self-creation. Health as release sits uneasily with both medical discourse and with the medicalised conceptions of health found in everyday life.

Health as release – an interpretation

In the limited space remaining I can only suggest the directions that an interpretation of the release modality might take. First, it is important to note that although there are people who speak mostly one or the other language, a significant number of those I interviewed speak both, at one point declaring the importance of controls, and at another expressing a longing to be free of disciplines.

As with self-control, there are practical or instrumental reasons why health is understood in terms of release. Health, this time defined more generally as well-being or 'feeling good' (almost always involving a somatic as well as a psychological component) may be maintained or improved through releasing activities and states of mind. Listening to people talk about health is to hear of considerable pressures in their lives, often cited as the source of physical tension, pain, or exhaustion. Several people talked about emotional strain, distress, or apprehension. Frequently, these and other emotional-social problems were linked with specific diseases of illness episodes, or were seen as threats to physical health. Repeatedly, I heard the lists of anxieties we have come to expect: money and future security (most frequently), employment, job or school performance, personal safety, concerns about children. As one low-income woman speculated with regard to the relationship between anxiety about money and hypertension, 'Everybody has the same thing – frustration. . . . We got to worry trying to get money; they got to worry about trying to keep it.' Many complained about not being able to relax, citing factors such as being too busy, too much work, the difficulties of managing both work and domestic responsibilities, their own personality, or simply 'too tired'. Most of these people would probably find absurd the suggestion that they find time for health-promoting activities such as jogging. Finding time for 'the self' may be an impossible dream for some of these highly pressured people (for example, single working mothers).

Release as a cultural theme

The question raised earlier about the metaphorical features of health as self-control can be asked about release as well. Is release simply a practical orientation toward achieving psychosomatic health? Or is talking about health in this way an opportunity to give expression to one of our culture's most fundamental symbolic categories, one of our most widely shared values? Again, the latter kind of interpretation is not opposed to nor does it exclude the former.

Every culture organises releases from its normal renunciations or 'moral demand systems' (Rieff, 1966). Occasionally, celebrations of release can turn against the social order, but typically release is a means by which societal tensions are managed.

For an economy that normally requires ever greater levels of consumption, a symbolic order based on self-control is ruinous. Rather than delay gratification, the imperative is to indulge. Rather than deny the self, the premise is instant contentment. Social institutions are mobilised to produce a personality structure compatible with consumption. Whereas production requires a structuring of time to the industrial clock, consumption must reorganise non-working time into 'leisure' and 'lifestyle' – a transformation into time available for buying and using an endless array of products. The sign of our culture, projected on billboards and television screens, is unambiguous: the 'good life' means a life of consumption.

I have argued that health is a symbol through which various concepts of individual and social well-being are given expression. Here I am suggesting that the discourse of health as release can be understood in part as a representation of historically specific values of and mandates for release. The assumption is that cultural mandates, particularly crucial ones such as the one that yokes release to consumption, are internalised and reproduced through key concepts such as health; concepts which thus function as metaphors for those mandates. I am not arguing that *the* meaning of health as release can be understood in these terms, any more than health as self-control can be interpreted as merely a reflection of the cultural mandates for discipline and control. None the less, these dominant cultural meanings are a good place to begin one's interpretation. But it is only a beginning. Symbols are appropriated for a multitude of individual purposes that in turn the analyst must attempt to understand in specific historical and subcultural contexts.

The opposition

'All of my self-control is used up not smoking cigarettes; therefore I don't have self-control for anything else. All my energy is used up . . . so I treat myself to everything I always wanted to eat.'

There are two opposing mandates, two opposing approaches to the attempt to achieve well-being. The opposition is structural. At the level of the social system it is a principal contradiction. The culture of consumption demands a modal personality contrary to the personality required for production. The mandate for discipline clashes with the mandate for pleasure. 'Put a little weekend in your week!' reads the beer advertisement. Employers in industries experiencing high levels of on-the-job or lunch-time drinking are not likely to be happy with alcohol promotions that undermine the symbols of self-control and discipline associated with the work ethic (the week) with symbols of release from those controls (the weekend). Release extended to the shop floor is subversive.

The contradiction in structure leads to a conflict in experience. As in the soft drink ads that portray young, athletic bodies, one must consume and stay thin at the same time. The omnipresent command, 'Eat!' is countered by the moral imperative to control eating. Indeed, food becomes a central metaphor for our dilemma. Indulgence in eating is infused with guilt while denial of food elicits the feeling of deprivation. Constant dieting engenders a persistent desire to 'indulge one's appetite.' Both feast and fast become images of health and disease.

The new health and fitness consciousness is also an embodiment of the opposition. The standard fare in most health clubs is an elixir of pleasure and pain. The body is reconstructed to the rhythms of your favorite music – 'Jamnastics is a fun way to get your heart beating and your body toned.'

The new health consciousness belongs to neither control nor release. People often speak of the necessity for 'balance' or the avoidance of 'extremes.' And certainly, each symbol and its corresponding experiences find their power in opposition, an opposition that is perhaps basic to human life. The specific content of these forms, however, a product of living cultures, raises questions as to their easy integration. The contemporary mandates for control and release, reflecting a basic contradiction in the social body, mitigate against such a balance. The pursuit of health is bound to reproduce that contradiction.

Vertical oppositions: some notes

I have argued that health is a metaphor for generalised well-being. It is a concept that references key aspects of our cultural order. Concurrent with practical reasons for our conceptions of health, which are themselves symbolically ordered, other socially structured systems of meaning are given expression through 'health.'

But the foregoing commentary oversimplifies. The cultural modalities of control and release that play themselves out in our bodily experience should not be understood in a unitary fashion. Our concepts of our bodies and our understandings of health do not simply replicate cohesive or unitary categories. Dominant cultural notions shape our concepts of health in complex relations with meanings that emerge from concrete physical-emotional-social experiences. These experiences do not simply conform to cultural mandates. The body is not only a symbolic field for the reproduction of dominant values and conceptions; it is also a site for resistance to and transformation of those systems of meaning. Cultural meanings are not only shared or given; they are fragmented and contested. They are contested because social life is divisive as well as cohesive. The body is a social body and the social body is fractured. Not only are systems of domination themselves contradictory, experiences of class, sex, race, and age also rupture meaning. Modes of perception and symbolic forms common to the entire society are filtered through hierarchically arranged social relations and the concrete experiences associated with one's position within them. Because of those experiences, we not only internalise dominant codes, values, or categories; we resist them, substituting our own meanings, transforming them, often putting to 'subversive' use symbols intended for quite another purpose.

Self-control and release understood as resistance, like their function as cultural mandates, must be seen as two sides of the same coin. It is the same society that paradoxically makes it difficult for us to attain control over the conditions that shape our everyday lives while concurrently undermining our capacity for 'healthful' release from imposed and internalised controls. That the body is the site for resistance should not be surprising. The mandates of control and release are experienced physically. Power imposes its agenda and achieves its objectives through our bodies. Certainly the political struggle for well-being must extend beyond our individual bodies. But to ignore the effects of power on our bodies is to miss a crucial arena for the exercise of power and for its transformation. Our bodies are social bodies. We need to become more aware of how our bodies are both the metaphor and the substance of our struggle against domination. Only then will we be able to move our submerged and individual gestures of resistance toward more collective and consciously political ends. 'Health' is but one dimension.

References

Crawford, R. (1980) 'Healthism and the medicalization of everyday life', *International Journal of Health Services*, **10**, 365–88.

Haley, B. (1978) *The Healthy Body and Victorian Culture*, Cambridge, Harvard University Press.

Rieff, P. (1966) *Triumph of the Therapeutic: uses of faith after Freud*, New York, Harper & Row.

Whorton, J. (1982) *Crusades for Fitness: the history of American health reformers*, Princeton, NJ: Princeton University Press.

The Expressive Style of a Motor-bike Culture*

PAUL E. WILLIS

This article is based on a research programme that concentrates on the role of pop music in the life style of two groups – 'hippies' and 'motor-bike boys' – in Birmingham, England. The fieldwork on which this article is based was conducted at a motor-bike club during 1969–70. The club has now closed and the group of motor-bike boys I worked with has dispersed. I have changed the names of all individuals referred to.

The fundamental argument I want to put forward is this. Whereas 'deprived' minority cultures do not use verbal codes to express their meaning, they do have complex feelings and responses which are expressed in their own culturally resonant way. Essentially these groups have forms of expression quite as varied and rich as those in apparently more 'accomplished' cultures, but in a mode which makes them opaque to verbally mediated inquiries and therefore vulnerable to gross minimisation in conventional accounts.

In this article I shall indicate what some of these 'opaque' expressive styles are in the case of the motor-bike boys, and go some way towards unpacking their meaning in relation to the central life-values of the motor-bike culture.

Clothes as expression

The dress of Bill-the-Boot, Sammy, Slim Jim and Bob (a group of bike-boys within the larger motor-bike culture that I studied) was not primarily a functional exigency of riding a motor-cycle. It was more crucially a symbolic extension of the motor-bike, an amplification of the qualities

---

*This is an abridged version of a chapter in Benthall, J. and Polhemus, T. (1975) *The Body as a Medium of Expression*, Allen Lane, pp. 233–52.

inherent within the motor-bike. The strict motor-cycle apparel, i.e. that most designed to eliminate the discomforts of riding the motorcycle, had the opposite effect. It tended to close down and minimise the natural qualities of the motor-bike. Thus, the conventional clothing of Percy consisted of a helmet, goggles, waist belt, tightly closed-in neck, gloves and large woollen socks. Generally, this conventional gear was water-tight and warm, to minimise the obvious discomforts of driving in the English climate. Also, it was generally free from all but essential accoutrements, and was pulled in tightly without open flaps, so as to minimise wind-resistance. In this conventional dress Percy was thus tightly packaged in, and given the maximum protection from the inherent dangers and discomforts of the motor-bike. The special characteristics of the motor-bike, its openness to the elements, its instability, its speed, the free rush of air, were minimised as far as possible, so as to render the motor-cycle a neutral form of transport.

The other members of the group, the motor-cycle boys, kept the same basic elements within their style but *transformed* them by small though crucial modifications. To start with, helmets and goggles were never worn. They knew quite well that helmets were advisable for safety, if only because a national safety campaign of the time, with posters across the nation, was aimed at encouraging motor-cyclists to wear helmets. The slogan read 'You know it makes sense'. (Helmets have since been made compulsory in Britain.) The reason they did not wear them was that helmets and goggles would have significantly limited both the *experience* and the *image* of motor-cycling. Helmets and goggles destroy the excitement of the wind rushing into the face, and of the loud exhaust-beat thumping the ears. The point of fast driving was the experience, not the fact, of speed. For those who have never ridden on a motor-cycle, it may not be clear that high-speed riding is an extremely physical experience. At high speeds the whole body is blown backwards.

The absence of gloves, goggles and helmet means that the equivalent of a high gale-force wind is tearing into exposed and sensitive flesh. Eyes are forced into a slit and water profusely, the mouth is dragged back into a snarl, and it is difficult to keep it closed. There is no disjunction whatsoever between the fact and the experience of speed, and physical consequences are minutely articulated with control decisions of the motor-bike. There is no sense in which the rider is protected by a panoply in which he has some calm to make protected decisions about events in the world out there. The motor-bike boy is in the 'world out there' and copes with handling his motor-bike at the same time as feeling the full brunt of its movement in the natural physical world. Furthermore, the motor-bike boy makes no attempt to minimise the drag effect of the wind. Jackets are partly open and are not buttoned down around the throat, belts are not worn, there's nothing to keep the jacket close to the skin, trousers are not tucked away in boots and socks, there is nothing to prevent wind tunnelling up the sleeves. Adornments of the jacket and free-flowing neckties add, although fractionally, to the total drag, an unnecessary drag that would be avoided by conventional motor-cyclists.

The motor-cycle as expression

The motor-cycle itself was not designed for aerodynamic efficiency. All of the motor-cycle boys in the group, except Percy, preferred large cattle-horn handlebars which required an upright sitting position with hands and arms level with the shoulders. This considerably increased drag, and ironically limits the top speed of the motor-bike. But it improves handling ability and increases the sensation of speed dramatically. The conventional motor-cyclist does exactly the opposite; he lowers the handlebars and puts the foot-rests further back, so that the body can lie virtually flat along the bike and present the minimum surface for wind resistance.

Thus the motor-cycle boys – that is Slim Jim, Bill-the-Boot, Sammy, Bob, in contradiction of the typical conventional motorcyclist, Percy – were concerned to *open out* the inherent characteristics of the motor-cycle. The clothing and style and riding and acceptance of risk accentuated the physical exhilaration of speed, and the gut reaction to danger. With the conventional motorcyclist, the qualities of the motor-cycle are closed down. The rider is completely impersonalised and hidden from view. The whole outfit is a carefully worked out, and carefully put together, attempt to muffle the effects and characteristics of the motor-bike; it is the technological answer to the problems technology has created – uniformity, anonymity, featurelessness encircle the rough, roaring, dangerous qualities of the motor-cycle. The motor-cycle boys accepted the motor-bike and allowed it to reverberate right through into the world of human concourse. The lack of the helmet allowed long hair to blow freely back in the wind, and this, with the studded and ornamented jackets, and the aggressive style of riding, gave the motor-bike boys a fearsome look which amplified the wildness, noise, surprise and intimidation of the motor-bike. The bikes themselves were often modified to accentuate these features. The high cattle-horn handlebars, the chromium-plated double exhaust pipes, the high exuberant mud-guards gave the bikes an exaggerated look of fierce power. More particularly, it was common practice to remove the baffles from the silencer box on the exhaust, in order to allow the straight-through thumping of the exhaust gases from the cyclinder to carry their explosion directly into the atmosphere.

This illuminates a crucial aspect of the motor-cycle culture both in its image and experience. In this culture, human flesh and sensibilities exist in a very special relationship to mechanical power. Where the conventional motor-cyclist and car-driver are, to some extent, shielded from the ferocity of mechanical power, the motor-bike boy accepts it, controls it and attempts to make it his own. There are two things here: one is the flesh wrestling with and controlling mechanical power, precisely overcoming the unease produced by powerful machines; the other is the appropriation of that power within the human zone of meaning, the symbolic extension of the motor-bike into the human world. Mechanical qualities were recognised, appreciated, extended and transformed into human qualities.

Death as expression

Death on the motor-bike held a particular awe and even attraction for the motor-bike boys; it held a privileged position in the symbolic world of the motor-cycle.

> BILL-THE-BOOT I think it's the best way. I'll have a bike until I'm thirty-five, you know. I think it's the best way to die . . . I'd like to go quickly mind you out like a light, 'bang' . . . fast like about a hundred miles an hour . . . hit a car, you know . . . smash straight into something.
>
> P.W. What are the chances do you think of having a serious accident?
>
> BILL-THE-BOOT Oh, well, I'm a nut-case you know on a motorbike, it might do, I've had some near misses, you know, through crash barriers, and I've had concussion and things like that without a crash helmet.
>
> P.W. But did that make you think?
>
> BILL-THE-BOOT No, funnily enough it didn't, everybody else said 'I bet that's made you think' . . . You see that's why I think I may die on a motor-bike.

Such interest in the motor-bike should not be taken as signifying a morbid fascination with death, or as a random quest for excitement or kicks (as, for instance, in drug-use). This would be to misunderstand their relationship to the motor-bike. Firstly, it was not the case that they had a simple death-wish which the motor-bike could efficiently minister to. The notion of skill and experience on the motor-bike, which was widely valued, was precisely about *avoiding* unnecessary accident. To have died through stupidity or obvious incompetence would not have been meaningful. Death came only after physical limits had been pushed to the full, after the body had made massive attempts to control the machine.

Thus they did not have a submissive attitude to the motor-bike, but an assertive attitude that stressed the importance of control over the machine; if the machine wouldn't be subject to the dictates of their will, then it was to be distrusted, not valued:

SAMMY No . . . the motor-bike don't frighten you.

BILL-THE-BOOT If the bike handles well, the bike will never beat you, if it handles bad, it frightens you, that's all.

P.W. Frightens, what does 'frightens' mean?

BILL-THE-BOOT No, scared, I mean. Like if I've got a bike and it don't handle well, I won't go fast on it, but if it'll do everything you want it to, well that's it you know.

Secondly, the motor-bike was not a random source of danger and excitement, but was located well within the common-sense world, and was responsive to ability and co-ordination in the physical world. In several ways – in its image, in its difficulty of mastery, in its precise functioning, in its predictable response – the motor-bike puts beyond doubt the security and physicality of the motor-bike boy's world.

Social interaction and bodily style as expression

At a simple physical level the bike-boys were rough and tough, certainly by conventional standards. Many social exchanges were conducted in the form of mock fights, with pushing, mock punches, sharp karate-type blows to the back of the neck. All of the groups (excepting Percy) had been in several fights and spoke of the occasions with some enjoyment.

However, their style was masculine and tough in more developed ways than the simply violent. This style, or ambience, within the culture could be described simply as the notion of 'handling oneself', of moving confidently, in a very physical and very masculine world. At one level this was the ability or potential ability to 'handle oneself' in a *real* fight situation. At another level, the same physical propensities were symbolically expanded into a rough kind of bonhomie. Movement and confidence in movement were the key to their style.

To be quite clear about the nature of this masculine style, it must be stressed that it owed nothing to the conventional notion of the healthy masculine life. Participation in organised sport, for instance, held very little attraction for the bike-boys; their view of the appropriate manly scope of action did not include the wearing of shorts and the obeying of formal rules, nor was athletic ability taken as evidence of masculinity. Attempts to channel their aggressive and robust style into formal sports situations generally met with disaster precisely because it misunderstood the nature of, and the difference between, the two kinds of masculinity. Where individuals did become involved in sport, by and large it was to spoof the whole thing. Rules and conventions were ignored, old sweaters and jeans were often worn instead of neat sports clothing. They would not engage in any safe channelling off of aggressive feelings that might have endangered the normal course of life. Masculinity and aggression were mixed in with normal life. To have siphoned these things off in a formal and organised way would have been to deny their identity.

Music and related activities as expression

The musical quality the motor-bike boys universally disliked was slowness and dreariness; the quality they prized in their preferred music was speed and clarity of beat – a general encouragement to movement and dancing. The antidote to boredom was always movement, particularly dancing, and this in turn relied on the strong beat. As Bill said, 'That's all you need.' The importance of being able to dance to the music was stressed time and again. The consistent taste for strong beat, fast tempo and danceable atmosphere is a direct extension of the motor-bike boys' attitudes and style in general life. In a masculine, aggressive, extrovert world, relying above all on movement and confidence, the qualities appreciated in music were bounce, movement and exuberant confidence.

There seemed to be an integral connection between rock music and riding fast. The experience of riding fast was incited by the feel of the rhythm in the head; all the qualities of fast dangerous riding, with the emphasis on movement and masculinity, summed up, and were part of, the similar qualities of the music. This became a generalised quality of the culture as a whole. Dancing had a similar, though less dramatic, function; it went with the music, it extended its range, expressed the same thing but in another mode. The same extension occurred from dancing to the bike; where dancing is stretched to the full, or is unavailable, then riding takes over as an extension of that mood and feeling.

BOB I kind of get a rhythm in my head, and try and beat it on my bike kind of thing, you can hear a record in your head while you're riding.

BILL-THE-BOOT If you hear a fast record you've got to get up and do something, I think. If you can't dance any more, or if the dance is over, you've just got to go for a burn-up.

Here there is an explicit kind of statement about the escalation from dancing to riding for the same kind of emotional feeling. There were several half-explained, sometimes obscure, statements pointing in a similar way towards the connection between rock music and riding the motorcycle:

BOB It helps like, the sound of the engine . . . try and get a beat in my head, and get the beat in my blood, and get on my bike and go.

SAMMY If I hear a record, a real good record, I just fucking whack it open, you know, I just want to whack it open.

BOB I usually find myself doing this all of a sudden [moving head up and down] with my feet tapping on the gear or something stupid like that.

In a more violent way, and particularly for Sammy, fighting was an extension of emotion associated in the first place with music. In a telling comment Bill said of Sammy, 'he can't dance you see; I get up and dance, he gets up and hits'. For him fighting had a relationship with pop in the sense that fighting was a playing-out of emotion embodied by the music; it would not have happened without the music, in a sense *was* the music.

There were several comments about fighting and pop music, which clearly show that it is neither pop music nor fighting which is being talked about, but a fusion of the two in relation to a dominant feeling; remember again that aggression and 'handling oneself', movement, bravado and courage were in-group values. Fighting too, fired by a primitive rhythm, was a quintessential expression of those qualities:

BILL-THE-BOOT . . . if the dance is over, you've just got to go for a burn-up.

SAMMY That's like me, we were at the Guardian Angel's dance and whenever a good record came on with a big beat I had to get up and hit some fucker, or do summat. It did, it sent me fucking wild . . .

These are highly specific ways in which pop music played an expressive role in the motor-bike culture. In much less definable, but still real ways, pop music coloured the whole cultural style, whose confidence and muscularity seemed to owe something to the tradition of early rock 'n' roll.

Conclusion

I have suggested in this essay that in the motor-bike culture the body, clothes, interaction, functional and expressive artifacts are used to express, confirm and resonate a whole cultural world and its intricate meanings. None of these expressive modes would be thought of as 'cultural' by middle-class and received standards, and yet within their own matrix and precise location they can hold tight, complex feelings and responses. That these expressions are buried in a life process, and hidden from a casual view, does not invalidate them: rather it is a mark of their unpretentious role as truly participatory elements of a living human culture. At a more general level I would like to propose a few ideas of a more provocative nature. They are only partly related to the preceding analysis, and I cannot bring to them here any weight of empirical evidence; but they may well serve to sharpen the debate. I suggest that the expressive life of a minority culture, in opposition to the main and dominating culture, is likely to have certain specific characteristics:

1 It is likely to use a code which is not fully understood by the main culture.
2 It is therefore unlikely to express its innermost meanings in a verbal way. To do this would be to risk destruction or incorporation by the main culture which has the mastery of, and exerts its power through, language.
3 It is most likely to express its meanings through some configuration of the visual, the bodily, the stylistics of movement and interaction, the use of functional objects, and the appreciation of anti-high-art expressive artifacts.
4 It is likely to use these protected modes of expression to state its opposition, marginal or full, to the main dominating culture. Its survival depends, in part, on the inability of the main culture, its agencies or commercial interests, to understand or reproduce those meanings and the style of their statement.
5 Though all the above elements may be present in a culture, it will not thrive and grow unless the expressive style allows a crucial sense of enhanced personal attractiveness and the development of some kind of collective mystique. The visual, non-verbal basis of such a culture is likely to be the basis of such attractiveness and distinctiveness.

I could speculate that the main middle-class culture is based on the head, language and cerebrality, and that minority opposition cultures are based on the body, style and the non-abstract. We must consider the possibility that the body is used in certain minority cultures to express coded, and partly hidden, opposition to the dominant culture surrounding them – it is *because* these codes of expression are largely passed over, or misinterpreted, by the middle classes and their agencies of control that they can, and are allowed to, play such a vital part in the generation of minority cultures.

16

The Myth of the Perfect Body*

ROBERTA GALLER

A woman was experiencing severe abdominal pain. She was rushed to the emergency room and examined, then taken to the operating room, where an appendectomy was performed. After surgery, doctors concluded that her appendix was fine but that she had VD. It never occurred to them that this woman had a sexual life at all, because she was in a wheelchair.

I saw a woman who had cerebral palsy at a neuro-muscular clinic. She was covered with bruises. After talking with her, it became clear that she was a battered wife. I brought her case to the attention of the medical director and social worker, both progressive practitioners who are knowledgeable about resources for battered women. They said, 'But he supports her. Who else will take care of her? And besides, if she complains, the court might take custody of her children.'

As a feminist and psychotherapist I am politically and professionally interested in the impact of body image on a woman's self-esteem and sense of sexuality. However, it is as a woman with a disability that I am personally involved with these issues. I had polio when I was 10 years old, and now with arthritis and some new aches and pains I feel in a rather exaggerated fashion the effects of aging, a progressive disability we all share to some degree.

Although I've been disabled since childhood, until the past few years I didn't know anyone else with a disability and in fact *avoided* knowing anyone with a disability. I had many of the same fears and anxieties which many of you who are currently able-bodied might feel about close association with anyone with a disability. I had not opted for, but in fact rebelled against the prescribed role of dependence expected of women

---

*This chapter was first published in Vance, C.J. (ed.) (1984) *Pleasure and Danger: Exploring Female Sexuality*, Routledge and Kegan Paul, pp. 165–72.

growing up when I did and which is still expected of disabled women. I became the 'exceptional' woman, the 'super-crip,' noted for her independence. I refused to let my identity be shaped by my disability. I wanted to be known for *who* I am and not just by what I physically cannot do.

Although I was not particularly conscious of it at the time, I was additionally burdened with extensive conflicts about dependency and feelings of shame over my own imperfections and realistic limitations. So much of my image and definition of myself had been rooted in a denial of the impact of my disability. Unfortunately, my values and emphasis on independence involved an assumption that any form of help implied dependence and was therefore humiliating.

As the aging process accelerated the impact of my disability, it became more difficult to be stoic or heroic or ignore my increased need for help at times. This personal crisis coincided in time with the growing national political organization of disabled persons who were asserting their rights, demanding changes in public consciousness and social policy, and working to remove environmental and attitudinal barriers to the potential viability of their lives.[1]

Disabled women also began a dialogue within the feminist community. On a personal level it has been through a slow process of disability consciousness-raising aided by newly-found 'sisters in disability', as well as through profoundly moving discussions with close, non-disabled friends that we, through mutual support and self-disclosure, began to explore our feelings and to shed the shame and humiliation associated with needing help. We began to understand that to need help did not imply helplessness nor was it the opposite of independence. This increased appreciation of mutual interdependence as part of the human condition caused us to re-examine the feminist idea of autonomy versus dependence.

Feminists have long attacked the media image of 'the Body Beautiful' as oppressive, exploitative, and objectifying. Even in our attempts to create alternatives, however, we develop standards which oppress some of us. The feminist ideal of autonomy does not take into account the realistic needs for help that disabled, aging – and, in fact, most – women have. The image of the physically strong 'superwoman' is also out of reach for most of us.

As we began to develop disability consciousness, we recognized significant parallels to feminist consciousness. For example, it is clear that just as society creates an ideal of beauty which is oppressive for us all, it creates an ideal model of the physically perfect person who is not beset with weakness, loss, or pain. It is toward these distorted ideals of perfection in form and function that we all strive and with which we identify.

The disabled (and aging) woman poses a symbolic threat by reminding us how tenuous that model, 'the myth of the perfect body,' really is, and we might want to run from this thought. The disabled woman's body may not meet the standard of 'perfection' in either image, form, or function. On the one hand, disabled women share the social stereotype of women in general as being weak and passive, and in fact are depicted as the epitome of the incompetent female. On the other hand, disabled women are not viewed as women at all, but portrayed as helpless, dependent children in need of protection. She is not seen as the sexy, but the sexless object, asexual, neutered, unbeautiful and unable to find a lover. This stigmatized view of the disabled woman reflects a perception of assumed inadequacy on the part of the non-disabled.

For instance, disabled women are often advised by professionals not to bear children, and are (within race and class groupings) more likely to be threatened by or be victims of involuntary sterilization. Concerns for reproductive freedom and child custody, as well as rape and domestic violence often exclude the disabled woman by assuming her to be an asexual creature. The perception that a disabled woman couldn't possibly get a man to care for or take care of her underlies the instances where professionals have urged disabled women who have been victims of brutal battery to stay with abusive males. Members of the helping professions often assume that no other men would want them.

Disability is often associated with sin, stigma and a kind of 'untouchability.' Anxiety, as well as a sense of vulnerability and dread, may cause others to respond to the 'imperfections' of a disabled woman's body with terror, avoidance, pity and/or guilt. In a special *Off Our Backs* issue on disabled women, Jill Lessing postulated that it is 'through fear and denial that attitudes of repulsion and oppression are acted out on disabled people in ways ranging from our solicitous good intentions to total invisibility and isolation'.[2]

Even when the disabled woman is idealized for surmounting all obstacles, she is the recipient of a distancing admiration, which assumes her achievement to be necessary compensation for a lack of sexuality, intimacy, and love. The stereotype of the independent 'super-crip,' although embodying images of strength and courage, involves avoidance and denial of the realities of disability for both the observer and the disabled woman herself.

These discomforts may evoke a wish that disabled women remain invisible and that their sexuality be a hidden secret. However, disabled (and aging) women are coming out; we are beginning to examine our issues publicly, forcing other women to address not only the issues of disability but to re-examine their attitudes toward their own limitations and lack of perfection, toward oppressive myths, standards, and social conditions which affect us all. Jill Lessing urges that we move away from this kind of thinking, the ideology which upholds an ideal type of human body and which regards anyone less than perfect as not fully human, 'with a political commitment as strong as our responsibility to fight racism, classism and sexism in ourselves as well as others'.[3]

In more direct and personal terms, to be a feminist with disability consciousness, or to be a friend or lover of a woman with a disability, you need to be aware of and include the limitations that disability places on her and on you. You must honor the reality of her oppression in the able-bodied world. You must join with her in the fight against external constraints and social injustice in the fields of employment, housing, and transportation accessibility. Feminist events should be accessible, and feminist issues expanded to include the specific concerns of disabled women.

Assumptions of asexuality, personal undesirability, and physical impossibility are perpetuated through the absence of sexual information, guidance, encouragement or social opportunity provided to disabled females growing up. Parents, educators, and health professionals remain generally silent on the subject but the message is loud and clear. *The lack of 'perfection' is equated with the lack of entitlement to sexual life.* Because some disabilities limit mobility, increase levels of fatigue and/or pain, cause loss of sensation or sensory impairment, or create a need for assistance, disabled women may require special awareness, sensitivity, and creative alternatives to enable them to enjoy their sexuality. Finally, after pressure from the disabled community, sex therapists, educators, rehabilitation workers and providers of birth control have begun to specifically direct their services to the needs of the disabled woman and make them accessible to her. Beyond overcoming the realities of physical limitations, however, attitudinal barriers must be made conscious and confronted, if sexual fulfillment is to be a possibility for disabled women.

Even in the changing political climate of women challenging traditional options, if a disabled woman should decide to opt for a non-traditional or independent lifestyle, such as single motherhood, a professional career, or lesbianism, she is often not regarded as having made a choice but is perceived as not having a choice. For disabled women, 'lifestyle, sexual preference and personal decisions are viewed as consequences of the disability rather than as choices'.[4]

By emphasizing the external restraints, social stereotypes and perceptions of others, I do not mean to minimize the significance of the internal world of the disabled woman or her own sense of self-esteem and personal worth. Parallel to women's feelings about their fatness, disabled women also often have a tendency to blame themselves, or imagine that if only they were different, better, and perfect, they would be good enough to do the impossible.[5] Sometimes, like fat, disability can stand for everything a disabled woman feels to be bad about herself and is the focus of low self-esteem, embodying feelings of being damaged, inadequate, unworthy and unlovable.

As women, we all know that constantly running into external barriers reduces a sense of self-worth. The expectations of others become part of the self-concept and self-expectation. This may perpetuate a psychological sense of invisibility, self-estrangement, powerlessness worthlessness, and lack of sexual entitlement among disabled women.

Society's standards of beauty and acceptability are embedded in our initial interactions with parents, caretakers, and health practitioners as they look at, comment about, and handle our bodies. In this way, external standards become internal realities. Too frequently our own bodies become our enemies. This is as true for non-disabled as it is for disabled women. If we are to be capable of seeing a disabled woman as a person instead of her disability, we must confront these feelings in ourselves. It is not easy to face our own limitations honestly, but to the extent that we are able to accept and make peace with the loss, pain, and vulnerability associated with our own lack of perfection, the freer we will be of myths which oppress us and with which we may oppress others.

Perhaps it is time for us all to 'come out' and express our feelings about our bodily 'defects.' Together as women, all with imperfections, limitations, vulnerabilities, strengths and weaknesses, desires, fears and passions, we need to accept and embrace the human condition and move in the direction of being able to live and love in our imperfect bodies.

Notes

1. Disabled women bear the disproportionate economic, social, and psychological burden of what it means to be disabled. Data and an excellent discussion of disabled women's extensive oppression (as compared to non-disabled women and disabled men) are provided in Michelle Fine and Adrienne Asch, 'Disabled women: sexism without the pedestal', *Journal of Sociology and Social Welfare*, July 1981. Their studies reveal that disabled women are more likely than disabled men to be without work: between 65 per cent and 76 per cent of disabled women are unemployed. Disabled women also earn substantially less than disabled men. For vocationally-rehabilitated men and women, the mean annual incomes are $4188 and $2744, respectively.

   Disabled women generally receive inadequate training for personal self-sufficiency and suffer the brunt of labor-force discrimination. Disabled men are more likely than women to be referred to vocational schools or on-the-job training and are somewhat more likely to be college-educated. As a result, women are less likely to find a job post-disability. Those women who do are more likely to absorb a cut in pay than disabled men and are more likely to live in families with incomes at or below the poverty level.

Disabled women are less likely to be married: they marry later and are more likely to be divorced. A greater percentage of female heads of households than male heads of households are disabled. There is a general social neglect of the sexual and reproductive roles of disabled women, because public opinion assumes disabled women to be inappropriate as mothers or sexual beings.

Asch and Fine explore how these stark social and economic realities, the impact of a hostile economy and a discriminatory society bears heavily on the disabled women's self-image. They cite research indicating that disabled women are significantly more likely to have negative self-perceptions and to be viewed negatively by the general public than are disabled men.

While Asch and Fine substantiate the double discrimination which disabled women face, they portray the disabled woman as neither helpless nor hopeless victim. Their perspective is that virtually all of the difficulties imposed by disability which is often painful, frustrating and degrading, stems from the cruelty, discrimination, ignorance of others and the neglect of disabled people by major economic and social institutions not from the disability per se.

While they certainly acknowledge that much remains to be done to insure that disabled women can live with independence and dignity, they also stress the strides individuals have made to challenge disability-specific constraints and cite the collective struggle of disabled women (and men) who are organizing and fighting against unjust economic and social conditions.

2. Jill Lessing, 'Denial and disability', *Off Our Backs*, Vol. xi, No. 5, May 1981, p. 21.
3. Ibid.
4. Adrienne Asch and Michelle Fine, (1981) 'Disabled women: sexism without the pedestal', op. cit.
5. Carol Munter (1984) 'Fat and the fantasy of perfection', in Vance, C.J. (ed.) *Pleasure and Danger: Exploring Female Sexuality*, pp. 225–231.

17

The Social Construction of Child-rearing

REX STAINTON ROGERS

'And she brought forth her firstborn son, and wrapped him in swaddling clothes, and laid him in a manger; because there was no room for them in the inn.'

Some of the best-known words in the English language, Luke 2:7 taken from the King James' translation of the Bible. A scene re-enacted in countless images: in more than a millennium of Christian Art; in traditional nativity plays and their degenerate progeny relegated to the primary school; in ancient folk-craft and in the plastic kitsch of a Modern Christmas.

From that text and those images, anyone who has had even the most secularised upbringing within a notionally 'Christian' culture has acquired a story of child-rearing in biblical times. Like all 'history' that past is a representation retold for its own times. 'No room at the inn' can be recast now (and no doubt is, by those 'trendy vicars' beloved of the right-wing press) into a message about our present concerns over the impact of homelessness on young families. For the first generation of readers of the King James' translation of the Vulgate, Jesus in swaddling clothes took his place in *Europe* – he became English, a country child in a familiar byre. Artists too, positioned Jesus in their own culture – a kinder in Germany, a bambino in Italy. They also iconographised Jesus by their own representational conventions – in other words, constructed an image using 'body language' to convey a message to the audience, just as would a modern advertising agency in promoting disposable nappies. As a result, Jesus is typically shown not swaddled but express-ively free of limb and body – able to show by his attitude that love for his mother that his viewers were meant to feel. Only where that response to a mother was not required were artists able, routinely, to swaddle biblical babies in the Lucan fashion. So it is that Moses, the abandoned baby, floats down the canvas in his mini ark bandaged from head to toe like the Egyptian mummies his adopters were destined to become. In Exodus 2:3 there is no mention of swaddling clothes – Moses, too, for the artists of High Christian Europe, had become a European baby. Every history informs us about the present in which it was created as much, if not more, than about the historical past it purports to reflect.

When people talk now about child-rearing, how it varies over historical time, from culture to culture or class to class, they too are telling us a great deal about our own society, its ways of looking at things, its concerns and preoccupations. To us, the active, expressive baby Jesus relating to his mother seems more 'natural', more 'normal', more 'desirable' than the swaddled condition of baby Moses. All that says is that our classical images of Madonna and Child tell a story of mother-infant relations we both tell and try to bring into being in our own time, while Moses seems more like a 'case for the social workers'. Yet, swaddling babies was in 13th to 16th century Europe a standard procedure and many other cultures did or do adopt similar practices (practices for them eminently 'natural', 'normal' and 'desirable'). Of course, how child-rearing has been represented in the past (or is in our own time) is no golden road to understanding practice. Not least, as feminist researchers have brought to our attention, because most history is his story – not the story of the women who were (and are) the primary rearers in most cultures past and present, and seldom the story of girl children either.

For most of human history, child-rearing, in all its variability, was largely governed by ordinary (folk) knowledge. Children grew up to rear children as they had been reared – as still goes on among surviving traditional peoples today. Our Modern (Western) world of care-givers who turn to and experience the ever-changing intervention of expert knowledge and its practitioners is a product of an economic and social revolution that began around two hundred years ago and is far from universal in its impact even today. Central to that revolution was the emergence of a belief that human betterment (the improvement of the conditions of young and old alike) could be achieved and could only be achieved through the pursuit of knowledge and its application in society. This 'Humanistic Project' saw the bringing into being of both the academic disciplines of the child and childhood as we know them today (e.g. developmental psychology, paediatrics, child psychiatry, educational psychology, sociology) and the welfarist practices that sought to intervene in child-care (e.g. social work, and the institution of statutory protections in the areas of health, work, and education). When Solomon said (Proverbs 22:6) 'Train up a child in the way he (sic) should go: and when he is old, he will not depart from it.' he spoke with traditional authority buttressed by the warrant of God – a folk wisdom robust enough to survive the complex transition from a tribal Asiatic Judaic context to the nation states of pre-Industrial Christian Europe. Yet, by the middle of the 19th century, the promise of a *science* of child-rearing', something which could uncover the *laws* underlying such training, pinpoint the interventions needed to correct matters when the 'way' went wrong, heralded a dramatic change in authority over child-rearing and child-care. Care-givers became increasingly responsible not to God but to the State and its agents, and, thereby, children became a national responsibility.

When we, then, consult a library today about child-rearing, what we find is the accumulative product of around 150 years' work in the academic and practitioner disciplines of childhood. Over the years, that work has variously told us that:

- childhood masturbation is a cause of untold physical and psychological damage *and* that it is harmless;
- too much cuddling damages children's adjustment *and* that you cannot cuddle your child too much;
- young children should never leave their mothers *and* that nursery education is positively beneficial;
- 'mongoloid idiots' are ineducable and best institutionalised *and* that 'Down's Children' thrive in families and can be integrated into mainstream schooling;
- 'mothers are always to blame' *and* that 'mother-blaming' is a patriarchal conspiracy;
- children are fragile and irreversibly damaged by aversive early experiences *and* that children are hardy and capable of overcoming adversity.

These same children have been presented to us as:

- biological blue-prints unfolding through maturation;
- almost infinitely flexible receptacles of specific socialisation practices;
- a seething mass of unconscious sexuality and aggression;
- elaborated puppies undergoing house-training;
- a set of inner traits of disposition and ability;
- a mind striving for knowledge – a biological computer.

Care-givers can perhaps be forgiven if they sometimes treat the latest twist to the best part of a century of such contradictory advice and diverse theorising with more than a grain of salt! After all, Science has usually been sold on the promise of bringing order out of confusion, not the reverse. Small wonder perhaps, that the child expert and his or her comeuppance is a popular figure in jokes, comedy sketches and cartoons –the child psychiatry book becomes not a source of advice on discipline but the means of applying that discipline a posteriori. But, behind the humour, there is also fear. The child expert has power over the care-giver and may use it (or abuse it). It is not hard to see how the popular press mines this twin vein of distrust in its reporting of child protection work: the social worker and the paediatrician do not just make errors but threatening errors – mistakes that could devastate not just in other families but also in our own.

Confusion and concern are not confined to popular culture. Scholars themselves (some of whom are also care-givers, of course, and have lived the confusion as well as studied it) are far from in agreement about how to evaluate the Humanistic Project of a *science* of child-rearing. Yet only if that knowledge is being properly built up can the social worker or the paediatrician be expected to get things 'right'. Over the past twenty years or so, there has been an increasing interest in studying how social scientific knowledge-making comes about and work with children has been one of the most popular areas of interest. Roughly speaking, we can break down this work into two main readings of the history of the science of child-rearing. They are profoundly different one from the other.

The first, the more traditional, and probably the more widely held, is that we are dealing with the story of the march of any kind of scientific knowledge. This interpretation argues that the apparent confusion is illusionary. Looked at more closely, it is a reflection of the gradual refinement of theory. Less satisfactory models of the child and of child-rearing are replaced by better ones as a result of an ever-improving pool of empirical findings based on evolution in methods of data collection. We are, in short, moving ever closer to the truth – *the* facts about child-rearing – and thereby to a technology for the production of better childhoods and better children.

The second reading of the history of the science of child-rearing, and the one I adhere to, offers a very different picture. This sees knowledge itself as a product of human activity – as the jargon has it, as a social construction. Facts are not things-out-there waiting to be found out, they are brought-into-being. Freud, say, did not so much discover the Oedipus Complex as *invent* it in a social process with his patients and the culture they all shared. Hence, the social constructionist reading argues that it is not the confusion in this area which is illusionary but the search for a science of child-rearing itself! This is a fairly dramatic claim and one which, if taken seriously, argues that what is needed is not 'more of the same' ('more research', 'more time to find the answers') but a fundamental reappraisal of the questions and a pondering upon how it is that we come to ask them and what we bring into being when we try to answer them. It is that agenda I now wish to explore.

If we are told that someone is rearing maggots or guppies or beagles, it can reasonably provoke the question 'why?' which carries with it a range of greaterly or lesserly plausible expected answers such as: for fun; as pets; for research; out of interest. Clearly, that doesn't work over children. 'Why are you rearing children?' is the kind of question we are not used to answering (unless perhaps we are professional carers). On the other hand, 'Why are you rearing your children *that way*?', although not perhaps the most polite of enquiries can at least be answered: 'So that they grow up to be non-sexist'; 'So that they can cope with a racist world'. The questioner may challenge the project and/or the means to achieving it but all of this now lies within the realm of the sensible. What this tells us is that child-rearing always raises both instrumental (how) and terminal (why) elements and both are subject to moral evaluation. This is equally true for the formal study of child-rearing. Researchers and their audience bring, to any research, ideas that are full of moral (and often ideological) content. To begin, child-rearing is studied not just (and often not primarily) in terms of the immediate process but for what it is hoped to, supposed to (or feared to) bring about when the child reaches adolescence or adulthood. Research takes on board, often without examination, ideas about what it is that we should become as we grow up. These ideas, of course, are themselves social constructions. Research was once done to discover why some boys didn't grow up masculine enough, it is now more likely to be done to discover why some boys grow up into sexist men. Not only can such research never be objective, it frequently reflects concerns that are very obviously products of their time. Anyone who puts in a research application today for funds to study 'the unmarried mother and her child' would be laughed out of court. Forty years ago it would have been seen as a highly important study 'addressing a major social issue of our time'.

Whenever 'issues' and, even more so 'problems' (as in 'the problem of the latch-key child') drive research, the research that results addresses constructed questions and thereby shapes the kind of answer we get. To pose 'the problem of the latch-key child' is to seek the 'feared-for' at the level of individual children: are they, say, less 'well-adjusted?' This brings two kinds of difficulties. First, what is adjusted? Does it, for example, mean 'like the researchers' children'? Secondly, it is also not to ask other questions: 'why is Britain so poorly equipped in after-school facilities?' Of course, that is a 'political' question but so too, of course, is the idea that 'problems' exist in individuals as though individuals existed independent of societal structure.

This brings us to another important plank in the social constructionist critique of the scientific study of child-rearing – we can never gain knowledge outside of the definitions and principles that guide our search for knowledge. How we define what childrearing is, how we decide what elements within it matter in terms of outcomes and, how we determine what outcomes matter, shape what we can come to know about it. Just to add to the complications, in a society in which 'research' feeds into ordinary understandings (and hence into care-giver conduct) through mass communications, to research something is frequently also to change it. This can be seen most easily by example. Right now we are in the midst of the development of concern about a 'problem', child abuse. As a result, our notions of child-rearing are changing, we can ask – as not many years ago we could not – whether particular childbearing practices are abusive and what the consequences of that abuse are. In turn, care-givers (and those who monitor them, like paediatricians and social workers) are changing their practices or at least coming to look at them in a different light. The belief that child abuse (and in particular child sexual abuse) severely damages the young leads us to look for evidence in later life of those 'feared-for' outcomes. It also brings into being particular ideas about what children are like (e.g. innocent victims), about what care-givers are like (prone to greater or lesser degrees to become perpetrators) and about those who once experienced abuse (survivors). Directly in front of us, the whole question of child-rearing has changed, and with it new ideas begin to gain currency: that children are endowed with rights that can be violated; that care-givers do not have rights 'over' the child but responsibilities to the child. The knowledges we are now building up are no more absolutely true than were the knowledges we had before this shift. What has happened, is that we have changed the questions. With our shifted questions and shifted knowledges, not just our own child-rearing practices come to seem different to us, but so too do those we find in history and in the study of other cultures. Hence, social constructionists argue that knowledge of child-rearing can never be absolute because we can never get outside of the social world to study it. Truth is always local and contingent, our truth reflecting our social world and its concerns.

Which brings me to the stage in my constructionist sermon for looking at a slightly less well-known passage from the Gospels. It concerns the point in cultural terms where Mary's baby becomes a true person to his society. This is, by the way, not the moment of birth (as is generally the case in current secular terms, e.g. in law) but his point of naming, when he becomes Jesus:

> And when eight days were accomplished for the circumcising of the child, his name was called JESUS. (Luke 2:21)

By some contemporary notions of abusive child-rearing, Jesus was, thereby also abused – he acquired a 'non-accidental injury'. You may or may not agree, you may find the very raising of the question offensive and I have no intention of prescribing how your judgement ought to go.

What I would encourage you to do is to explore your arguments and to recognise how your moral, religious, political (even, perhaps aesthetic) world views enter into them. It may help the process if you try following this paragraph through again as if Jesus had been a girl!

Research cannot tell us which are good child-rearing practices and which are bad – unless it includes moral, religious and political (i.e. non-scientific) preassumptions like the importance of an 'ethnic or religious identity'. These are always open to dispute and reinterpretation. I suspect most of you will find it easier to support a policy of Catholic adopters for 'Catholic' babies than Satanist adopters for 'Satanist' babies (unless your name is Rosemary, perhaps). In other words, child-rearing and its evaluation are always the product of persons-in-culture, our understandings cannot help but tell us about ourselves. Many constructionists would go so far as to say that it is by how we evaluate the social world that we come to a sense of who and what we are. The self and the sense of self are themselves also socially constructed. Of course, if the judge as well as the judged are socially constructed, then by shifting the judged we may also shift the judge. This puts the onus for change towards better childhoods onto each one of us (increasingly, as they gain in cultural competence, that includes children and young people themselves), it is not a matter for 'experts' alone. Academics (like developmental psychologists) or practitioners (like social workers) have no special resources for making *moral* or *political* decisions about child-rearing beyond those that are accessible to our culture in general. Just as we have only one Earth in trust to all of us, so too for our culture. In child-rearing, as in everything else, in the words of the old Gospel song 'We're gonna reap just what we sow'.

References

James, A. and Prout, A. (1990) *Constructing and Reconstructing Childhood*, London, Falmer.

Scarre, G. (ed.) (1989) *Children, Parents and Politics*, Cambridge University Press.

Stainton Rogers, R. and Stainton Rogers, W. (1992) *Stories of Childhood*, Hemel Hempstead, Harvester-Wheatsheaf.

18

Policing the Family? Health Visiting and the Public Surveillance of Private Behavior*

ROBERT DINGWALL and KATHLEEN M. ROBINSON

Health visitors are public health nurses whose main work has traditionally been the unsolicited routine visiting of all families with young children for the purposes of health screening and health education. The history of their occupation provides a case study in the conditions under which the surveillance of domestic behavior in a liberal democracy becomes possible, of the working practices that sustain it and of the ideological movements that can destroy it. If home care is to be shaped by the felt needs of the carers and the cared, it will be argued that such a proactive system of population surveillance is essential. The search for need must be an overriding objective of social policies and organizational designs.

This objective was a major influence on the development of health visiting in Britain from the 1880s to the 1980s. It never gained wide acceptance in the United States, as illustrated by the failure of the attempt to provide a coherent system for child health and welfare through the Sheppard-Towner Act in the 1920s (Rothman, 1981; Halpern, 1988). The opposition remains as fierce as ever. In 1975, for example, there was a celebrated exchange in *Pediatrics*. The journal had

*This is an abridged version of a chapter in Gubrium, J.F. and Sankar, A. (1990) *The Home Care Experience: ethnography and policy*, Sage, pp. 253–73.

published a commentary article by C. Henry Kempe, the leading pediatrician and researcher on child abuse, advocating health visiting on the British model as the key to effective child protection. It was the way to discover need in those too young to articulate it for themselves and whose caretakers might have a vested interest in denying its existence. Kempe anticipated the obvious objections:

> Visits by the health visitor do not deprive the members of the family of their civil rights but do guarantee that the civil rights of the child will be recognized and protected . . . [they] do not significantly infringe on the parent's right to privacy but demonstrate that society has the obligation to ensure access to the child during the first years of his life rather than waiting until he enters school. . . . If the plan is made egalitarian and universal, it would obviate the concern that it is a repressive program for those who are poor or from minority groups. (Kempe, 1975 pp. 693–694)

This article brought such fierce responses that the editors and publishers felt obliged to print a defense of the principle of free debate in professional journals. The views of Dr. Herbert Rubinstein from New York are typical:

> It is despicable that the Academy would be party in the propagation of such totalitarian-egalitarian views. . . . Those who feel they can, because of their own inclinations, subjugate others should become dictators, not healers. Those who feel they want to force changes in child-rearing should become social workers, not scientists. Those who feel parents must be forced to raise their children in a preconceived beneficial manner should become terrorists, not educators. (Rubinstein, 1976, p. 577)

Similar voices were heard in Britain at the beginning of the twentieth century when health visiting acquired state sponsorship.

Policing the home

By the beginning of the twentieth century, paid visitors could be found in most of the major industrial areas of Great Britain. The following decade (1910) saw the term *health visitor* generally adopted as a label for these employees; by 1918, all local public health departments were obliged to provide this service.

Health visiting was given additional impetus as an instrument of state policy by the perceived need to replace the manpower losses of World War I, and its reach was gradually extended to middle-class families during the 1920s. This strengthened the universalistic aspects of health visiting, while also becoming more firmly medicalized with the restriction of recruitment to registered nurses and its increasing identification as a nursing speciality. These features were largely unaffected by the establishment of the National Health Service, and its basic ideological justification remained unchanged. Indeed, one of the last acts of the Council for Education and Training of Health Visitors (CETHV), the accrediting body for training programs before its absorption in 1980 by a new council regulating all branches of nursing, was to reassert the primacy of the search for unmet need through the home visit in terms used almost a century before:

> Our original employers sent health visitors into communities which had obvious and desperate health needs. It was left to the individual worker to search for and identify the health needs of individual families. Without this painstaking and time-consuming search, the identification of individual need could not have been made with any precision, nor appropriate remedies applied. . . . As health needs have become less overt, search was and is even more importantly now, the source of all health visiting. . . . There is no other group in the health or the social services with the tradition of visiting people in their own homes so that health needs may be identified before health problems develop. (CETHV, 1977, pp. 26, 29)

What does this search look like in practice? How is it distinguished from the sort of investigation that might be conducted by a police officer, social security official, or social worker from child protective services? How is it actually possible for state agents to enter the private domain of the family?

The home visit

The data collected were taken from a sample of 28 transcripts of *primary visits* – that is, home visits made on or about the tenth day after the birth of a new baby.[1] The family will have been visited daily by a midwife up to this time as part of the clinical follow-up to the actual delivery, whether the birth took place in a hospital or at home. This was the first post-natal contact with a health visitor. Fifteen health visitors participated in the study, recording their own work with equipment supplied by the researcher in order to minimize observer effects. The community in which they were working was generally affluent, but the families in the sample range from relatively poor agricultural workers to professionals who commuted to jobs in London.

The health visitor's entry to the house is a key point for analysis. In a liberal state, unannounced official agents do not have the power to force entry. However, the theory of tutelage (Donzelot, 1980) provides that a refusal of access to the health visitor may cause the family to be treated as disreputable and consequently referred to other agencies, like the police or child protective services, who do have access to such powers.

The summons below is a simple device based on the caller's identity as a health visitor (HV):

> *HV*: Sarah Dawson, the health visitor. Hello. It's Mrs. Jones. I'm Dr Arthur's health visitor. Shall I go up?

If the person at the door is hesitant, the identity might be repeated but not elaborated:

> *HV*: Hello there, I'm Erica Tate, the health visitor. . . . Is your wife in? Erica Tate, the health visitor.

Sometimes, even the label of health visitor is unnecessary.

> *HV*: Hello, how are you? Is Sue in or is she busy or . . .?

These summonses have certain notable features in this context: for example, their cursory character. Although the health visitors do not enter without an invitation from the person who opens the door, there is no attempt to 'sell' the visit. They do not attempt to explain their presence or to justify their entry. Indeed, their behavior implies an expectation of entry, even an entitlement.

What did the health visitors actually *do* with their role as orchestrators? This is where the data, at least superficially, are most surprising. There is no apparent evidence of any grand scheme or purpose, unlike say an encounter on the doorstep with a Jehovah's Witness or a double-glazing salesman. Much of the interaction has a somewhat desultory character. This is best seen through an examination of the movement from one topic to another in the course of the interaction.

Sacks (1972) has summarized the way in which topic organization works in ordinary conversation:

> A general feature . . . is movement from topic to topic, not by topic close followed by a topic beginning but by a stepwise move, which involves linking up whatever is being introduced to what has just been talked about, such that, as far as anybody knows, a new topic has not been started, though we're far from wherever we began. (pp. 15–16)

With this system, the actual content represents the preferred outcome of the parties. This does not mean, however, that the content was designed in advance but, rather, that at each decision point (at every turn), continuation was organized to the parties' satisfaction by a selection from the range of options seeming to be legitimately available. By definition, then, a conversation cannot *pursue* an agenda. An agenda *may* be covered in the course of a conversation, if it goes on long enough or the agenda is brief, but it is more likely that one of the parties will have to breach the convention of stepwise transition and indicate a specific subject as a preferred topic. This would involve special procedures to block opportunities for stepwise movement.

The health visitors seemed to concentrate on the maintenance of the encounter as an end in itself with, at most, the negative objective of preventing their attempt to mimic a conversational form and a 'friend of the family' relationship from overly diluting the thematic orientation to childbirth and motherhood with general conversational topics. Agenda-oriented talk was rare and generally occurred as a justification for a breach of stepwise transition, anticipating the questions, 'Why this, why now?' Several examples refer to the completion of paperwork:

HV: Can I just fill in some paperwork?
HV: Now I've brought the card and all the bits and pieces.
HV: I must fill in my card.

The absense of work on content, however, is most apparent at the points where the interaction lapses, like those places in an ordinary conversation where it 'runs out of steam' and requires a move from one or other party to restart it. This is one of many examples:

HV: And how long does he sleep during the day? Does he go over four hours?
M (   ) he he has done=
HV: =he has done. [Ye:s Ye:s]
M: [(   ] wake him up
HV: You do, yes, that's a good idea, I think. (1.7) Ye:s (1.2) Well, Shirley (the midwife) said something about his weight.
M: She wasn't very happy with it [[(I don't think)]
HV: [Ye:s Ye:s]

The health visitor's reluctance to introduce a new topic is marked by the pauses and the elongation of the 'Ye:s' in her third turn. It might be thought that this would create space for mothers to raise their own concerns but, in fact, as here, they rarely take the chance.

This brief summary illustrates the basis for our contention that the main objective of the modern home visit by health visitors is simply to visit. The encounter is not used to conduct any clear and systematic health assessment or health education, although these goals may be pursued covertly or opportunistically. The health visitor may, for instance, test a child's motor development by engaging him or her in play, but the element of assessment in the activity is unlikely to be made explicit. Equally, she may take a mother's remark as an occasion to give advice on smoking or diet, but she is unlikely to make this a positive objective of the encounter. Indeed, the most difficult topics are conspicuously absent. Health visitors never seem to ask, 'Have you felt anger toward the child? Does she cry a lot? Have you felt like shaking her? Does your husband (or boyfriend) shout at her? Does he come home drunk?'

The modern politics of health visiting

If these arguments are correct, they raise some rather obvious questions about the value of an expensively trained and reasonably well-paid professional going into homes simply for the sake of it. In the absence of recordings from past health visitor/client interaction, we cannot state conclusively whether this apparent lack of content is simply a modern phenomenon. However, there are reasons for thinking that health visitors may once have had a much more conscious agenda. The widespread reports of early hostility to health visitors, for example, suggest that they might well have behaved in an investigative fashion with obviously disreputable clients (Smith, 1979, p. 117; Lewis, 1980, pp. 106–107).

Some clues as to a possible change may, however, also be found in the changing tone of public statements by health visiting's leaders. We have already noted the CETHV's view of the centrality of the search as needed for the work of health visitors. They characterized this as 'activity that is purposeful, unique, focused on health, self-initiated, expert and non-stigmatizing' (CETHV, 1977, p. 27). It involved the systematic screening of populations to identify needs and then to work with those affected, both as individuals and as groups, to change either personal or collective behavior.

Compare this with the approach now advocated by the then-general secretary of the Health Visitors Association (Goodwin, 1988). The CETHV had acknowledged the importance of searching along various dimensions of need – normative, felt, expressed, and comparative, in a categorization derived from Bradshaw (1972, p. 69). The new health visiting, however, only recognizes those felt and expressed needs which are validated by health care professionals. This is reflected in three particularly significant changes. First, the health visitor's objectives will now be determined by reference to an annually compiled community health profile based on epidemiological data. Second, the health visitor/ parent relationship will be put on a contractual basis, which will provide for home visiting only by prior agreement. As a result, the main worksite will shift from the home to the clinic, where screening, group education, and self-help programs will be carried out and parents will be expected to take principal responsibility for initiating health-related actions in relation to their children.

The cumulative impact of these changes amounts to a considerable ideological shift in the basis of health visiting. Instead of beginning from her experience of visiting individuals and aggregating this to map the needs of a community, the health visitor will now start from the official picture of the community and seek to find the individuals who fit its categories, as documented by those data on mortality, morbidity, and related factors that others have considered worth collecting. The result will be to exclude other views of need, particularly those that may arise from what is, in effect, the systematic ethnographic study of a community by an expert in public health.

The language of contract in British health and social services has been imported from the United States, where its combination of authoritarianism and populism reflects the values of a very different society. As Nelken (1988) has pointed out, its abandonment of the vision of universal concern and provision may seem consumer oriented. In practice, however, it forces the recipients into a narrow conception of autonomous individualism. Here, it leads to the discarding of any ideal of client advocacy, that the state might have any duty to see that the voices of those unable to speak for themselves can be heard. Such an activity would be an illegitimate extension of state power and contribute to the perpetuation of dependency. Autonomous clients can and must speak for themselves in the formulation of their contracts with the state.

The new health visiting exemplifies a critical weakness of this contractual theory. Its practitioners will only assess children at times and places chosen and stage-managed by their parents. A child brought to a clinic can be cleaned, fed, and dressed for the occasion. Any peculiarities in the child's behavior can be attributed to the unfamiliarity of the setting. The point is not that parental care should routinely be treated as suspect, but that its inadequacies are most vulnerable to identification in the home. By treating the family as a self-sufficient unit of autonomous individuals, this strategy ignores the abundant evidence of physical, economic, and cognitive inequality. Its effect is to give priority to the views of those, such as parents and especially men, who have political access to the process of defining social problems and legitimate responses, neglecting those, such as children and, to a lesser extent, women, who do not.

The reliance on community health profiles compiled from existing data obliterates the intelligence that health visitors could furnish to the policy community about local perceptions of health and social need. If the National Health Service (NHS) does not receive this information, it can claim absolution from any obligation to respond. Where agenda-free home visits were a means of containing problems by not seeking to dig them up, the new style simply prevents them from coming to light by not looking for them at all. It is an ingenious method of cost containment at the expense of the poor, the housebound, and the inarticulate. Moreover, narrow financial motives for the limitation of public expenditures can be concealed behind a rhetoric of privacy that colludes with existing inequalities. The language of contract creates an illusion of self-determination that can be used to assign responsibility for the consequences to those whose 'choices' have had negative outcomes.

As the British experience has shown, population surveillance is not incompatible with liberal democracy. Indeed, as a number of areas demonstrated in the 1950s and 1960s, the health visiting model could be extended successfully to other disadvantaged groups, like the elderly and the chronically sick and disabled. But the acceptance of home visiting rested on a fragile basis. It arose out of assumptions by the British state about the need for healthy human resources for military and industrial purposes. Once warfare became a matter of technology, rather than numbers, and employment was a matter of surplus, rather than scarcity of labor, the concern inevitably became diluted.

The rash claim of the welfare state that it had abolished poverty undermined further the legitimacy of health surveillance. It began to open up the possibility that the condition of the poor resulted from their own choices rather than their structural circumstances. If they failed to articulate their needs or to use the available services, that was their problem, an attitude which, in turn, limited the collective obligations of others to those who might otherwise be seen as paying the price of their own prosperity.

Home visiting could be revived as a valid instrument of social policy only in the context of its redefinition as an element of the democratic process, as the means by which a liberal state guarantees fundamental entitlements to all citizens. Surveillance as a technique carries no inherent moral charge. As Dingwall and Eekelaar (1988) have argued elsewhere, the public/private opposition is a false dichotomy. The existence of a private sphere is conditional on the self-restraint of the public. To the extent that commercial privacy has perpetuated avoidable inequalities of gender, color, age, or whatever, state intervention has always been justifiable. Its extension to the family is the logical consequence. The search for need is the means of redressing the disenfranchisement of those excluded from the normal political process by age or infirmity.

While surveillance could be a vehicle for tyranny, as Dr Herbert Rubinstein saw, it could equally be a means of educating a polity, of bringing members of one class into contact with the conditions of another, and of confronting professionals with the realities beyond the cozy environments of their clinics, offices, or consulting rooms. The privatization of welfare is a screen erected by those who will not see. But democracy is a seamless web: a state that abandons its concern for the home life of its citizens in pursuit of a chimeric ideal of privacy is colluding in the perpetuation of everyday oppressions and inequalities that are ultimately likely to subvert its public order. The fate of home visiting is a key marker in the politics of welfare.

Note

1. Full details of the sampling and methodology can be found in Robinson (1986). The original transcripts were prepared according to the conventions of conversation analysis and will be presented here in a much simplified form.

References

Bradshaw, J. (1972) *A Taxonomy of Social Needs*. Oxford, Oxford University Press, Nuffield Provincial Hospitals Trust.

Council for the Education and Training of Health Visitors (1977) *An Investigation into the Principles of Health Visiting*. London, Author.

Dingwall, R. and Eekelaar, J.M. (1988) 'Families and the state: an historical perspective on the public regulation of private conduct'. *Law and Policy*, **10**, 341–361.

Donzelot, J. (1980) *The Policing of Families*. London, Hutchinson.

Goodwin, S. (1988) 'Whither health visiting?' *Health Visitor*, **61**, 379–383.

Halpern, S. (1988) *American Pediatrics: the social dynamics of professionalism 1880–1980*. Berkeley, University of California Press.

Kempe, C.H. (1975) 'Family intervention: the right of all children'. *Pediatrics*, **56**, 693–694.

Lewis, J. (1980) *The Politics of Motherhood*. London, Croom Helm.

Nelken, D. (1988) 'Social work contracts and social control'. In Matthews, R. (ed.), *Informal Justice?* London, Sage.

Robinson, K.M. (1986) *The social construction of health visiting*, Unpublished doctoral dissertation, CNAA/Polytechnic of the South Bank, London.

Rothman, S.M. (1981) 'Women's clinics or doctors' offices: The Sheppard-Towner Act and the promotion of preventive health care'. In Rothman, D.J. and Wheeler, S. (eds) *Social History and Social Policy*, pp. 175–202. New York, Academic Press.

Rubinstein, H.A. (1976) 'Letter: a protest about Kempe's views'. *Pediatrics*, **57**, 577.

Sacks, H. (1972, Spring) Unpublished lecture notes transcribed by Gail Jefferson, Lecture 5.

Smith, F.B. (1979) *The People's Health 1830–1910*. London, Croom Helm.

19

The Health of the Homeless

ELISE DAVIES

Introduction

> The weary Mole also was glad to turn in without delay, and soon had his head on his pillow, in great joy and contentment. But ere he closed his eyes he let them wander round his old room, mellow in the glow of the firelight that played or rested on familiar and friendly things which had long been unconsciously a part of him. He saw how plain and simple – how narrow even – it all was; but clearly, too, how much it all meant to him, and the special value of some such anchorage in one's existence. It was good to think he had this to come back to, this place which was all his own, and could always be counted upon for the same simple welcome
> (Kenneth Grahame, *The Wind in the Willows*, 1908).

A home is more than just a roof over our heads. It is a place of security and comfort; a place to rest and relax and care for ourselves and our children; an anchorage in our existence.

Unfortunately a growing proportion of our society is excluded from the stability that a home can offer. The 'homeless' are a large and diverse group with varied and multiple needs, all of whom are denied a decent home in which they can afford to live.

The homeless include families living in 'bed and breakfast' and other kinds of temporary accommodation; single homeless people living on the streets, in squats, and in night shelters; women and children in refuges; long-term patients in institutions and hospitals, who cannot be discharged as they have nowhere to live; and the 'hidden homeless' who are living in overcrowded conditions with relatives and friends, or in decaying council housing, or in appalling conditions in the private rented sector in shared houses and bedsits (known as houses in multiple occupation).

A recent report by the Faculty of Public Health Medicine (1991) states that 'decent housing is a basic need and a prerequisite for a healthy life.'

Homelessness – a growing problem

The homelessness statistics produced quarterly by the Department of Environment show that the number of accepted homeless cases for 1991 was 145,790 households (DOE, 1991a) – an estimated 435,000 people.

This figure is vastly understated, since it excludes the much larger group who do not fulfil the 'official' homelessness criteria. These are homeless young people; childless couples and individuals; people living in overcrowded and dangerous conditions in the private and public housing sectors; people sleeping rough; and those who are declared 'intentionally' homeless.

The underlying cause of all homelessness is the gross imbalance between the need for decent, affordable housing and the *supply* of it. In their *Review of the Homelessness Legislation* (DOE 1989), the Government appear to acknowledge a continuing need for subsidised rented housing. However, current housing policies call into question the Government's commitment to providing this.

Demand for subsidised housing is increasing. Whilst the overall population growth rate is quite slow, the number of individual households is increasing rapidly (DOE 1991b). The structure of traditional households is changing due to a variety of factors: more single-parent households; a high divorce rate; the desire and expectation of young people to leave their parents' home. In addition, the reduction in residential care for elderly people and physically and mentally ill or disabled people has increased demand for subsidised housing.

Local authorities, who have been the main providers of subsidised municipal housing for the last 60 years, have now been forced out of this role. The Government sees housing associations as the main providers of public sector housing for the future (DOE, 1989). But in spite of increased activity in recent years, housing associations have not been able to meet the need for low income housing.

Access to private sector housing, both rented and owner-occupied, is also a huge problem. Those who are socially and economically disadvantaged through unemployment, single-parenthood, age, disability, low pay and racial discrimination have the least housing choice. Renting a house or flat from a private landlord requires a deposit (no longer available through the Department of Social Security), and many landlords will not take people on state benefits. Even squalid bedsits and shared housing at the bottom end of the private rented market are in demand and rents are high.

The cost of all types of housing as a proportion of income has risen dramatically, but this is particularly evident in the owner-occupied sector. Buying a home is out of the question for many people, and high interest rates are forcing many who have bought their own homes into debt and eventual repossession and homelessness.

Faced with such a discrepancy between supply and demand for housing, many local authorities are becoming increasingly strict in their interpretation of the homelessness legislation. (See Arden, 1988, for a comprehensive review of the Homelessness legislation.)

Living in bed and breakfast

The occasional night in bed and breakfast as part of a holiday can be an exciting adventure for some families, but the establishments that profit from providing 'bed and breakfast' to homeless families are very different from the typical holiday B&B. They are frequently over-crowded, insanitary, dilapidated buildings which are lacking in basic amenities such as bathrooms, toilets and kitchens.

Homeless families living in bed and breakfast have to endure months and often years of living in stressful conditions usually in one room with all their possessions, such as the family in the following case study.

> Karen is a 21-year-old single parent with two children: Tom 10 months and Jasmine who is nearly 3. Karen has not got a job and she receives no maintenance from her ex-boyfriend, so the family are dependent on income support.
>
> They live in one room on the top floor of a hotel which is full of other families and single vulnerable people who have been placed by the council in bed and breakfast. Breakfast is served between 7.30 a.m. and 8.30 a.m. There are no other meals and no cooking facilities. Since both children are very poor sleepers, Karen is reluctant to drag them downstairs early in the morning for breakfast, so usually they all miss this. All their other meals are either take-aways, meals in cafés, or cold snacks.
>
> Jasmine's name is on the waiting list of several playgroups and nurseries, but she is highly unlikely to get a place because the facilities near to the hotel are grossly oversubscribed. She has become withdrawn and will not allow her mother out of her sight without becoming hysterical. She is very aggressive to strangers.
>
> Because of the variety of people living in the hotel Karen will not use the communal bathroom. She found evidence of intravenous drug use in the bathroom on one occasion and since then she has washed the children in a bowl in their room. She uses the public toilets which are situated over the road from the hotel. She has deliberately kept Jasmine in nappies so as not to have the problem of trying to toilet train a child in bed and breakfast.

Karen is desperate to be allocated permanent accommodation, but she has arrears on the charge levied by the council on households in bed and breakfast, and will not be offered anything else until the debt is paid. With so little money coming in, and the expense of take-away meals Karen says she has no chance of paying this. She thinks the council will eventually stop paying her bed and breakfast charges and she will lose her chance of permanent accommodation.

Like Karen and her children, those who live in bed and breakfast find it difficult to maintain proper nutrition (HVA/GMSC, 1989). They often need to rely on very expensive take-away food or food which can be stored and prepared without refrigeration or equipment. Some families organise their own cooking facilities in their rooms, but this poses an accident risk to young children and a serious fire risk (Drennan and Stern, 1986). Some guesthouse rooms are so hazardous that young children cannot be left unsupervised even for a moment. For parents who do not have the support of another adult this can mean that children have to go with them, even to the toilet.

Living in one room makes play and recreation almost impossible for all family members. Babies and toddlers are forced to spend much of the time strapped in chairs or in cots due to lack of space and dangerous surroundings, resulting in developmental delay and behavioural problems (Drennan and Stern, 1986).

Schoolchildren have nowhere to play or to do their homework. Stairs, landings and any communal areas become play areas, causing noise and inconvenience to other residents. Bed times are disrupted. Children often have to share beds with siblings or parents, and go to bed at the same time as their parents.

This results in tiredness and poor concentration at school, and their education suffers (HMI, 1990). They cannot invite their friends home, and may be living some distance from their school so they will find it difficult to maintain friendships. Schoolchildren suffer socially from the stigma of homelessness and can be ostracized by their peers.

Living in bed and breakfast puts great strain on relationships. Adults are unable to have any time alone, or with each other when the children are in bed. Lack of privacy means they cannot maintain a normal sexual relationship. Marital stress, depression, alcoholism and family breakdown are all prevalent among households living in this kind of accommodation (Drennan and Stern, 1986).

Harassment such as sexual and racial harassment by the landlord, staff or other tenants is also a problem. Problems of noise, lack of privacy, and fear and suspicion can cause isolation and distress to all occupants. Where there is a poor social mix the residents are less able to draw strength from each other, by sharing experiences or helping each other out. People become confined to their own small rooms and everything else is viewed as hostile.

Homelessness has profound effects on health and wellbeing. The actual event of becoming homeless may have been exacerbated by unemployment, ill health, or financial difficulties, thus morale and personal confidence are likely to be very low. Many households try every possible option before finally accepting that they are 'homeless'', and turning to their local authority for help.

The strict criteria that local authorities apply mean that the process of establishing whether someone is in fact homeless can be a dehumanising and humiliating experience. Once they have been placed in temporary accommodation they are at the mercy of bureaucratic processes. They have no control over where they must live or for how long, and information is rarely forthcoming. It is not surprising that low self-esteem and feelings of social rejection are so common.

Homeless and roofless

There has been a tendency to stereotype the single homeless as middle-aged vagrants, usually men, who often have alcohol dependency, and have 'chosen' to live in this way. In fact the 'roofless' are a diverse population, who may move in and out of different types of accommodation. They are likely to spend time sleeping rough; staying in night shelters or short-stay hostels; squatting or sleeping in empty garages and sheds, etc. The lengths of time they spend on the streets or in temporary shelter varies tremendously, and it is precisely because of their high mobility that this is an extremely difficult area to study.

The housing charity Shelter (1991) estimate that there are 2–3000 people sleeping rough in London, and up to 5000 in the rest of England. Stations, shopping precincts, doorways and subways are 'home' to a growing number of people in many of our towns and cities. There is a growing concern about the apparent increase in the number of *young* single homeless people. Shelter estimate that about 156,000 young people become homeless in Britain each year (Shelter, 1991). Centre-point (1988) estimates that there are 50,000 homeless 16 to 19 year olds in London alone.

The 1986 Social Security Act which came into effect in April 1988 has made access to accommodation very difficult for single homeless people, particularly 16 and 17 year olds who are not in full-time education or on a Youth Training Scheme, as they are not entitled to income support, and can be literally destitute.

The way in which housing benefit is paid can also prevent people securing accommodation. Housing benefit is paid *after* accommodation has been secured, but finding accommodation requires access to money in advance. The old 'board and lodging' payment was also abolished for many hostel-dwellers, greatly reducing their disposable income and making saving for a deposit for privately rented accommodation impossible.

The physical illnesses suffered by the roofless are varied. Cuts, gashes, broken bones and puncture wounds are all common, particularly among rough sleepers, since sleeping on the street carries a high risk of assault. Respiratory conditions such as bronchitis, asthma, and tuberculosis, are exacerbated by the conditions in which they live. Other problems include diarrhoea, malnutrition, and dental problems due to enforced poor hygiene, skin infections and infestations (Shanks, 1988).

Young homeless people are particularly vulnerable to involvement in prostitution (as a source of income), and intravenous drug use, and there is a great concern that needle-sharing and unsafe sex put young homeless people at considerable risk of AIDS (Faculty of Public Health Medicine, 1991).

There are studies which report high rates of psychiatric illness among the single homeless, particularly those found in common lodging houses (Single Homeless in London Working Groupo, 1987). Psychiatric surveys *do* reveal a high level of mental illness and alcohol problems among the roofless, leading some reports to conclude that their homelessness has been caused by psychiatric illness. But the reverse can also be true: homelessness can lead to mental illness. The loss of a home is a serious adverse life event, and the lack of stability, feelings of social dislocation, and the day-to-day reality of living on the streets can result in depression and isolation (Faculty of Public Health Medicine, 1991). The complicated effects of homelessness and psychiatric problems are evident in David's case.

> David is a 22-year-old who left home at 16 after the breakdown of his relationship with his stepfather. He has had intermittent periods of homelessness. He lived on the streets for 9 months, and then moved in to the council flat of a friend. The friend died and the tenancy was lost.
>
> As well as housing problems David has a long history of solvent abuse, chronic self-mutilation and depression. After the death of his friend David made several serious suicide attempts.
>
> David was housed in a low-support shared housing scheme which was organised for him through a psychiatric social worker, but he felt isolated and unable to cope. He left the scheme and spent a further period of time on the streets, and the occasional night in a short-stay hostel. He has recently moved into a bedsit in the private rented sector, but this type of accommodation does not offer David the intensive support he needs. Because of his difficulties he is unable to mix with the residents in the other bedsits, and it seems only a matter of time before he ends up back on the streets.

The factors which lead to a young person becoming homeless are multiple and varied, including wanting to get away from home or like David from an abusing parent; being thrown out by parents; moving to take up casual work or to look for work. Many street homeless young people have a history of being in care, either in institutions or in foster homes. (This figure is as high as 41% according to the Young Homelessness Group, 1990.)

The Children Act (1989) places a duty on Social Services departments to provide care and services to children 'in need'. Potentially this legislation could assist homeless young people, and particularly those who have been in care who are at high risk of becoming homeless, but its success depends on the co-operation and motivation of housing departments as well as Social Services. Young people without dependent children are not covered by the homelessness legislation unless they are proved to be 'vulnerable' through physical or mental illness. Age alone is unlikely to be considered as grounds for vulnerability.

Barriers to health care

All groups of homeless people face difficulties in gaining access to appropriate health care. The mobility of homeless groups is an important factor, particularly in registering with a general practitioner. Changes in the organisation of primary health care (the GP contract which came into force in April 1990) have created financial disincentives to GPs to register people who are likely to be moving on quickly. The homeless are predisposed by their circumstances to a higher level of ill health, and GPs who work in areas where there are high numbers of homeless people may find themselves unable to cope with the additional demands placed on their services. A recent survey by the Special Interest Group for Homelessness found that some health authorities denied the existence of homeless people in their area, and others concluded that they had no responsibility for the homeless, who 'by definition' could not be included in their resident population (Stilwell, 1991).

However, some health authorities have recognised the particular problems faced by homeless people, and have set up a wide variety of projects and initiatives to deal with them, for example by appointing specialist health visitors for the homeless. This is valuable but, as Stilwell (1991) points out, many of these projects have short-term special funding only.

Homeless people need advocates. There is now a wealth of evidence that homelessness has profound effects on health and wellbeing, but because they are a diverse population, and because of the isolation, stigma and sense of social dislocation which homelessness brings, homeless people are unlikely to complain and campaign for themselves.

Note

The case studies are true case histories although names have been changed to protect the identity of individuals.

I should like to thank all members of the Special Interest group for Homelessness for their support in the writing of this article, and Jackie Brookes and Fatima Akilu for supplying the case studies.

References

Arden, A. (1988) *Homeless Persons: The Housing Act 1985 Part III, third edition*. Legal Action Group.

Centrepoint (1988) *No Way Home. A survey of 16–19 year olds in temporary accommodation in London*. Centrepoint, Soho.

Conway, J. (ed.) (1988) *Prescription for Poor Health. The crisis for homeless families*. London; London Food Commission, Maternity Alliance, SHAC, Shelter.

Department of Environment (1989) *The Government's Review of the Homelessness Legislation*. DOE.

Department of Environment (1991a) *Local Authorities Action under the Homelessness Provision of the 1985 Housing Act Part III*. DOE quarterly returns.

Department of the Environment (1991b) *Public Household Projections England 1989–2011. 1989 based estimates*. London, HMSO.

Department of Health (1991) *The Health of the Nation: A consultative document for health in England*. London, HMSO.

Drennan, V. and Stern, J. (1986) 'Health visitors and homeless families'. *Health Visitor* Vol. 59, No. 11, pp. 340–342.

Faculty of Public Health Medicine (1991) *Housing or Homelessness; a public health perspective*. London, Royal College of Physicians.

Grahame, K. (1908) *The Wind in the Willows*. First published by Methuen & Co. Ltd.

Her Majesty's Inspectorate of Schools (1990) *A survey of the education of children living in temporary accommodation April–December 1989*. Department of Education and Science.

Health Visitors' Association and General Medical Services Committee (1989) *Homeless Families and Their Health*. London, British Medical Association.

Shanks, N. J. (1988) 'Medical morbidity of the homeless'. *Journal of Epidemiology and Community Health*, Vol. 42, pp. 183–186.

Shelter (1991) *Homelessness in England – the facts*. Shelter Fact Sheet.

Single Homeless in London Working Group (1987) 'Primary health care for homeless single people', in *London: A strategic approach*. London, Health Sub-group.

Stilwell, B. (1991) *Health Services for Vulnerable Client Groups*. Unpublished report produced for the Special Interest Group for Homelessness of the Health Visitors' Association.
Young Homelessness Group (1990) *Young Homelessness – A National Scandal*. London, YHG.

20

Familist Ideology and Possessive Individualism

GILLIAN DALLEY

The ideology of familism

A particular view of the family and the expected roles of its various members underlies a whole range of policies – especially, but not exclusively, policies related to caring. There is a consistency and a patterning in this that suggests a coherent ideology underlying these social forms. Fallers (1961) defined ideology very broadly as 'that part of culture which is actively concerned with the establishment and defence of patterns of belief and value'. This definition, while it omits discussion of 'establishment how' and 'in whose interests', does stress the *defence* of these patterns, which emphasises that ideology is something which is contestable. Thus dominant ideology is that which successfully establishes and defends its hegemony – overriding others' interests and buttressing those which it underpins.

In the present discussion, it is the ideology of familism – or familialism, as Barrett and McIntosh (1982) have termed it – which has established its dominance and operates as a principle of social organisation at both the domestic and public level, especially in the field of social care. And this has major implications for the position of women. As an ideological construct, 'the family' – the central focus of familism– underlies all contemporary forms of social organisation of daily living. This does not mean that all such forms are conscious or unconscious

---

*This is an abridged extract from Dalley, G. (1988) *Ideologies of Caring*, Macmillan Education, pp. 20–40.

approximations of the construct – but it is the standard against which all forms are measured and, importantly, judged. Thus within, and according to, the ideology of familism, non-family forms are deemed to be deviant and/or subversive. And, it is argued, because of the hegemonic nature of familism, assorted categories of individuals subscribe to, or have internalised, the values of that ideology even though its dominance may, objectively, run counter to their interests. And if they fail to achieve the required standard, then they perceive *themselves* as deviant.

The fourfold application of familism

Taking the ideology of familism as a starting point, an explanatory model can be constructed which accommodates a parallel pair of replications – one reproduced internally (within the domestic group) and the other externally (in the public sphere). Thus the principles underlying the social organisation of daily living (as demonstrated in patterns of residence, household membership, the domestic division of labour, relationships of domination and subordination) are replicated in the caring functions performed by that group (through the social organisation of care, provision for children and other dependent members of the group, the altruisim and self-abnegation typically expected of women and the manner of the social construction of dependency).

This internal pattern of replication is then reproduced in the public sphere; the ideology underpinning domestic relations becomes a major organising principle upon which social relations outside the domestic group are based. It governs major and fundamental cleavages between the public and private spheres, creating a gendered division of labour in which women for the most part are principally consigned to the private sphere – although drawn out into the public sphere acccording to the demands of capital, or when they are of intermediate status (single, or non-mothers – i.e. when they do not 'fit' the ideological premise of women as biological reproducers and social servicers). Or they may be marginal, peripheral workers; working part-time to augment the inadequate 'family wage' earned by the male breadwinner. And beyond the private-public division, within the public sphere itself, the ideological principle governs social relations there too: men's careers are structured on the premise that women will provide the servicing functions which allow men to pursue their career interests single-mindedly; certain female occupations reproduce the familial subordination/dominance model in relation to 'male' occupations – nurses/doctors, secretaries/bosses, and so on.

And just as the ideology supporting domestic organisation also validates the organisation of care-giving domestically, that same ideology reproduced in the public sphere of work and public affairs is also replicated in the field of social care. This can be demonstrated by examining policies designed for the public provision of care for chronically dependent people (both adults and children), and by looking at the position of women who, by implication, figure largely in those policies as carers.

This cluster of replications is well known; modern feminists over the past decade and more have demonstrated how the whole of domestic life is premised on the unequal division between men and women. Patterns of residence fragments and isolates individuals into small domestic units, dependent on the individual servicing of the household by women as wives and mothers; houses and flats are built only for such small units. The legal conditions under which residential accommodation is leased or mortgaged has tended, at least until very recently, to recognise this family group as the only acceptable unit of residence. Within the domestic unit, the division of labour is sharply drawn, as research studies show (Oakley, 1974). Relations of domination and subordination prevail – studies of domestic violence suggest that physical violence is less rare than defenders of the familial form would claim (Dobash and Dobash, 1980). Rather than its being an aberrant form of family life, it is perhaps an inevitable consequence of the structure itself.

Another aspect of subordination is manifested in patterns of resource allocation within families. Pahl (1980) has shown how frequently women receive unequal shares of family income, restricted by their menfolk's budgetary control. This is especially difficult where families are subsisting on low incomes, often on state benefits. In such circumstances, as in the case of Supplementary Benefit, where there are specific amounts designated for wives and dependent children, and where the man is deemed to be the breadwinner, the payment is made directly to him. It frequently depends on his whim as to how much money the woman receives, and yet more often than not it is she who is expected to provide for the family. Child allowances paid directly to the woman may well be the only source of income that a woman can lay claim to – hence the importance, past and present, of campaigns to make sure such allowances are preserved.

Intimately bound up with women's role within the domestic unit is their role as carers. The biological divisions of gender difference are capitalised on again. Thus men not only accumulate power and access to the public sphere, they also accumulate the servicing power of women. Their children (and by extension their other dependants) are cared for by their women; child care within the home is favoured and supported by expert opinion – Bowlby (1953) and Leach (1979) are widely cited by those favouring the home-centredness of women, suggesting that young children will suffer if separated from their mothers too soon. Even where integration of the child into an external social world is favoured, the child, it is argued, should be accompanied by its mother. There are many pre-school activities (the British Pre-school Playgroup Association groups are an example), taken up especially by middle-class mothers, which are structured precisely on the full participation of mothers as well as children.

Women are expected to provide care not only for their immediate dependants (their children and their ageing parents, but also frequently for their husbands' ageing dependants (that is, their parents-in-law). If they do not marry they are expected to give up participation in the public sphere of work and look after their dependent relatives alone. The National Council for the Single Woman and her Dependants (renamed the National Council for Carers and their Elderly Dependants in 1982) did not refer to the single woman without good reason. Indeed, in the case of the unmarried woman, rather than her being subordinate to a husband as in the case of her married sisters, she remains subordinate to the demands and expectations of her family of birth. Thus her single status does not confer any real independence from familial, domestic responsibility; there always remain latent demands on her freedom which can be activated at time of crisis.

Thus in the private or domestic domain, there is a twofold, unequal division between woman and men – first, in the social organisation of daily living and, secondly, in the social organisation of care-giving. This internal replication is then produced in the public sphere. In the external or public sphere of work, the division of labour whereby women are excluded from certain sectors, concentrated into others, or relegated to lowly status in yet others, is a reflection of the pattern of relations within the domestic unit – where women are largely concerned with servicing and maintenance roles and are frequently excluded from equal access to family resources. Men's work, for example, is organised on the presumption that their wives will provide supportive assistance – there is already a literature (Finch, 1983; Calland and Ardener, 1984) on the incorporation of women into their husbands' work. The clergyman's wife is an example. Large companies and political parties frequently vet men's wives to ensure their suitability in this supportive role. Where women work in the public sphere, they are frequently concentrated in 'female' occupations – for example, the 'caring' occupations, such as nursing, social work, teaching, health auxiliary work, which all depend on the supposed instinctive caring capacities of women; or the 'dextrous' occupations, such as small-scale electrical assembly work, which depend on the supposed innate aptitude of women to do intricate, complicated, manual work; or the mindless occupations, such as monotonous repetitive conveyor belt work, packing, cleaning, which depend on the supposed disinclination of women to apply themselves to intelligent forms of activity. The evident diversity of these three 'innate' female characteristics is rarely noted.

Familial ideology affirms these forms – it affirms that there is indeed something natural and appropriate about women's place being predominantly in the domestic sphere, that they have a natural inclination towards and aptitude for performing the monitoring, servicing tasks within the family setting. Further, it affirms as natural the dominance of men within the private sphere and, inevitably, in the public sphere – over which they have, or should have, it is believed, near monopoly of access.

Caring is perceived of as one of the integral functions of the domestic group so depicted – the caring for and socialising of children is seen as correctly taking place within the domestic sphere and it is a small step to extend this function of caring to include the caring for of other dependants, the chronically ill and disabled family members of all ages. And this, of course, presupposes the continuous presence (or activation of such a presence when necessary) of the woman in the family.

And where the private function of caring breaks down, and the public sphere takes on responsibility for the provision of care (which it has done on more than a residualist basis for centuries), the same ideology of familism is now reproduced. It is a mark of the hegemonic nature of familial ideology that, in recent years, it has become the foundation of public policy for care as well as of private care – at a time when the actuality of family *structure* has been demonstrated to be a fluid and shifting form (Gittins, 1985; Rimmer, 1981). Social care replicates, or is expected to replicate, the family form of care as closely as possible.

Recent policies relating to the care of those patient groups designated as 'priority groups' in current health service policy documents, exemplify this; they are based on a normative framework of 'family care as best'. This has two aspects: first, that for dependent individuals care is best provided for 'at home', and second, for the kinfolk of those dependent individuals, there is an overriding moral duty for them to provide that care. The policies are consciously articulating the ideology of familism – in recent years there has been a publicly achieved consensus between policymakers, practitioners and 'experts' from the academic world that the family model of care is the appropriate policy goal, and it is one which should be applied in all fields of dependency. It has figured prominently in the de-institutionalisation debate, so that the revulsion rightly felt towards the grossest examples of dehumanised institutional care has been directly linked with the view that the appropriate alternative in all cases is family-based care. Where that form of care is not available, then measures which are 'nearest approximations to that form' are introduced. An associated ethos of 'rights to surrogate family care if "own family" is unavailable' is fostered to legitimate these measures (Dalley, 1983). Propounders of the familist ideal favour it because for them it embodies notions of the family as haven, as repository of warm, caring, human relationships based on mutual responsibility and affection and thus a private protection against a cold, hostile, outside world.

The practical and unfortunate consequences of familism

Policies which enshrine these assumptions have consequences both foreseen and unforeseen. Amongst the foreseen are the direct consequences for women. They are the individuals expected to be available for caring. If dependent people are to be decanted from institutions into the community, back to their homes, there have to be people available to care. Caring in the community is regarded as a domestic function; women, according to the ideology of familism, form that category of individuals which pertains to the domestic sphere. Therefore it is a given that it is they who will do the caring. In practice, however, given the diversity of family and household structure, there may not be enough women available to provide the necessary care.

Thus the family model of care becomes infinitely flexible; it becomes the rationale for the dementing old lady being maintained in her home, living alone, perhaps with few relatives who might be able to visit or, more importantly, perform caring tasks. She is supported by a variety of professional services, coming in on a daily basis (or less frequently) – district nurse, health or geriatric visitor, GP, social worker, home help, meals-on-wheels deliverer to name the most likely – all of which confusion serves to exacerbate her dementia. Or perhaps she may be bused to the local psychogeriatric hospital for the day, returned at night to 'her familiar surroundings', locked in alone, until sometime the next morning the ambulance arrives again, to repeat the exercise, removing her to a more monitored environment. This care is called 'care in the community'; the fact that the woman sleeps in a bed in her own home at night is deemed to represent own-home care. At the other end of the scale, harassed health authorities close down large psychiatric hospitals or the geriatric wards of district hospitals only to build 60, 70 or 80 bed units on the same sites, often behind the same high walls, and call them 'homes', 'home-like' or 'community units'.

The same rationale is also used to justify the apparently endless moves of children in care from one foster family to another, interspersed by return to the family of birth, and indeterminate lengths of stay in children's homes (regarded as the most inappropriate forms of care, because they are 'institutions'). Equally, it becomes the justification for the return of children from care to parent or parents who live in isolation, lacking support from networks of kin or friends, and who present real threats to the physical and emotional well-being of their offspring.

At a more significant level, middle-class mothers, especially in the affluent south-east of England, turn to mother substitutes to care for their children. From *The Lady* (a monthly magazine for the genteel English middle classes) to the notice board in the corner shop, there are advertisements searching for either unemployed school-leavers, qualified nannies or homely 'motherly' ladies to care for the babies, toddlers and pre-school children of the middle classes. Substitute mothers are preferred over the alternative – collective child care in nurseries or nursery schools – because it mimics the family model of care closest.

Thus the justification in all these examples is that the solution to the problems of care must be based on approximations to the family model of care. Rather than the particular needs of particular patient or client categories being examined in their own terms, satisfaction of those needs is forced into a single mould labelled 'community care', whether the measures decided upon are appropriate or not. And the outcome of such measures frequently turns out to be inappropriate. Frail and confused elderly people live isolated and bewildered lives, out of contact with their peers and their kin; young children are moved from one setting to another lacking the very security and familiarity the policies were, apparently, designed to foster; the favoured sons and daughters of the middle class are cared for often by bored and frequently exploited teenagers who have little idea of the basic requirements of childrearing; community-based hospital care develops rapidly into the institutional form of care it was intended to replace.

There are further consequences. Alternative forms of care are denigrated or are declared redundant. Old people's homes, hospital-based geriatric provision, children's homes all become the focus of professionals' and policy-makers' opposition. Furthermore, the occupants of this form of care become stigmatised along with the residential units which accommodate them. Chronically dependent people – dependent either through old age, youthful infirmity or disability – become identified with the form of care provided; the people providing that care take on some of the stigma too. Care workers in institutional settings tend to be low-paid, lacking in qualifications, often of low morale and under-valued.

These then are some of the consequences of the penetration of familist ideology into so many levels and areas of social organisation. But why should that penetration be so all-embracing? How has this state of affairs come to be? It seems inevitable that answers have to be looked for in the past. It is clear that this tradition of familism has been firmly established for many generations. We are familiar with the expectations of 'womanly behaviour' as laid out in nineteenth-century literature; the idealised nuclear family model has been with us for many years. And its values and the goals it is said to stand for are linked clearly to those of a wider philosophical tradition – possessive individualism.

Possessive individualism and its relationship to familist ideology

Possessive individualism incorporates a number of related notions: the individual as an 'independent centre of consciousness' in Kant's terms; the notion of the self and self-determination; of privacy and freedom from intrusion. Along with these is the quality of posessiveness which is found 'in the conception of the individual as essentially the proprietor of his [sic] own person and capacities, owing nothing to society for them. . . . The human essence is freedom from dependence on the will of others, and freedom is the function of possession' (Macpherson, 1962, p. 236).

The principles of individualism are embodied in the ideals and aspirations conventionally assigned to the bourgeois family – the single-minded pursuit of self (family)-improvement, in both material and spiritual terms; the determination that the family, under the guidance of the head of the family – the husband/father, should be autonomous in thought and action, especially in relation to the upbringing and education of its children. The Bergers summarise it thus:

> . . . an emphasis on high moral standards, especially in sexual matters; an enormous interest in the welfare of children, especially their proper education, the circulation of values and attitudes conducive to economic sucess as well as civic peace; at least the appearance of religious faith; a devotion to the 'finer things' in life, especially the arts; and last but not least, a sense of obligation to redress or alleviate conditions perceived as morally offensive. (Berger and Berger, 1983, p. 17)

And while these ideals and aspirations were far removed from the reality of life, as experienced by the exploited and oppressed newly urbanised working class throughout the nineteenth century, the Bergers argue that gradually through time the concept of the bourgeois family first as a sort of 'ideal type' and later as a reality has been taken over by the working class. In fact, they argue, this has happened to such an extent that it is now the working class which defends the principles upon which the bourgeois family form is founded, while what they term the new 'knowledge class' consistently seeks to subvert and overturn them.

A Marxist view would suggest that this is a case of the subordinate class absorbing and taking on the values of the hegemonising dominant class. Certainly the contrast between working-class life and attitudes in nineteenth-century Britain as depicted, say, by Engels and Mayhew, and that of the present day is strong. Bourgeois ideals of marriage, careful upbringing and education of children, and the cultivation of a private domain of diligent self-improvement were far from the experience of the most down-trodden sections of the working class in Victorian Britain. In marked contrast is today's working class, from which a substantial amount of support in recent years has been drawn in both Britain and the United States for Thatcherite and Reaganite values of sturdy self-reliance and a rejection of 'moaning minnie' welfarism.

Whilst Marxism would regard this as an outcome of false consciousness, the Bergers applaud the bourgeoisie's colonisation of working-class value systems. They see the cleaving of the working class to the bourgeois values of individualism, as embodied in the nuclear family, as the means of preserving what is best in modern western society – preserving what they call 'the middle ground'. They expound at length on the manner in which the present-day working class has taken on the attitudes formerly espoused by the bourgeoisie – and indeed regard these new working-class attitudes as a bulwark against the encroachment of more subversive values. The modern professionals (social workers, therapists, teachers) who are the heirs of the nineteenth-century philanthropists and bourgeois 'good women' now police the working class in the name of values which are anathema to the old ethos of self-determination, self-reliance and family integrity. For the Bergers, it is necessary to take power away from such professionals and reinvest it in the hands of those best suited to hold it – honest, decent, hard-working parents. They cite professional attitudes to the role of women in the home as an example of what has gone wrong:

> . . . in the 1950s, social workers and other professionals were preaching the virtues of domesticity to their female clients. The good mother, it was maintained, stayed at home and devoted herself full time to the tasks of child rearing. Lower class mothers who were economically able to do so, were all too willing to follow such advice – only to be berated in the 1960s and 1970s by the same professionals who had now had their consciousness raised by the new feminist movement, for surrendering their autonomy as persons to the slavery of the household. (Ibid., p. 48)

Those more critical of the bourgeois ideal would agree that the ethos of familism has been absorbed by the working class but question, if this is so, who gains from it – especially since the ideal form of the nuclear family (father as breadwinner, domesticated wife as home-based service provider and diligent, obedient children) has rarely been the norm for large sections of the working class. Whilst the role of woman as biological reproducer is predetermined, her role as social reproducer and the extent to which she is involved in production is to a certain degree less fixed (though broadly circumscribed by structural forces). But it is the force of the ideology of familism, itself rooted in the individualistic principle, with its prescriptive assumptions about the 'natural' and 'right' position of women which chiefly circumscribes and constrains the actions and thought of all women, regardless of the wide and often opposed differences between their particular class, ethnic or status positions.

It is in seeking to counteract the pervasive strength of the ideology that feminists have looked for alternative principles upon which to base their struggle. Since they identify the possessive individualism which provides the base upon which familial ideology is constructed as the fundamental source of their subordination, they have looked for oppositional principles upon which to base strategies of challenge. Since they locate the central problem of women's subordination in western society as lying in the inner-directed male-dominated nuclear family, with its clear, gendered separation of domestic and public domain (where the crossing of this separation creates ambiguous and conflictual situations), they have consequently emphasised collective alternatives to the servicing and socialising functions of the family, and an unambiguous opening up of the public sphere to women as well as men.

References

Barrett, M. and McIntosh, M. (1982) *The Anti-social Family*. Verso, London.

Berger, B. and Berger, P. (1983) *The War over the Family: capturing the middle ground*. Penguin, Harmondsworth.

Bowlby, J. (1953) *Child Care and the Growth of Love*. Penguin, Harmondsworth.

Callan, H. and Ardener, S. (1984) *The Incorporated Wife*. Croom Helm, London.

Dalley, G. (1983) 'Ideologies of care: a feminist contribution to the debate', *Critical Social Policy*, Vol. **8**.

Dobash, R.E. and Dobash, R. (1980) *Violence against Wives: a case against patriarchy*. Open Books, London.

Fallers, L. A. (1961) 'Ideology and culture in Uganda nationalism', *American Anthropologist*, Vol. **63**, No. **19**.

Finch, J. (1983) *Married to the Job: wives' incorporation in men's work*. George Allen & Unwin, London.

Gittins, D. (1985) *The Family in Question: changing households and familiar ideologies*. Macmillan, London.

Leach, P. (1979) *Who Cares?* Penguin, Hardmondsworth.

Macpherson, C. B. (1962) *The Political Theory of Possessive Individualism*. Oxford University Press, Oxford.

Oakley, A. (1974) *The Sociology of Housework*. Martin Robertson, Oxford.

Pahl, J. (1980) 'Patterns of money management', *Journal of Social Policy*, Vol. 9, No. 3.

Rimmer, L. (1981) *Families in Focus: marriage, divorce and family patterns.* Study Commission on the Family, London.

21

Women in Banana Republics*

CYNTHIA ENLOE

It is always worth asking, 'Where are the women?' Answering the question reveals the dependence of most political and economic systems not just on women, but on certain kinds of relations between women and men. A great deal has been written about countries derisively labeled 'banana republics'. They are described as countries whose land and soul are in the clutches of a foreign company, supported by the might of its own goverment. A banana republic's sovereignty has been so thoroughly compromised that it is the butt of jokes, not respect. It has a government, but it is staffed by people who line their own pockets by doing the bidding of the overseas corporation and its political allies. Because it is impossible for such compromised rulers to win the support of their own citizens, many of whom are exploited on the corporation's plantations, the government depends on guns and jails, not ballots and national pride.

The quintessential banana republics were those Central American countries which came to be dominated by the United Fruit Company's monoculture, the US marines and their hand-picked dictators. Their regimes have been backed by American presidents, mocked by Woody Allen, and overthrown by nationalist guerrillas.

Yet these political systems, and the international relationships which underpin them, have been discussed as if women scarcely existed. The principal actors on all sides have been portrayed by conventional commentators as men, and as if their being male was insignificant. Thus the ways in which their shared masculinity allowed agribusiness entrepreneurs to form alliances with men in their own diplomatic corps and with men in Nicaraguan or Honduran society have been left unexamined.

*This article was first published in Enloe, C. (1989) *Bananas, Beaches and Bases*, Pandora, pp. 133–226.

Enjoying Cuban cigars together after dinner while wives and mistresses powder their noses has been the stuff of smug cartoons but not of political curiosity. Similarly, a banana republic's militarized ethos has been taken for granted, without an investigation of how militarism feeds on masculinist values to sustain it. Marines, diplomats, corporate managers and military dictators may mostly be male, but they tend to need the feminine 'other' to maintain their self-assurance.

One of the conditions that has pushed women off the banana republic stage has been the masculinization of the banana plantation. Banana-company executives imagined that most of the jobs on their large plantations could be done only by men. Banana plantations were carved out of wooded acres. Clearing the brush required workers who could use a machete, live in rude barracks, and who, once the plantation's trees were bearing fruit, could chop down the heavy bunches and carry them to central loading areas and from there to the docks, to be loaded by the ton on to refrigerator ships. This was men's work.

Not all plantation work has been masculinized. Generally, crops that call for the use of machetes – tools that can also be used as weapons – are produced with large inputs of male labor: bananas, sugar, palm oil. Producers of crops that require a lot of weeding, tapping and picking hire large numbers of women, sometimes comprising a majority of workers: tea, coffee, rubber.

Nor is the gendered labor formula on any plantation fixed. Plantation managers who once relied heavily on male workers may decide to bring in more women if the men become too costly; if their union becomes too threatening; if the international market for the crop declines necessitating cost-cutting measures such as hiring more part-time workers; if new technology allows some physically demanding tasks to be done by workers with less strength. Today both sugar and rubber are being produced by plantation companies using more women workers than they did a generation ago.[1] What has remained constant, however, is the presumption of international corporations that their position in the world market depends on manipulations of masculinity and femininity. Gender is injected into every Brooke Bond or Lipton tea leaf, every Unilever or Lonrho palm-oil nut, every bucket of Dunlop or Michelin latex, every stalk of Tate & Lyle sugar cane.

Like all plantation managers, banana company executives considered race as well as gender when employing what they thought would be the most skilled and compliant workforce. Thus although the majority of banana workers were men, race was used to divide them. On United Brands' plantations in Costa Rica and Panama, for instance, managers recruited Amerindian men from the Guaymi and Kuna communities, as well as West Indian Black men and Hispanicized Ladino men. They placed them in different, unequally paid jobs, Ladino men at the top (below white male managers), Amerindian men at the bottom. Amerindian men were assigned to menial jobs such as chopping grass and overgrown bush, thus ensuring that Ladino men's negative stereotypes of Amerindians – *cholos*, unskilled, uncultured natives – would be perpetuated. The stereotypes were valuable to the company because they forestalled potential alliances between Ladino, Black and Amerindian men over common grievances.[2]

Manager: It's easier to work with *cholos*. They're not as smart and don't speak good Spanish. They can't argue back at you even when they're right . . . Hell, you can make a *cholo* do anything.

Ladino foreman: My workers are [not] *cholos* . . . It's different here. Sure I can grab them [Ladino and Black male workers] and make them work faster; but the consequences will catch up with me tomorrow. We're not *cholos* here . . . you understand?

Guaymi worker: They used to have up to 200 of us crammed into shacks eating boiled bananas out of empty kerosene cans.[3]

To say, therefore, that a banana plantation is masculinized is not to say that masculinity, even when combined with social class, is sufficient to forge political unity. On the other hand, the presumption that a banana plantation is a man's world does affect the politics of any movement attempting to improve workers' conditions, or to transform the power relationships that comprise a 'banana republic'.

A banana plantation's politics are deeply affected not just by the fact that the majority of its workers – and virtually all of its managers and owners – are men, but by the *meaning* that has been attached to that masculinization. Even male banana workers employed by a foreign company that, in alliance with local élites, had turned their country into a proverbial banana republic, could feel some pride. For they were unquestionably performing men's work. They knew how to wield a machete; they knew how to lift great weights; they worked outside in close coordination with trains and ships. Whether a smallholder or a plantation employee, a banana man was a *man*.

> Touris, white man, wipin his
>   face,
> Met me in Golden Grove
>   market place.
>
> He looked at m'ol'clothes brown
>   wid stain,
> An soaked tight through wid de
>   Portlan rain,
> He cas his eye, turned up his
>   nose,

He says, 'You're a beggar man, I
    suppose?'
He says, 'Boy, get some
    occupation,
Be of some value to your
    nation.

I said, 'By God and dis big right
    han
You mus recognise a banana
    man . . .

Don't judge a man by his patchy
    clothes,
I'm a strong man, a proud man,
    an I'm free
Free as dese mountains, free as
    dis sea,
I know myself, an I know my
    ways,
An will say wid pride to de end
    o my days.

Praise God an m'big right
    han
I will live an die a banana man.[4]

In the 1920s when banana workers began to organize and to conduct strikes that even the US government and local élites had to pay attention to, their demands reached beyond working conditions to political structures. These workers' protests took on strong nationalist overtones: the local regime and foreign troops were as much the target of their protests as the plantation companies. But so long as banana plantation work was imagined to be men's work, and so long as the banana workers' unions were organized as if they were men's organizations, the nationalist cause would be masculinized. A banana republic might fall, but patriarchy remained in place.

Women weed, women clean

The banana plantation has never been as exclusively male as popular imagery suggests. It takes women's paid and unpaid labor to bring the golden fruit to the world's breakfast tables.

A banana plantation is closest to a male enclave at the beginning, when the principal task is bulldozing and clearing the land for planting. But even at this stage women are depended upon by the companies – and their male employees – to play their roles. As in the male-dominated mining industry from Chile to South Africa and Indonesia, companies can recruit men to live away from home only if someone back home takes care of their families and maintains their land. The 'feminization of agriculture' – that is, leaving small-scale farming to women, typically without giving them training, equipment or extra finance – has always been part and parcel of the masculinization of mining and banana plantations.[5] The male labor force has to make private arrangements with wives, mothers or sisters to assure them of a place to return to when their contracts expire, when they get fed up with supervisors' contemptuous treatment or when they are laid off because world prices have plummeted. Behind every all-male banana plantation stand scores of women performing unpaid domestic and productive labor. Company executives, union spokesmen and export-driven government officials have all preferred not to take this into account when working out their bargaining positions. International agencies such as the International Monetary Fund scarcely give a thought to women as wives and subsistence farmers when they press indebted governments to open up more land to plantation companies in order to correct their trade imbalances and pay off foreign bankers.

Once the banana trees have been planted, women are likely to become residents and workers on the plantations. Plantation managers, like their diplomatic and military counterparts, have found marriage both a political asset and a liability. On the one hand, having young male workers without wives and children has advantages: the men are in their physical prime, they are likely to view life as an adventure and be willing to tolerate harsh working and living conditions. On the other hand, young unattached men are more volatile and are willing to take risks if angered precisely because they will not jeopardize anyone's security aside from their own. This makes the married male worker seem more stable to a calculating plantation manager. He may demand more from the company in the form of rudimentary amenities for his wife and children, but he is more likely to toe the company line for their sake.[6]

Women are most likely to be employed by the banana companies if the plantation cannot recruit men from a low-status ethnic group, like Amerindians in Central America, to do the least prestigious and lowest-paid jobs. In all sorts of agribusiness, women tend to be given the most tedious, least 'skilled' jobs, those that are most seasonal, the least likely to offer year-round employment and those company benefits awarded to full-time employees. Weeding and cleaning are the quintessential 'women's' jobs in agriculture, both in socialist and capitalist countries.[7]

Bananas today are washed, weighed and packed in factories on the plantations before being transported to the docks for shipment overseas. Inside these packing houses one finds the women on the modern banana plantation. They remove the bunches of fruit from the thick stems, an operation that has to be done carefully (one might say skillfully) so that the bananas are not damaged. They wash the bananas in a chemical solution, a hazardous job. They select the rejects, which can amount to up to half the bananas picked in the fields. Companies often dump rejected bananas in nearby streams, causing pollution which kills local fish. Women weigh the fruit and finally attach the company's telltale sticker on each bunch. They are paid piece-rates and foremen expect them to work at high speed. In between harvests they may have little work to do and not receive any pay. At harvest time they are expected to be available for long stretches, sometimes around the clock, to meet the company's tight shipping schedule.[8]

Tess is a Filipino woman who works for TADECO, a subsidiary of United Brands, Philippines. She works on a plantation on the country's southern island, Mindanao. A decade long war has been fought in the area between government troops and indigenous Muslim groups pro-testing against the leasing of large tracts of land either to multinational pineapple and banana companies or to wealthy Filipino landowners, who then work out lucrative contracts with those corporations. Tess herself is a Christian Filipino. She, like thousands of other women and men, migrated, with government encouragement, to Mindanao from other islands in search of work once the bottom fell out of the once-dominant sugar industry. She works with other young women in the plantation's packing plant, preparing bananas to be shipped to Japan by Japanese and American import companies. She is paid approximately $1 a day. With an additional living allowance, Tess can make about $45 a month; she sends a third of this home to her family in the Visayas.

Tess uses a chemical solution to wash the company's bananas. There is a large, reddish splotch on her legs where some of the chemical spilled accidentally. At the end of a day spent standing for hours at a time, Tess goes 'home' to a bunkhouse she shares with 100 other women, twenty-four to a room, sleeping in eight sets of three-tiered bunks.[9]

Many women working on banana plantations are young and single, and, in the Philippines, often have secondary-school or even college educations. They may be the daughters of male employees, or they may be recruited from outside. They are subjected to sexual harassment in the packing plants and can be fired if found to be pregnant. The life of a banana washer is dull and isolated: 'We have no choice than to stay here. First, the company is quite far from the highway and if we . . . spend our fare what else would be left for our food?'[10]

Large banana companies – Geest in Britain, United Brands, Del Monte and Dole in the United States and Japan's Sumitomo – also require workers at the other end of the food chain, in the countries where they market their bananas. The docks, the trucks and the ripening plants reveal how company managers shape the sexual division of labor. Stevedores in every country are thought of as doing a classic 'man's' job, though again ethnic politics may determine which men will unload the bananas from the company's ships. Today in Japan, where immigrant labor is being increasingly relied upon to do the low-status, low-paid jobs, Filipino men do the heavy work of transferring bananas from ships to trucks. The job has become so closely associated with the fruit that to be a longshoreman in Japan is to be a 'banana'. Women are hired in all the consumer countries to weigh and sort at the ripening plant before the fruit heads are ready for the supermarket. Food processing is as feminized – as dependent on ideas about femininity – as nursing, secretarial work and sewing.

Women are hired by the banana companies to do low-paid, often seasonal jobs that offer little chance of training and promotion; some involve the hazards of chemical pollution and sexual harassment. But many women still seek these jobs because they seem better than the alternatives: dependence on fathers or husbands (if they are employed), life on the dole (if work is not available), work in the entertainment industry around a military base, subsistence farming with few resources, emigration.

Many women are heads of households and take exploitative jobs in order to support their children; other women see their employment as part of being dutiful daughters, sending part of their meager earnings back to parents, who may be losing farm land to agribusinesses. Neither women nor men working on any plantation – banana, tea, rubber, sugar, pineapple, palm oil, coffee – are simply 'workers'. They are wives, husbands, daughters, sons, mothers, fathers, lovers; and each role has its own politics. The politics of being a daughter, a mother or a wife allows First World and Third World governments to rely on international plantation companies, which in turn are able to recruit and control women workers and win the consumer loyalty of women buyers. 'Daughter', 'mother', and 'wife' are ideas on which the international political system today depends.

Notes

1. Belinda Coote, *The Hunger Crop: Poverty and the Sugar Industry*, Oxford, Oxfam, 1987; Herbener Bossen, *The Redivision of Labor: Women and Economic Choice in Four Guatemalan Communities*, Albany, SUNY Press, 1984; Noeleen Heyzer, *Working Women in South-East Asia*, Milton Keynes and Philadelphia, Open University Press, 1986.
2. Philippe Bourgois, *Ethnic Diversity on a Corporate Plantation*, Cambridge, MA, Cultural Survival, 1986.

3. Ibid., pp. 10–11.
4. 'The Banana Man', song written by Jamaican writer Evan Jones in 1952, reproduced in *Whose Gold? Geest and the Banana Trade*, London, Latin America Bureau, 1987, p. 12.
5. On the feminization of agriculture and its developmental consequences, see Esther Boserup, *Women's Roles in Economic Development*, London, George Allen & Unwin, 1970; Barbara Rogers, *The Domestication of Women: Discrimination in Developing Societies*, London, Kogan Page, 1980.
6. Philippe Bourgois, Department of Anthropology, Washington University, St Louis, in correspondence with the author, October 2, 1986.
7. See Susan Bridger, *Women in the Society Countryside*, Cambridge and New York, Cambridge University Press, 1987; Sharon L. Wolchik and Alfred G. Meyer, editors, *Women, State and Party in Eastern Europe*, Durham, Duke University Press, 1988.
8. Elizabeth U. Eviota, 'The articulation of gender and class in the Philippines', in Eleanor Leacock and Helen I. Safa and contributors, *Women's Work*, South Hadley, MA, Bergin & Garvey, 1986, p. 199.
9. Sr Mary Soledad Perpinan, 'Women and transnational corporations: the Philippines experience', reprinted in Daniel Schirmer and Stephen R. Shalom, editors, *The Philippines Reader*, Boston, South End Press, 1987, p. 243.
10. Quoted in the slideshow, 'Bananas', produced by a progressive Filipino organization in the early 1980s. See 'Women of Dole', originally published in *Womenews*, Vol. 3, No. 1, January–March, 1986, reprinted in *Philippine Women*, NY, Women's International Resources Exchange, 1987. On Castle and Cook's banana and pineapple operations in the Philippines, see Dorothy Friesen, *Critical Choices: A Journey with the Filipino People*, Grand Rapids, MI, William B. Eerdmans Publishing Co., 1988.

22

The Sense of Coherence as a Determinant of Health*

AARON ANTONOVSKY

Pathogenic thinking and its consequences

The fundamental assumption of the pathogenic paradigm, until this very day is that the normal state of affairs of the human organism is one of homeostasis and order. Homeostasis is occasionally disrupted by microbiological, physical, chemical, and/or psychosocial stressors, vectors, or agents. Regulatory mechanisms – neuropsychological, immunological, endocrinological – come into play in the organism's effort to restore homeostasis. Sometimes these mechanisms are inadequate and disease results. Therapy then seeks to reinforce, enhance, or replace the regulatory mechanisms.

What have been the consequences of the dominance of this paradigm in thinking, research, and action – consequences that remain even when it is expanded to include psychosocial variables? Six phenomena can be noted:

1. We have come to think dichotomously about people, classifying them as either healthy or diseased.

2. Thinking pathogenically, we have almost inevitably taken as our focus of concern a specific pathologic entity: heart disease, or cancer, or schizophrenia. Even those concerned with prevention are channeled, intellectually and institutionally, into prevention of disease X, Y, or Z. We formulate hypotheses related to the specific dependent variable. We seek specific immunities and specific cures.

---

*This is an abridged version of a chapter in Matarazzo, J.D. *et al.* (1984) *Behavioural Health: an overview*, Wiley, pp. 114–129, reviewed and updated for this Reader by the author.

3. In parallel fashion, the pathogenic paradigm has constrained us to search for the cause or, if enlightened by the concept of multifactorial causation, the causes of disease X. The notion that stressors are ubiquitous, that pathogens are endemic in human existence (see Dubos, 1965) is an alien notion. In other words, prime attention is given to the bugs – as noted earlier, to the specific bugs related to disease X – and not to generalized capacities for coping with bugs.

4. Particularly in the field of stress research, which is a central concern of behavioral health but not unrelated to the 'cleanliness is godliness' precept, the pathogenic orientation has led us to assume that stressors are bad.

5. The pathogenic paradigm underlies the ambience that Dubos (1960) has so cogently warned against, 'the mirage of health'. Wars against diseases X, Y, and Z are mounted. Toughminded scientists, concerned with the 'magic bullet', are little attracted to the soft pleasantries of what the behavioral scientists have to offer. Moreover, they control the resources, for it is they who, in the general image, have pulled off the miracles. So, presumably, we move closer and closer to utopia.

6. Finally, pathogenesis has given overwhelming priority to the case or, in considering prevention, to the high-risk group. It tends to ignore what methodologists call deviant cases. We do not ask about the smokers who do not get lung cancer, the drinkers who stay out of accidents, the type As who do not have coronaries. Much more important, we do not study, as Brown (1981) puts it, 'the symptoms of wellness.'

Thinking salutogenically

What are the consequences of adopting what I have proposed to be called a salutogenic paradigm, which suggests that the normal state of affairs of the human organism is one of entropy, of disorder, and of disruption of homeostasis? What are the consequences of positing that the great mystery to be studied is that of health?

First, salutogenesis opens the way for a continuum conceptualization of what I have called health ease–dis-ease. The total population becomes the focus of concern, since none of us are categorized as healthy or diseased. Rather, we are all somewhere between the imaginary poles of total wellness and total illness.

Second, seeking the mystery of health, we are freed from the isolation of being limited to a particular disease entity. We come to communicate with all others working on the mystery. We begin to deal with the generalized factors involved in movement along the continuum, not just the factors specific to this or that disease entity.

Third, assuming that stressors are ubiquitous, we turn our attention away from the potential pathogen and from the specific answer to a given pathogen and become concerned, in research and in practice, with the resources that are valuable in coping with a wide range of pathogens and stressors. In doing so, we anticipate the emergence of new pathogens.

Fourth, we avoid hysteria about stressors and the gimmicks and instant cures that often accompany such hysteria. The question becomes not 'How can we eradicate this or that stressor?' but 'How can we learn to live, and live well, with stressors, and, possibly even turn their existence to our advantage?'

Fifth, recognition of the limited utility of wars against diseases X, Y, and Z, of the search for utopia, leads us to focus on the overall problem of adaptation, of the perpetual struggle for sources of adaptation, negative entropy – of input into the social system, the physical environment, the organism and lower-order systems, down to the cellular level to counteract the immanent trend to entropy. This paradigm not only serves as a countervailing force to biological scientists working on diseases; it opens the way for real cooperation between all scientists and practioners.

Sixth, the salutogenic paradigm continually focuses on the deviants, on those who make it against the high odds that human existence poses. It posits that we all, by virtue of being human are in a high-risk group. We come to ask questions at all points of the continuum.

It is essential at this point that a misunderstanding be avoided. I am not proposing that the pathogenic paradigm be abandoned, theoretically or institutionally. It has immense achievement and power for good to its credit. I have attempted to point to its limitations, to the blinders involved in any paradigm.

The sense of coherence

The very core of the salutogenic paradigm is the focus on successful coping, on what may well be called behavioral immunology. Once one adopts the paradigm, one begins to seek those forces and characteristics that are negentropic, that successfully screen out or do battle with the entropic forces.

The question is no longer 'What keeps one from getting sicker?' but 'What facilitates one's becoming healthier?' wherever one is at any given time on the health ease–dis-ease continuum.

Considerable attention has been given in the literature to a wide variety of coping variables. They have largely been conceptualized as buffers, mitigating the effects of stressors and muting the damaging effects on health. The list of these coping variables is long, ranging from money through knowledge to certain coping styles. The current vogue is social supports. What characterizes most of these studies is not only their failure to relate the coping variables under consideration to other coping variables – or, as I have called them, generalized resistance resources – but also their failure to translate the variables to a higher order of abstraction, which would provide a theoretical explanation of how the organism copes successfully to reinforce health.

The search for an overarching explanatory variable led to the sense of coherence (SOC) construct, whose original formulation appeared in Antonovsky (1979). This formulation was based on the assumption that, by late early adulthood (about age 30), individuals develop a generalized way of looking at the world, a way of perceiving the stimuli that bombard them. In the course of work designed to develop an operational index representing the SOC considerable refinement of the original definition was introduced (1). The SOC is now defined as:

> The sense of coherence is a global orientation that expresses the extent to which one has a pervasive, enduring though dynamic feeling of confidence that (1) the stimuli deriving from one's internal and external environments in the course of living are structured, predictable, and explicable; (2) the resources are available to one to meet the demands posed by these stimuli; and (3) these demands are challenges, worthy of investment and engagement. (Antonovsky, 1987, p. 19).

The three components of the SOC are called comprehensibility, manageability and meaningfulness.

Components of the sense of coherence

The *comprehensibility* component is indeed closest to the original formulation. It refers to the extent to which individuals perceive the stimuli that confront them as making cognitive sense, as information that is ordered, consistent, structured, and clear – and, hence, regarding the future, as predictable – rather than as noisy, chaotic, disordered, random, accidental, and unpredictable. No implication is made as to the desirability of stimuli. When people see the world as comprehensible, it does not mean that they are Panglossian, but only that they see it as understandable. It does not mean that they are unwilling to enter open-ended situations, but that when they do so, they have confidence that sense and order can be made of the situations.

The *manageability* component refers to the extent to which people perceive that resources are at their disposal that are adequate to meet the demands posed by stimuli. There is some similarity to White's (1963) concept of the sense of competence, which he defines as the sense in the living organism of 'its fitness or ability to carry on those transactions with the environment which result in maintaining itself, growing, and flourishing.' At first glance, it seems related to Kobasa's control component (Kobasa *et al.*, 1981) – people's belief in their ability to influence the course of events – and to the obverse on Seeman's concept of powerlessness (Seeman and Anderson.[2]). Both these concepts, however, directly derive from Rotter's (1966) internal locus of control measure, and in this they differ from my understanding of manageability. 'At one's disposal' may refer to sources under one's own control – the Kobasa, Seeman, and Rotter understanding – but it may also refer to resources controlled by legitimate others – friends, colleagues, god, history – upon whom one can count. No implication exists that untoward things do not happen in life. they do; but when people are high on manageability, they have the sense that, aided by their own resources or by those of legitimate others, they will be able to cope and not grieve endlessly. Moreover, there will be no sense of being victimized by events or of being treated unfairly by life.

The *meaningfulness* component of the SOC is, in a sense, the emotional counterpart to comprehensibility. When people say that something 'makes sense,' in cognitive terms they mean that it is ordered; in emotional terms, however, they mean that they care. People who are high on meaningfulness feel that life makes sense emotionally, that at least some of the problems and demands posed by living are worth investing energy in, are worthy of commitment and engagement, and are challenges that are welcome rather than burdens that they would much rather do without.

The SOC and health: avoidance, appraisal, and active coping

Wherever people are located at any time on the health ease–dis-ease continuum, the theory presented here hypothesizes that the stronger their SOC, the more likely they are to maintain that location or improve it. There is a distinct analogy (in due time it may become more than an analogy) to Burnet's (1971) concept of immunological surveillance, 'perpetually patrolling the body, as it were, for evildoers' (p. 157). The research evidence suggesting that this hypothesis is plausible is summarized in chapter 6 of Antonovsky (1979). Two relatively minor ways and one major way can be suggested to explain how this works.

First, the stronger their SOC, the more people can *avoid* threat or danger. They are more likely to engage in activities that are health-promoting and to avoid those that are health-endangering. People's belief that life is meaningful (which, not incidentally, gives them a good reason for wanting to be healthy in order to be able to function optimally), that they have the resources to manage, and that life is ordered and predictable provides a sound basis for such behaviors. It is worth investing in smoking cessation efforts, exercise, good nutrition, and the like, because they believe that these efforts will pay off. They are less tempted by the 'it can't happen to me' mode of thought. Of course, some people become faddists, but this tendency is held in check by the pragmatic criterion of whether a behavior pays off. People with a weak SOC, however, have neither the motivational nor the cognitive basis for the active coping, positive or negative, that the avoidance of threat requires.

Second, the stronger their SOC, the more likely it is that, confronted by the innumerable stimuli that cannot be avoided, people will appraise the stimuli not as threats or dangers that paralyze and lead to negative self-fulfilling prophecies, but as opportunities that offer meaningful rewards, as challenges worthy of investment of energy, and as situations that can be managed well. The woman who concludes that, given the specific life conditions under which she lives, she cannot go out to work and must continue being a housewife, will seek, if she has a strong SOC, to focus her energies on childrearing. The recent widower who has had a happy marriage will, together with the pain and sadness, be able to 'give up,' and restructure his life. People with a strong SOC, confronted with a potentially noxious situation, will be more able to define or redefine the situation as one to which they need not succumb, one that is not necessarily noxious.

Whatever the possibility of avoiding threat, however, or of redefining situations as non-noxious, life inevitably confronts us with noxious stimuli, with threats, with stressors. How does a strong SOC function negentropically? I suggest that this is the heart of the matter. It is here that we must turn to the concept of generalized and specific resistance resources, a concept that will be more fully discussed in the later section on the sources of the SOC. For present purposes, the crucial point is that resistance resources – defined as agencies that facilitate coping with pathogens – are potentials. They must be transformed kinetically before they can function to combat and overcome pathogens. The antibiotic is of no use unless it is taken appropriately. The friend is of no use unless there is communication. Clear cultural norms are of no use until they are applied to the concrete situation. Money is of no use until it is spent. Surely, people differ in the potential resources available in them. Beyond this, however, they differ significantly in the readiness and willingness to exploit the resources that they have at their potential disposal. This is what distinguishes between people with a stronger and a weaker SOC. The former will search very hard for the coping resources that are potentially available; the latter are more likely to 'give up' (this time in Engel's sense), and say 'Neither God, nor in myself, nor anyone else can help me.'

Sources of the SOC

In my original formulation, I characterized the SOC as 'enduring though dynamic.' It was envisaged as an orientation that emerges out of childhood, adolescence, and early adulthood, at the end of which the individual has become located at some point of the SOC continuum. The two questions to be dealt with in this section are, first, what factors shape a person's location and, second, what *dynamic* means.

The SOC construct emerged from a search for a parsimonious answer to the question '*How* do resistance resources seem to eventuate in good health?' as shown by substantial data. Rather, the data, gathered largely in answer to the pathogenic question, show that the absence of resistance resources eventuates in poor health?' – as seen, for example, in my own work on poverty and social class (Antonovsky, 1967). this search led to a specification of the commonalities of resistance resources – that is, the characteristics that are shared by the different phenomena that are labeled resistance resources. The definition of such resource had to be such that it would not lead to tautology – that is, defining a resistance resource as something that is empirically found to be related to health. Such findings do not answer the fundamental theoretical question of *how*.

The proposed answer to what resistance resources have in common is that they repeatedly provide life experiences that have three characteristics: consistency, an underload–overload balance, and participation in decision making. It is argued that having money or belonging to the upper class, having a clear ego identity, living in a stable society, having a clear religious stance, having social supports, and so on, all provide such life experiences.

Consistency refers to the extent to which a given life experience fits other previous or contemporary life experiences. Does a given behavior result in the same consequence as it did the last time the person manifested such behavior? Can the person make accurate predictions about what is likely to take place? Do social responses to the person in life area A contradict social responses in life area B? Do people relate to the person in one way today and in a different way tomorrow? Do significant others interact with the person in complementary or similar fashion? From our earliest childhood through the end of our lives, all our life experiences can be characterized as being to some degree consistent with one another. The core of this notion is the extent to which a person's life is laden with surprises for which there is no reasonable explanation. The greater the consistency of our life experiences, the more our lives are predictable. Note, here, the close link to the comprehensibility component of the SOC.

The *underload–overload balance* refers to the extent to which the life experiences we undergo – which always involve some demand – are appropriate to our capacities. Again, from birth, we are confronted by demands, emerging from both the internal and the external environments, to which we are called upon to measure up. Over and over again, we experience a greater or lesser degree of success. We can be bored or we can be overwhelmed; or we can repeatedly confront tasks that call on us to exert our energies, skills, knowledge, abilities, and potentials so that the tasks can be coped with successfully.

Much of the literature stresses the significance of overload. Underload is just as significant, however. When we are not called upon, or do not call upon ourselves, to do anything – when we have nothing to manage – our personal and role identities wither. Emptiness is no less dangerous than overload. When our life experiences are just about right in making demands on us, however – even, perhaps, with a slight leaning in the direction of overload, leading to the discovery of hitherto untapped energies and talents – our SOC is thereby strengthened. Note, here, the close link to the manageability component of the SOC.

Life experiences can be seen as having a third major dimension, one that I intuitively included in my original discussion but only began to understand later. Many life experiences can be consistent and balanced but not of our own making or choosing in any way. The question arises whether, with respect to any life experience, we have taken part in choosing to undergo that experience, in judging whether the rules of the game are legitimate, and in solving the problems and tasks posed by the experience. When others decide everything for us – when they set the task, formulate the rules, and manage the outcome – the experience inevitably remains alien and vicarious to us. It is important to stress that the dimension is not control but *participation in decision-making*. What is crucial is that people approve of the tasks set before them; that they have considerable performance responsibility; and that what they do or not do has an effect on the outcome of the experience. This formulation thus has room not only for the largely autonomous person but also for the loyal party member, the religious believer, the work group participant, and the child in a certain kind of family. Repeated experience of this kind of participation provides the basis for the meaningfulness component of the SOC.

Conclusion

By adopting a salutogenic orientation, we are guided and pressured to confront a central problem of behavioral health – namely, fostering a way of looking at and interacting with the world, which can be intractably difficult and stresstul – that will promote our movement toward the health pole of the health ease–dis-ease continuum. This outlook, called the sense of coherence, is a construct that purports to give meaning to the many empirical findings linking generalized and specific resistance resources to health. The construct, gives us a parsimonious and powerful way of analyzing many life situations and – by confronting the issues of consistency, underload–overload balance, and participation in decision making – possibly making programmatic advance. It offers no easy answers, particularly because it raises issues relating to the basic social structures and value systems of Western societies.

Notes

1 The 29-item SOC questionnaire has to date been translated into 14 languages and has been or is being used in well over 100 studies. What is common to these studies is the analysis of coping strengths among such diverse samples as homeless women in California, cancer patients in Stockholm, Norwegian adolescents and Flemish caregivers to the elderly.
2. Seeman, M. and Anderson, C. *Alienation and alcohol: The role of work, mastery and community in drinking behavior*. Unpublished manuscript, University of California at Los Angeles, Department of Sociology, 1981.

References

Antonovsky, A. (1967) 'Social class, life expectancy and overall mortality', *Milbank Memorial Fund Quarterly*, **45**, 31–73.
Antonovsky, A. (1979) *Health, Stress and Coping*. San Francisco, Jossey-Bass.
Antonovsky, A. (1987) *Unraveling the Mystery of Health*. San Francisco, Jossey-Bass.
Brown, V.A. (1981) 'From sickness to health: an altered focus for health care research', *Social Science and Medicine*, **15A**, 195–202.
Burnet, M. (1971) *Genes, Dreams and Realities*. New York, Basic Books.
Dubos, R.J. (1960) *The Mirage of Health*. London, Allen & Unwin.
Dubos, R.J. (1965) 'The evolution of microbial diseases'. In Dubos, R.J. and Hirsch, J.G. (eds) *Bacterial and Mycotic Infections of Man* (4th edn). Philadelphia, Lippincott.
Kobasa, S.C., Maddi, S.R. and Courington, S. (1981) 'Personality and constitution as mediators in the stress-illness relationship', *Journal of Health and Social Behavior*, **22**, 368–378.

Rotter, J.B. (1966) 'Generalized expectancies for internal versus external control of reinforcement'. *Psychological Monographs*, No. 80.

White, R.W. (1963) 'Sense of interpersonal competence: two case studies and some reflections on origins'. In White, R.W. (ed.) *The Study of Lives*. Chicago, Aldine.

Part III

HEALTH ON WIDER AGENDAS

Introduction

The articles in this final section reflect the diversity of views about future directions for health and wellbeing. They also link health to wider debates in contemporary political life. Conflicts about health – how it is to be conceptualised, constructed, experienced, safeguarded – cannot be viewed in isolation, for they connect to more profound and wide-ranging struggles between different social philosophies. Health is moving on to wider agendas at a critical time of turbulence and uncertainty in welfare, and the tensions in welfare philosophy mirror the choices, risks and tensions which health policies also need to address. The articles that follow examine some crucial areas of debate, and offer commentaries and visions about health and wellbeing in the future.

The first two articles highlight current debates in health and welfare about consumerism and the limits of individualism. Chapman and Egger consider the advantages of using commercial advertising techniques to persuade people not to smoke. They argue that advertising is a powerful medium for influencing lifestyle behaviour and that health educators should employ similar techniques to 'sell' their product – a healthy, non-smoking lifestyle.

The article by the World Health Organisation Health Education Unit, in contrast, reviews the lifestyles debate within a broader social constructionist framework. A post-medical era is envisaged, in which lifestyles become the focus for the attainment of health and wellbeing. Healthy and unhealthy lifestyles are seen as the outcome of a range of influences which include psychological factors and social conditions. Victim-blaming conceptions of lifestyle, the article suggests, must be countered by emphasising the impact of living conditions on individual behaviour.

The next cluster of articles highlights the tension that exists between personal freedom and collective responsibility in relation to one highly controversial issue: transport policy. It is used to illustrate some of the difficult choices facing health as it moves on to wider agendas, and to

215

explore how far campaigners will succeed in pushing health issues higher up the social agenda. In a 1975 paper, reproduced here, Hillman set out 'social goals' for transport that gave priority to equity and sustainability rather than unlimited personal freedom and growth. In his 1992 retrospect, Hillman explores some of the implications of not accepting these goals: global pollution, health risks, rapid consumption of finite resources.

Much of the debate about transport and health centres on the role of the private car, which Hunt argues now constitutes a major, yet largely unnoticed, health hazard. Hunt notes that a continued focus on individual driver inadequacies (or pedestrian responsibilities) distracts our attention from those wider political and economic interests which promote car production, purchase, and car use and abuse. It is time, she argues, for health educators to highlight the public health implications of private cars.

In contrast, Bayley indicates how private cars might promote wellbeing. Some of the magnetic appeal of individual car ownership is captured in his article. Bayley points out how private cars have been celebrated as the symbol of personal freedom, and the embodiment of their owner's status and virility. In an echo of Willis's earlier comments about motor-bikes, Bayley recognises that cars also make powerful personal and cultural statements.

Debates about individualism, collectivism, equity and social justice have moved centre stage in health, but they are still difficult to interpret. The article by Beattie offers an opportunity to explore several different approaches to conceptualising and formulating health, and to planning and intervening in health matters. Beattie explores how different health narratives connect to other distinctive features of the cultural landscape. He highlights how modes of thought and intervention in health can be linked to different intellectual traditions and reminds us of the interconnectedness of health, wellbeing and the wider politics of social welfare.

The final group of articles, drawn from politics, philosophy and literature as well as health, explores prospects of health and wellbeing in contemporary society. Not surprisingly, in view of the conflicting opinions about how to achieve health and wellbeing, the readings are diverse. The contribution by Popay *et al.* reflects a growing dissatisfaction with current policy-making approaches which emphasise economic growth as the key to social progress and better health. The authors call for a fundamental reappraisal of wealth creation in industrialised societies, in which the health costs and hazards of economic 'growth' are fully quantified. The current economic equation – wealth creates health – needs to be superseded by more ecologically based, health promoting policy approaches.

This theme – of the need for new insights and visions if the health of future generations is to be safeguarded – informs the next four articles. The first, by Williams, explores the prospects for reformulating agendas for political action by acknowledging and embracing contemporary social movements. Williams suggests that peace, ecology and feminism have provided contemporary politics with the most significant insights and innovative approaches. Together, he argues, they offer the potential for a new kind of radical politics, and the resources for 'a journey of hope' to a more peaceful, just and sustainable future. Robertson, reflecting on the place of work in future society, maps out three alternative scenarios: the superindustrial 'HE' vision, the social and personal adaptation 'SHE' vision, and the 'Business-As-Usual' approach. He suggests that health and wellbeing is most likely to be achieved if the work style of the future becomes 'ownwork' for all as in the SHE vision, characterised by personal choice and control.

The third of this group of articles suggests that a 'Green' future, achieved through sustainable global development, will offer most in the way of health, Gee points to the interrelatedness of our environment and our health. World poverty, famine, pollution and global warming and not just environmental disasters; a stricken planet cannot sustain, let alone promote, health. Health in the future depends on achieving fundamental shifts in values, resources and power. Pietroni offers another powerful vision of health in the future, one in which spiritual values and holistic practices will be uppermost in medicine. Growing interest in ecological principles, and greater open-mindedness towards alternative health beliefs and practices together signal, Pietroni suggests, a 'greening' of medicine.

The Reader ends on a note of hope and of homage to lay voices. The final article, by Ursula LeGuin, is a celebration of lived experience. The older woman at the centre of LeGuin's essay, the 'Space Crone' of the title, symbolises human endeavour. Through her struggles and survival she offers the prospect of a better and healthier future.

23

Myth in Cigarette Advertising and Health Promotion*

SIMON CHAPMAN and GARRY EGGER

> Well he can't be a man cause he doesn't smoke the same cigarette as me . . .
> (M. Jagger and K. Richards, 'Satisfaction')

There is no logically necessary link between smoking and manhood. In fact one might suggest the opposite. Yet the ironic certainty in the Rolling Stones' lyric illustrates the power of an image forged through deliberate and consistent association. Advertising is perhaps the most prolific vehicle for such image making in capitalist societies. It is made more efficient through the built-in process of evaluation obtained through sales records, which are often used to 'fine-tune' subsequent messages.

Advertising is often used to promote and sell products and services which in the long term may be harmful to human health. On the other hand it has been used sparingly in promoting health, probably because the reaction of health professions in general to advertising has been to regard it as 'soft', 'pop' and without an established base. Yet it should be through awareness rather than disdain of these techniques that health promoters operate.

Health education and promotion in the mass culture of the 1980s require efficient public health communication. An understanding of the principles and techniques involved in commercial advertising could provide a potentially powerful means of improving those modern health problems such as smoking that have a large behavioural component. If

*This is an abridged extract from Davis, H. and Walton, P. (eds) (1983), *Language, Image and Media*, pp. 66–86, Oxford, Blackwell.

people can be persuaded to take up smoking by advertising, perhaps they can be also persuaded to give it up.

Myth in advertising

Adverisements can be argued to have a mythical dimension which parallels aspects of the nature and functions of myth in traditional societies. In modern society, the place formerly occupied by traditional and overt mythology has been supplanted by many disguised mythologies (Eliade, 1957; McLuhan, 1959). The correspondence in popular commitment to old and modern myth systems is clear – advertising surely influences as many people today as were influenced by traditional myths in pre-industrial societies. As Maranda has explained, there is little difference in the metamorphosis of a beast into a handsome prince whether it be communicated as a fairy story or as a deodorant advertisement (1972, p. 16).

Advertising is one of the richest sources available for surveying the state of modern mythology. The truncated form that advertising takes necessitates a concentration of symbolism and imagery for the sake of economy in communication. This enables one to quite readily attempt to dissect the essence of the communication because of the relatively small number of elements being used. It is of course possible to analyse a mythical dimension in any public form or institution – fashion, humour, the news, etc. (Smith, 1979).

In popular usage, the word 'myth' is often used to refer to beliefs or opinions that are demonstrably false. In anthropology, it is used independently of any truth function. We are using 'myth' in the latter sense to refer to any real or fictional story, recurring theme or character type that appeals to the consciousness of a group by embodying its cultural ideals or by giving expression to deep, commonly felt emotions. In this way, to describe an element of social life as 'mythical' is to refer to the way that it is somehow *culturally distinctive* as both a meaningful and expressive element of the culture or subculture in question.

Mythological analysis can in this way, serve as one approach to the description of social ideologies. Like Lévi-Strauss we are 'concerned to clarify not so much what there is *in* myths' as the function of myth in 'conferring a common significance or unconscious formulations which are the work of minds, societies and civilisations' (1969, p. 12).

Promises for problems

Of all the illustrations, photographs and words that might be used to make up copy in advertising, why is it that particular scenes and actors in their special poses are selected rather than all possible others? In turning the pages of a magazine or watching a 30-second commercial, the 'reading' of an advertisement and the myths within it are 'exhausted at one stroke' (Barthes 1973) or read 'at a flash' (Goffman 1978, p. 27). Like traditional myths, they aim at causing an immediate impression. 'It does not matter if one is later allowed to see through the myth, its action is assumed to be stronger than the rational explanations which may later belie it' (Barthes 1973, p. 128).

In tobacco advertising, like all advertising, the fundamental problem that an advertisement seek to redress is that, for whatever reason, not enough people are choosing the product of concern. It will seek to redress this either by bringing the product to the consumers' attentions, or by trying to change the impression of the product and its associations. Conceptually, the whole venture of developing an advertisement may be considered in terms of there being a *problem* to which the advertisement will need to offer a *promise* which will be energized or made salient by a *myth* (Chapman, 1979). (See Table 23.1.)

The problem that an ad will offer a promise about may be one or a combination of two things:

(a)   negative qualities or associations of the actual product;
(b)   negative qualities or associations in or about users or potential users of the product.

So for example, cigarette sales may be down or not high enough because of widespread beliefs about their role in the aetiology of cancer, their stale smell or their role in halitosis. Such facts or beliefs about tobacco

TABLE 23.1   **Framework for decoding advertisements**

Problem	Negative qualities or associations in product as seen by consumer	Negative qualities or associations in user or potential user of product (popular views about smokers of particular brands; common personal worries; anxieties)
Promise	Positive aspects of product	Positive aspects of user of product and the product's part in attaining these aspects
Myth	The role of the product expressed as a metaphor for a cultural myth	The essence of the sort of person who uses the product, their basic qualities, needs and place in the world: as such, a mythical portrait

are problems to the company in the sense of (a) above. Similarly, in the sense of (b) above, there may be some consensus that smokers of particular brands characteristically behave, dress, or simply *are* a certain way that is felt as negative by people who are not (or hope that they are not) that way themselves. Schoolchildren have little difficulty in dramatizing differences between 'Mr Marlboro' and 'Mr Benson and Hedges', which may mean that many have internalized stereotypes for such smokers. Advertising may influence brand loyalty either positively or negatively: positively in the case of those attracted or identifying with an image; negatively in the case of those who are turned off or away from a brand by its image.

The third aspect to this framework is the part played by myth, and may be best approached by asking of any advertisement: 'Why does this particular promise *work* for this readership.' Generally speaking, a literal interpretation of any advertisement is commensurate with the promise being offered, while a metaphorical interpretation shows the way to the mythological force behind the promise that makes it culturally distinctive and meaningful to its reader. This deeper, mythological aspect of the process may sometimes be unconscious in the work of the advertiser. Interviews with former employees of the industry have revealed that the mythological/ideological aspects of the advertising process do not always occur to those involved in the production of advertisements. Their perception of their work concurs with Hall's comments on the day-to-day practical/technical routinizations of their tasks whereby supposedly ideologically neutral considerations of graphic design, good taste or 'eye-catchiness' govern what is finally produced (Hall, 1977). The process is better understood not as any attempt at deliberate, sophisticated manipulation of mythological themes, but rather as a case of the advertiser bringing his own humanity and socialization into the process through use of the 'naturally' appealing, taken-for-granted things of life, the way things *are*.

Myth resolves contradiction

The conglomerate of images presented by all brand advertising covers the range of smoking personae encompassed by all different smokers of different brands. Brand advertising and the consumer behaviour that may be generated by it fulfils a totemic function in differentiating smokers and others' perceptions of them. As pointed out by Williamson.

> Advertisements appropriate the formal relations of pre-existing systems of differences. They use distinctions existing in social mythologies to create distinctions between products. (1978, p. 27)

How and why would tobacco companies benefit from participating in the mythical process by providing expressions of sentiments meaningful to smokers? What is there in such expressions that results in new recruitment of smokers and increased brand loyalty? Myths may be studied as either *mirroring* or *constituting* a social condition (Armstrong, 1959). Cassirer's notion of the function of myth as expression may be explained a stage further by the introduction of this idea: that in the mass expression of commonly held sentiments or character ideals, the public form thus acquired serves as a mirror that can only be said to be somehow intrinsically gratifying to those who see their desired self-image or sentiments on various issues reflected back to them.

Further explanation would necessitate resource to psychoanalytic theories of the human condition – of why mirrors (metaphorical/social and literal/glass) are so popular. Lévi-Strauss, for example, makes an appeal for a 'group instinct': 'Just as music makes the individual conscious of his physiological rootedness, mythology makes him aware of his roots in society. The former hits us in the guts; the latter we might say appeals to our group instinct' (1969, p. 28). So when a smoker views an advertisement that *appeals*, one might explain this as perhaps a process of his being gratified through seeing certain aspects of real or sought-after self-identity, attitudes and fantasies objectified and somehow made more real through virtue of the constitutive nature of the physical advertisement itself.

Lévi-Strauss, in *Structural anthropology*, argues that the purpose of myth is to provide a model of thought capable of overcoming contradiction generated by society or human condition. This notion is compatible with the problem-promise approach to understanding advertising described earlier, and with Langholz Leymore's use of the Exhaustive Common Denominator (ECD), a basic structuralist analytical process involving the reduction of signifying surface presentations to binary opposite substructures. Langholz Leymore writes that, like myths, advertising:

> . . . acts as an anxiety reducing mechanism. This is done first by re-stating, on the deep level, the basic dilemmas of the human condition; and second by offering a solution to them. It re-iterates the essential problems of life – good and evil, life and death, happiness and misery etc. and simultaneously solves them. (1975, p. 7)

Cigarettes, their use and their users are rife with contradictions which advertising attempts to resolve by placing their resolution in apposition to the product or user. Cigarettes (that are easy to obtain) are placed in apposition to cherished or desired values, moods or situations (that are difficult to obtain or experience). The desirable values, moods and

situations are located within certain social settings, e.g. the sophisticated, international 'world' of the jet-setter, or the rugged, free, masculine 'world' of the cattle-rancher. These social settings or 'worlds' are
referent systems.

Elements of content of the advertisement that evoke the referent
system are called *signifiers* by Saussure. Thus in the examples above of
the sophisticated, international world of the jet-setter and of the rugged
cattle-rancher the signifiers may be a Concorde jet, and a horse, cowboy
gear, etc. respectively. It is pointed out that any given advertisement has
theoretically an inexhaustible number of signifiers, but that invariably
only a limited number are selected out in the decoding process as being
significant. For example, in the Marlboro advertisement we list four
signifiers (Marlboro man; cowboy hat; stables; and Marlboro smoking
gesture). It could be argued that more pertinent signifiers are shown but
not listed as significant by us. Why have we not listed his sideburns, his
poker face, the hair on the back of his hands and so on?

Our selection is really a shorthand approach in recognition of
Goffman's elegant description of this methodological impasse that
would otherwise plague all decoding of photographs with copious
listings. He writes:

> The student can exploit the vast social competency of the eye and the
> impressive consensus sustained by viewers. Behavioral configurations which
> he has insufficient literary skill to summon up through words alone, he can
> yet unambiguously introduce into consideration. His verbal glosses can serve
> as a means to direct the eye to what is to be seen instead of having to serve as a
> full rendition of what is at issue. the notion of a 'merely subjective response'
> can then be academically upgraded; for clearly part of what one refrains from
> studying because the only approach is through verbal vagaries has a specific
> nature and is precisely perceived, the vagary being a characteristic of one's
> literary incapacity, not one's data. (1978, p. 25)

In decoding advertisements one can use the three-tiered 'problem–
promise–myth' framework (Table 23.1) as a guide in following the steps
of the makers of advertisements. This will be best achieved by first
examining the advertisements for *signifiers* which will then allow for
extrapolation to *referent systems*. In utilizing this approach, it is necessary
to constantly project one's thinking into the various realities of people
reading these advertisements, into part of what folklorists and myth-
ologists call the 'ethnographic context'. One must imagine oneself as
both pleaser and pleased; as those offering solutions and those in need
of them. Barthes would approve. He wrote:

> If one wishes . . . to explain how [myth] corresponds to the interests of a
> definite society, in short, to pass from semiology to ideology . . . [one must

focus on] the reader of myths who must reveal their essential function . . . If he receives it in an innocent fashion, what is the point of proposing it to him? (Barthes 1973, p. 129).

Example: Marlboro

The recurrent signifiers in Marlboro ads are the 'Marlboro man', horses (usually being rounded up), open spaces and the distinctive smoking gesture of the Marlboro man's mouth. All of these signifiers are found in the mythical 'Marlboro country', a place that is better understood as a metaphor for freedom than as any literal rural Utopia.

Most people who see Marlboro advertisements (and who smoke Marlboro) are urban dwellers. The advertisements are not designed for people who are like the Marlboro man, but for those who would like to be like him. Marlboro advertising is perhaps the most blatantly escapist of all cigarette advertising. It offers translation of the harried, rushed and crowded urban man to the open spaces, freshness, elemental toughness and simplicity of Marlboro country.

The Marlboro man himself is a man of few words. Unlike Hogan of Winfield, or the sophisticates of Benson and Hedges, he displays neither wit nor sophistication but is rather the 'strong, silent type' with quiet confidence and inner resources. As such it is likely that he acts as a model for many men who have little to say in social situations; lighting up a Marlboro signals to others and reassures the smoker that he is really a person of some depth: like a Zen master, he only speaks when absolutely necessary.

It is in this context that the Marlboro 'way' of smoking is particularly interesting. If one asks a group of schoolboys to role-play 'how a Marlboro smoker smokes' and 'how a Benson and Hedges smoker smokes', we see the task almost always presents no difficulty, and the differences are marked. The Marlboro smoking style is full of determination, facial grimacing and suggests that a drag from a Marlboro is not child's play. One definitely knows that a 'decent' cigarette is being smoked. In short, it is a tough smoke for tough men.

Schoolboys probably choose Marlboro for its escapist promise as well as its promises of power and control. The Marlboro man rounds up horses that haven't seen a man for months (so one advertisement explicitly claims). They are quite wild, yet are rounded up helplessly. There is an analogous role reversal portrayed here in the schoolboy situation. They see themselves as young men being belittled, ordered about, rounded up, placed in uniforms and made to conform by teachers and parents who still view them as children. The role of the Marlboro man is obviously an attractive alternative. (See Table 23.2.)

TABLE 23.2   Summary of Marlboro advertising

Signifiers:	Marlboro man; cowboy hat; stables; Marlboro smoking gesture.
Referent systems:	wide open spaces; the tough, free life of the cowboy.
Problems:	trapped in urban artifice; rushed, ordered, powerless, insignificant; lost for words.
Promises:	freedom; power; signal to others one's inner strength. product as restorer of freedom and potency
Myths:	product as restorer of freedom and potency
Binary opposites:	free : trapped
	strong : weak;
	independent : dependent;
	powerful : powerless.
Exhaustive common denominator:	Marlboro smokers : others
	≃ winners : losers.

Hero myths

Heroes typically rise from the common ranks and achieve success as winners. As Henderson (1964) has pointed out however, mythological heroes are of many and varied form. Their function is to assist the immature ego through a trying stage of development to where it can stand alone. As such, different types of heroes have different appeal at varying stages in ego development. Henderson uses North American Winnebago mythology to illustrate the appeal of the trickster myth as exemplified by the hare and the fox to the early adolescent. Trickster characters are subtle, fun-loving, mischievous, unthreatening and uncomplicated. Unlike the superhuman image of some hero myths, the trickster is more accessible as an identity model to the perceiver. He is not extra-ordinary. Yet he can compete with the extraordinary or super-human and invariably come out on top. Because he is not superhuman, the trickster is easily identifiable by the young adolescent who can not yet relate to power and strength beyond his or her own capacity.

The Marlboro man, is a winner through inner strength. Like Hercules of classical mythology, the Marlboro Man conquers the odds expected on a voyage to maturity by meeting them head-on. The Marlboro appeal is likely to be to the older adolescent (i.e. 15+).

Myth and anti-smoking campaigns

Health appeals aimed at attacking advertising appeals are doomed to failure. Orthodox health appeals, with their theme of delayed gratification (i.e. postponement of premature death perhaps 40 years hence), and their incitement to those identity-seeking young wishing to show strength by defying the odds, must suffer the fate of Goliath in the hands of the all-conquering David. A number of conclusions about anti-smoking education arise from this.

First, it should be obvious that rational information-based appeals aimed at preventing smoking amongst adolescents will not succeed (Thompson, 1978). Adolescents know from their own experience of smoking that its adverse consequences will arrive, if at all, in the distant future. 'Future rewards for current deprivations' is the antithesis of the essence of advertising (except perhaps insurance and bank advertising), which promises instant gratification.

This is not to suggest that informational approaches do not work with more mature audiences. The implication for future campaigns therefore may be that while research shows a definite need for still more health information related to smoking, this should be aimed at a more mature audience, i.e. over 30 years of age. Appeals directed at the young need to be more concerned with image and less with knowledge.

Second, while every effort should be made to restrict cigarette advertising that appeals to the young, there is little to be gained by attacking the image perpetuated by cigarette promoters. The trickster has a thick skin and the hero, by definition, always wins. Non-smoking appeals can aim to replace these images, not destroy them. They can utilize similar techniques to develop an image around the non-smoker, although not one in which adult motivations (i.e. health, longevity) are used to appeal to sub-adult audiences. The adolescent who chooses not to smoke, unlike his smoking peer, has no established mythological image structure with which to identify. The task is to develop one.

References

Armstrong, R.P. (1959) 'Content analysis in folkloristics'. In de Sola Pool, I. (ed) *Trends in Content Analysis*. Urbana, University of Illinois Press.

Barthes, R. (1973) *Mythologies*, selected and translated by A. Lavers, St Albans, Paladin.

Chapman, S.F. (1979) 'Advertising and psychotropic drugs: the place of myth in ideological reproduction', *Social Science and Medicine*, **13**, 751–764.

Eliade, M. (1957) *Myths, Dreams and Mysteries*. New York, Harper Torch Books.

Goffman, E. (1978) *Gender Advertisements*. London, Macmillan.

Hall, S. (1977) 'Culture, the media and the ideological effect'. In Curran, J., Gurevitch, M. and Woollaccott, J. (eds) *Mass Communication and Society*. London, Edward Arnold.

Henderson, J.L. (1964) 'Ancient myths and modern man'. In Jung, C.G. (ed) *Man and His Symbols*. New York, Dell Publishing.

Langholz, Leymore, V. (1975) *Hidden Myth: structure and symbolism in advertising*. London: Heinemann.

Lévi-Strauss, C. (1969) *The Raw and the Cooked*. New York, Harper and Row.

Maranada, P. (1972) *Mythology*. Harmondsworth, Penguin.

McLuhan, M. (1959) 'Myth and mass media', *Daedalus*, **88**, 329–348.

Smith, R.R. (1979) 'Mythic elements in television news', *Journal of Communication*, **29**, 51–57.

Thompson, E.L. (1978) 'Smoking education programmes, 1960–1976', *American Journal of Public Health*, 68–250.

Williamson, J. (1978) *Decoding Advertisements*. London, Marion Boyars.

Lifestyles and Health*

HEALTH EDUCATION UNIT, WHO

The increasing emphasis on promoting health and improving lifestyles

In the 19th century, great improvements in health were brought about by what might be called 'engineering methods' – the building of safe water supply and sewerage systems in the towns and the use of mechanized agriculture to provide cheap food for the urban population. Such methods of improving health are still important in the poorer parts of the region. The first 60 years or so of the 20th century could be termed the 'medical era', in which allopathic medicine emerged as the dominant approach to health care: this was based on mass vaccination and the extensive use of antibiotics and is still the main approach in some parts of the region. Now, however, the industrialized parts of the region have entered upon a 'post-medical' era, in which physical wellbeing is undermined by certain types of individual behaviour (e.g. smoking), failures of social organization (e.g. loneliness), economic factors (e.g. poverty, over-eating) and factors in the physical environment (e.g. pollution), that are not amenable to improvement by medicine, which now has in many parts of the region only a limited capacity to effect further improvements in health. Whereas in the 'medical' era health policy has been concerned mainly with how medical care is to be provided and paid for, in the new, 'post-medical' era it will focus on the attainment of good health and wellbeing.

The debate on lifestyles and their impact on health is an expression of the search for ways of meeting the new situation, in which chronic conditions, particularly cardiovascular disorders and cancer, make up the bulk of morbidity, and psychological disorders such as depression and the repercussions of stress are becoming increasingly important.

*This is an abridged version of an article that was first published in *Social Science and Medicine*, Vol. 22, No. 2, pp. 117–124, 1986.

At first the key to preventing many of these conditions was considered to be a change in the health behaviour of the individual and it is of course true that excessive drinking and smoking, overeating and faulty nutrition, lack of exercise and misuse of drugs and other medicines, have a deleterious effect on wellbeing and health. Much more controversial is the question of *why* unhealthy lifestyles have become so widespread and what practical conclusions should be drawn from the knowledge accumulated in the past decade about this situation, especially since industrialized countries are exporting unhealthy life-styles to the poorer parts of the world. Researchers are now acknowledging that the standard risk factors do not explain everything and are beginning to study the combined influence of lifestyles, psychological factors and social conditions on human wellbeing as a basis for their concepts. With poverty still present and health contrasts due to socioeconomic inequalities even increasing in some parts of the Region, it is one of WHO's responsibilities to ensure that the lifestyle concept is used not as a blanket explanation in which the victim is always blamed, but as a means of stressing how great an impact living conditions have on individual wellbeing and health behaviour.

The meaning of lifestyles

There is almost no agreement either in theory or practice as to what constitutes a 'lifestyle'. Some use it to denote a number of health-relevant patterns of consumption and general living, but often in too broad and general a way to enable specific health consequences to be determined. Others use 'lifestyle' in a sense implying that the individual has chosen particular types of behaviour and particular habits of his own free will: here the term refers to individual types of behaviour that are hazardous to health and does not leave room for clear differentiation between a particular habit that is injurious to health and a specific lifestyle.

In the regional strategy and the target document, the term 'lifestyle' is taken to mean a general way of living based on the interplay between living conditions in the wide sense and individual patterns of behaviour as determined by sociocultural factors and personal characteristics. The range of behaviour patterns open may be limited or extended by environmental factors and also by the degree of individual self-reliance. The way in which an individual lives may produce behaviour patterns that are either beneficial or detrimental to health. If health is to be improved, action must be directed at both the individual and environmental factors affecting lifestyle.

For example, there is extensive evidence of relationships between socioeconomic status (including occupation) and morbidity, disability and mortality, and between level of education and health maintaining practices and health status.

Another potential source of confusion in attempts to detect associations between daily living habits and morbidity and mortality is a stressful life situation due to causes other than insufficient income or an unhealthy work environment. Stressful events or situations have often been found to have adverse effects on health and persons exposed to them may become more neglectful of health.

It has also been shown that social intercourse and support help to reduce the deleterious effects of stress, perhaps by influencing health behaviour.

Finally what people believe about health affects their attitude to healthful behaviour, their utilization of preventive health and screening services, their behavioural responses to illness and even the degree to which they report illness.

One working definition of lifestyles that attempts to cover the multitude of background factors, reads as follows:

'Lifestyles are patterns of (behavioural) choices made from the alternatives that are available to people according to their socio-economic circumstances and to the ease with which they are able to choose certain ones over others' [1].

This definition links the consciousness, experiences and behaviour patterns of individuals and social groups to identifiable structural patterns within a given society, and thus provides a basis for health policy decisions, health promotion and health education.

For the purposes of analysis lifestyle has to be defined in relation to collective and individual experiences and to conditions of life. The range of options open to an individual is confined to the area in which the two groups of factors overlap.

The lifestyle of a social group comprises a range of socially determined patterns of behaviour and interpretations of social situations, developed and used jointly by the group to cope with life.

An individual's lifestyle is made up of the standard reactions and behaviour patterns that are developed through processes of socialization. They are learned through social interaction with parents, peer groups, friends and siblings or through the influence of schools, the mass media, etc. They are continually interpreted and tested out in social situations and are therefore not fixed once and for all but subject to change based on experience and reinterpretation. the lifestyle of an individual provides a framework for different sorts of behaviour: choice of a particular behaviour pattern will depend on his cognitive and emotional make-up and the constraints and contradictions of the surrounding social world. Thus research on the effects of lifestyles on health is bound to be an extremely complex matter.

Since no individual lives for himself or herself alone, and no social group exists without links to the near and far environment and without reference to its tradition and culture, there must be identifiable elements within the social system that transmit its broad values down to the level of daily behaviour. These elements are institutionalized in various forms (kinship, family, school, religion) and act as intermediaries between the lifestyle of a society and the lifestyles of the groups and individuals that make it up.

The lifestyle of a society as a whole will be affected by modernization and social change and these will reach different groups at different points in time and space (thus accounting for the North–South differences within and between countries). Essential features of modernization are (a) the segregation of work from private life, with a resultant increase in anonymity, (b) a dichotomy between the public and the private sphere leading to new forms of social isolation, (c) the splitting of life into distinct and separate areas, leading to increased segmentation of experience and (d) the increasing adoption of urban lifestyles. Despite the economic growth and individual emancipation made possible by these developments it seems that apathy and unsettledness are becoming ever more common in modern societies or those undergoing the process of modernization. Especially when they are exported to the developing countries the ideas, images and models of 'modern' conduct lead to overexpectation of a better life and to disintegration and disruption of the old society – with massive repercussions on physical and mental health.

Individual behaviour occurs against a background of past experience, stresses, social relationships and knowledge within the cultural, political and economic environment characteristic of the society concerned. Many factors they know to be detrimental to health cannot be affected by individuals. It must also be borne in mind that the attainment of health in a society in which some social groups (e.g. women, the elderly, the poor) are systematically at a disadvantage is problematical. A healthy community cannot be based on exploitative, i.e. unhealthy, human relations.

A new macro-perspective: scenarios for health

People differ in the place they give to health, as compared with other concerns in their lives, and the same applies to societies. In many traditional societies, for example, illnesses are considered to be due to the intervention of supernatural beings conveying a spiritual message to the individual and the group he lives in, rather than to pathogens or other material factors. In late industrial societies, health tends to be defined biologically and dealt with medically. Personal concern with health is usually in response to ill health and the health services and health professions are mainly employed in dealing with injury and sickness. A different society or a different set of personal values might give high priority to establishing and maintaining good health. Health considerations would play an important part in decisions about work, housing, planning, energy policy, economic policy, and other aspects of life.

In determining what research on lifestyles can contribute to the attainment of health for all by the year 2000 the scenario technique may be useful. A scenario is a description of a possible pattern of future development. It is based on the possibility that an existing trend or set of trends will become predominant. It is unlikely that any one scenario will actually be fulfilled in every detail. The future is more likely to contain elements from different scenarios. Scenarios simply provide a more or less systematic way of imagining and working out possible challenges, opportunities and other relevant developments in the future, as a basis for present decisions. They can also help determine which of today's tendencies should be regarded as favourable to the end in view – in this case the encouragement of healthy lifestyles.

Many very different futures can be imagined. However, below three such scenarios for health have been outlined as examples and related to possible changes in the social environment and in social values.

In a 'traditional' scenario, health will continue to be given a comparatively low priority both by society and by individuals. Instead of the creation of a healthy society and the enjoyment of a healthy personal life being regarded as priority goals, the approach to health will continue to be remedial and to some extent preventive, but not positively promotive. The health services will continue to be primarily sickness services, and people who take a positive approach to their personal health will be exceptions to the norm.

The 'technological' scenario for health is based on the rapid advancement and extensive use of medical technology to solve health problems. Genetic screening will help to eliminate genetic diseases and handicaps: organ transplants and spare-part banks will make it possible to repair the human body: new drugs will control mental health, cure mental illness and prevent cancer, obesity, additions, senility and viral diseases; computer monitoring will ensure that patients comply with the medication prescribed. Computerized medical records, containing data on the physiological, emotional, social and economic aspects of everyone's life, will enable physicians, surgeons and other medical and health technologists to deal quickly and effectively with their patients' problems. People will be able to relax in the knowledge that their health will be well cared for, so long as they trust the experts and follow their advice – not only about medication and treatment but also about diet, work, leisure activities and other aspects of life. In this scenario, in short, the health care system will be the preserve of the medical profession, and more and more prolems will be treated medically. Health-promoting behaviour will probably gain some ground, but the increased dominance of health care by the medical profession will mean that great stress will continue to be laid on remedial measures, with prevention in second place.

The 'ecological' scenario for health, on the other hand, is based on personal and social responsibility and a positive concept of health. People will take personal responsibility for their own health: they will discharge that responsibility in a spirit of individual self-help and mutual aid, and will actively insist that society provide a health-promoting environment.

Interest in nutrition and environmental public health will become widespread. The psychosomatic aspects of health will also be given much higher priority. The causes of illness-inducing stress will be tackled. People's capacities for self-understanding, self-reliance and mutual support by various means will be systematically developed. People will learn to accept and manage better than they do now the stressful transitions from one stage to another in their lives. Small-scale information technology will be used to enable people to decide for themselves when they should call for professional medical advice or help. The emphasis will be on wellness rather than disease.

A new micro-perspective: coping, risk behaviour and control

As already stated, whatever path is chosen to attain better health will be subject to constraints. Large parts of the individual's responsibility for his own life have been handed over to anonymous bodies, to social and state agencies. Sometimes it seems that what is left is too much to give up, yet not enough for us to take responsibility for our own lives again. It is this model of modern life that we are exporting to the developing world in the form of patterns of production and consumption that change the structure of everyday life. Individuals are made aware that there is little they can do that will affect the social situations and conflicts with which they are confronted or contribute to any kind of solution. To risk health is sometimes the only way to continue functioning or at least to cope with the requirements of everyday life.

Coping behaviour itself is beginning to emerge as a major factor in lifestyles and one that influences health in a subtle and complex fashion. People try to cope with their problems in three basic ways:

- they try to alter their perception of the problem.
- they try to control the stress to which the problem gives rise, or
- they try to change the situation that has created the problem.

It is obvious that in situations beyond individual control, the second variant will be the most common (resulting in often dangerous forms of risk and health behaviour as described below) and that the way of coping will depend on the way of looking at the world, the values and the social and economic resources available of the social group concerned. Long-term problems tend to have a particular adverse impact on health and for that reason for those social groups – the elderly, women, the poor – faced with most uncertainty and most problems the freedom of choice in respect of health practices will be significantly less, if it exists at all.

Feelings of powerlessness are a major factor in the causation of risk behaviour. Any decision on how to act or react in a social situation is determined by what risks are considered acceptable but acceptability is not always based on rational criteria and is not always subject to individual control.

The notion of 'health risk' has been gradually expanded by the medical system. For example, in the ever-increasing intervention of medicine in childbirth, people have consistently lost part of their freedom to opt for a particular type of behaviour and/or treatment. Studies of alternative services show that one of their special attractions for the public is that they have adopted a different concept of risk, in that the persons concerned are involved in the decision-making process and are allowed to make the final choice.

A further positive aspect of risk behaviour is the role it plays in establishing an identity and testing the control the individual has over the environment and self: this aspect of risk behaviour is of major important when trying to understand why young people adopt patterns of behaviour that involve risks for their health: only too often such patterns are merely dubbed 'irresponsible' rather than being considered as necessary in a period of transition from one stage of life to another.

Finally, risk behaviour may constitute a way in which the individual can compensate for conflicts that arise in everyday life and regain the physical and psychological ability to face up to them again. The risks are taken personally, with an eye to individual benefit not to the degree of social acceptance or rejection they may provoke.

Often such behaviour patterns are highly acceptable in our culture and are promoted by mass media, advertising and tradition: 'You need a drink'. 'Take a pill'. 'Have a cigarette', etc. are phrases suggesting that escape from conflict situations by risk behaviour is a matter of conformity and is therefore socially acceptable. The individual benefit of risk behaviour lies in this escape, however short-term it may be. Attempts to influence individuals to adopt healthier forms of behaviour must allow for the fact that their present behaviour is not merely a matter of free choice: it may more often be a desperate reaction in an attempt to find a way to deal with individual problems as well as the problems of society.

In this respect research findings that point to the influence of variables such as self-esteem or people's perception of internal or external control over their own lives are becoming increasingly important for health promotion.

Major settings for intervention

The lifestyle approach does not imply that the preventive measures and the health philosophy of the social reformers of the 19th century are no longer worth considering. On the contrary, their idea that environmental conditions are responsible for much mass disease is particularly important and relevant today.

The two important objectives are:

(a) to try to control not only physical and biochemical risks but also risks arising from the social environment:
(b) to encourage and support those factors in the environment that cushion the individual and help him/her to cope (the social structure).

Lifestyle interventions must be based on the co-operation and full participation of the individuals and groups concerned, since if they were dominated by professionals they would not be health-promoting in the new sense.

In view of the effect of nutrition, housing, transport problems and poverty on individual and community health, and the fact that these areas cannot be influenced by separate individuals, action for change will have to be carried out at local and national government levels. Such action can only be effected by individuals working collectively (in a trade union, for example) and only if they are capable of assuming responsibility for their environment. This demands a level of knowledge and skill that most people do not have and if wider social change is to be brought about steps must be taken to train people to take responsibility.

Lifestyles are established or altered as a consequence of structural environmental and personal forces. Successful intervention, therefore, must first accept that the social forces already at work in influencing health for the better are of paramount importance. This means that ways must be found of strengthening the influence of factors conducive to healthy lifestyles. The public should be informed of the merits and demerits of the various options open to them and resources should be made available to make the option chosen possible.

Conclusions

The essence of health promotion is choice. If, in the process of promoting lifestyles conducive to health, one tyranny, i.e. undue emphasis on health, is substituted for another, then the whole process will have failed. People must be free to refuse and this must be a prime requisite for all intervention strategies: at the same time people should assume their social responsibilities towards each other.

A code of ethics is needed which should comprise general principles, rules for their practical application where appropriate and for their adaptation to specific situations, and illustrative examples.

Planning for health promotion and healthier lifestyles should bear in mind the principles listed above and care should be taken to ensure that no unintended effects are produced by the programmes of action decided upon.

A new perspective is needed on lifestyles and health promotion, one which places them firmly in the context of broad social trends and define them as inherently social in origin and in growth. This would reflect an ecological model of health, not a purely medical, behavioural, sociological, environmental or political one. It would recognize that health is affected by a multitude of factors and that it is a public good.

There is now an opportunity to take an objective look at the broad policy implications of our work on lifestyles and health promotion. We have reached the age of responsibility.

Note

1. Milio, N. (1981) *Promoting Health through Public Policy*. F.A. Davis, Philadelphia.

25

Social Goals for Transport Policy*

MAYER HILLMAN

Introduction

The overriding objective of public policy should be to improve the quality of life for all members of society. The setting out of explicit social goals to which the public subscribes is a prerequisite in the pursuit of this objective. It would seem that a consensus does exist on most of the basic goals,[†] even though they are rarely enunciated – the furtherance of equity, the maintenance of maximum personal freedoms compatible with similar freedoms for all members of society, the abolition of causes of unnecessary suffering, responsibility to posterity, the minimization of waste (particularly of finite resources) and the improvement of the social and physical environment.

In my view these goals are as relevant to transport policy as they are to other areas of public policy. Indeed it seems impossible to determine what relative significance to attach to the criteria of efficiency, cost effectiveness, energy needs or environmental preservation used to evaluate the efficacy of transport policies in the absence of clearly defined goals. I believe that failure to formulate and then pursue such goals accounts in large measure for the qualitative decline in the urban environment coinciding with rising transport 'affluence'. How well in fact do present transport policies match up to these goals?

---

*This abridged version of an article was first published in 'Transport for society', *Proceedings of the Conference of the Institute of Civil Engineers*, pp. 13–20, 1975.
[†]I have deliberately not attempted to order these goals, to suggest that they are mutually exclusive or wholly compatible, or to imply that the list is comprehensive, but I would claim that they are complementary in many respects.

Equitable distribution of costs and benefits of transport

The great majority of people have a need to travel in their daily lives, and at the same time an aversion to the intrusion caused by motorized traffic. Therefore it may be posited that one of the principal social goals of transport planning should be to ensure that the benefits of safe and convenient access to people and places, and freedom from the 'costs' of motorized traffic should be distributed as fairly as is practicable; the *status quo* should only be changed if such change improves the condition of those groups in society with the greater need.

Since the Second World War the growth of motorized travel has been associated with a widening of the gap between those able to live and work in surroundings free from traffic nuisance and those exposed to it, and the rising mobility of those with the optional use of a car has been achieved by effectively reducing the mobility of those without such use.[1] Yet this latter group is now and always will be a majority of the population, including the young and most of the elderly, the disabled and the poor. These people are largely dependent on walking (and sometimes cycling) and on public transport – travel methods which have steadily declined in quality, convenience and availability as car ownership and use have risen. Paradoxically these travel methods impose the least social and environmental costs on society.[2] For these reasons one could have expected government policies to promote them.

In the same way that transport planning policies have largely ignored consideration of the equitable distribution of transport's benefits, so policies on the distribution of its disbenefits can be seen to be inequitable in application. The channelling of traffic to reduce its environmental costs by the creation of environmental areas, and the designation of lorry routes in urban areas, frequently result in a further diminution of amenity for those whom it is least fair to penalize – people living on the main roads – as they are already subject to an unfair share of the public nuisance costs of traffic.[3]

Maintenance of personal freedoms

The second social goal, and one closely related to that of equity, is concerned with the rights of individuals to maximize their freedom of action. This is an instinctive desire, and indeed there can be little doubt that it is the freedom-giving potential of the private vehicle that largely accounts for the dramatic post-war increase in traffic. However, concomitant with this increase there has been a decline in the ability of certain groups in society with low or no access to private vehicles to exercise their freedoms.

The growth of traffic has created a condition in which children in particular have sustained a dramatic loss of independence as parents have increasingly felt obliged to impose restrictions on them. This has resulted in a considerable circumscription of their freedom as individuals, compared with the freedom enjoyed by their parents and even more by their grandparents. Recent surveys have shown that, on average, parents will only allow their children to cross main roads unaccompanied at the age of eight, to travel by bus at the age of nine and to cycle on the roads on their own at the age of ten,[4] but far from this being recognized as an unfortunate development requiring changes in transport policy in view of this inroad into children's basic freedom, parents are often admonished for not accompanying their young children. Children's inability adequately to perceive traffic danger is viewed as sufficient reason for denying them this freedom: the Department of the Environment specifically excludes them from traffic counts taken to establish the need for pedestrian crossings. It is odd that children are obliged by law to go to school but the law gives them no protection on their way.

Theoretically, older children are able to get around like adults once they become free of parental constraints. However, the same surveys show that teenagers prefer to lead lives independent of their parents as their interests often do not overlap.[2] The consequence of this is that, in common with adults who have no car of their own, they rely on walking, public transport or in some cases cycling. The significant difference is that even if both parents have cars, a teenager is not necessarily mobile – he can hardly be taken to the cinema with his girl friend and later collected!

Mothers of young children have another disadvantage which effectively represents a loss of their freedom. About half the mothers of primary schoolchildren feel obliged to accompany their children to school and often to the playground, and to their children's friends and leisure activities, principally because of a fear of road accidents.[5] Able-bodied adults accompanying able-bodied children because of fear is one of the more disturbing and wasteful by-products of the motorized society.

Pensioners are another substantial group of people who are at a disadvantage as a result of current transport planning. Most of them have never been able to own a car and only about one in five holds a driving licence.[6] Moreover, few of them have access to a car because of their low income; only 6% of one-person households and 30% of two-person households where the head of household is 65 or over, own cars.[7] This low level of potential access to a car is reflected in a greater dependency on walking and public transport. Indeed pensioners are the most frequent users of buses, other than people in non-car-owning households who go out to work; yet a recent survey recorded that the pensioners who have some difficulty in walking – comprising one third of those questioned – use buses less often and make more of their trips on foot.[5] The apparent anomaly is explained by the fact that if they have some difficulty in getting about on foot they have even more problems in reaching the bus stop, in waiting for the bus, and often in riding it.

At the same time many people have had to put up with a decline in the quality of their environment due in particular to the increse in traffic noise and air pollution, and this too could be viewed as a diminution of their freedom. In this respect there is a need for a greater awareness of the fact that each journey in a motorized vehicle necessarily makes life marginally worse for people living along the route taken – and therefore the longer the journey the greater is the communal loss of amenity. Similarly the gain in freedom due to the saving in travel time of people able to use newly constructed roads is often achieved by the denial of the more basic freedoms of other people – the right to enjoy peace and quiet in their homes or to be able to continue to live in them.

This issue is a highly emotive subject as it has been the tradition in Britain to minimize trespass on personal freedoms. Where it can be seen, however, that the exercise of this freedom deprives others of theirs – and particularly where the freedom is more basic – then there must first be appeal to public consideration and conscience. If this fails, however, it is surely the function of government to intercede.

Abolition of causes of unnecessary suffering

The third social goal for transport planning relates to the most basic freedom: the preservation of physical health, of mental welfare and more essentially of human life. Past and current policies have failed lamentably, evaluated according to this measure. Indeed, the appalling toll of casualties on the roads of Britain – close on one million people killed or seriously injured in the past ten years – is a single sufficient proof of the unacceptability of proceeding with these policies. Account should be taken not only of the large number of people whose lives are physically affected but also of the much larger number of people bereft or distressed following these 'accidents'. The policy makers who tacitly concede such a level of suffering bear a heavy responsibility, for road accidents are both predictable and preventable.

Analyses of the small variations in type and numbers from year to year reveal this predictability. For instance, cars are consistently involved in over two thirds of urban road accidents, and pedestrians (about half of them children) account for 40% of the total.[9] Given the continuation of present policies therefore, a further one million people are likely to be killed or seriously injured on the roads in the next ten years.

It is apparent, however, that the great majority of road accidents are preventable, for both the lower speed limits and the lower traffic mileage recorded in 1974 when compared with 1973 resulted in a reduction in the number and severity of accidents – a cause and effect relationship confirmed in studies of traffic speed and accident severity. It is perhaps ironic that the temporary lower limits were introduced to discourage unnecessary consumption of energy but not of lives!

If one goal of transport policy were to be the minimizing of risk to life, then it is clear that a considerable step could be taken by introducing a far lower speed limit, of perhaps 20 mile/h in urban areas – and enforcing it.

Responsibility to posterity

The fourth social goal is concerned with morality in a different context, for policies need to be framed out of respect for the lives of future as well as present generations. Consideration of future needs is pertinent to present transport policies since the reserves of oil lying dormant for aeons of time will almost certainly be exhausted within the lifetime of our children, at present levels of consumption.[10]

The argument that technology will come to the rescue through the development of new forms of energy is suspect on two counts. First, a well argued case has been made to show that a switch by industry from oil use is not technically feasible, given the high costs and energy consumption required for a nuclear power programme and the limited time within which the transfer would have to be made.[11] Should this case prove correct the consequences for societies heavily dependent on energy-intensive life styles are serious indeed. Second, this most favoured energy source for the future has a built-in risk element in terms of the disposal of radioactive waste; this risk, for a minimum period of 25 000 years,[12] is one to which this generation has no right to expose future generations. The question has been asked *à propos* the value of public participation, 'How do you secure the participation of people who are either babes in arms or have not yet been born, for these are the people who will be the main recipients of most large-scale works?'[13] In the context of costs and risks, this question is even more pertinent at this juncture, for not only do current policies impose irresponsibly on future generations, they also discount the need of these generations for finite resources.

It is clear that the best use to which finite fossil fuels can be put is to provide for the essential needs of transport and agriculture in the world for a maximum number of years in order to provide the lead time to enable scientists to develop safe sources of energy which do not limit the options of future generations. Planning for a way of life which is increasingly dependent on motorized travel is no way to attain this objective.

Minimization of waste

A fifth social goal for transport planning policy, which is in many respects related to the previous goal, is to ensure that proper priorities are established for private and public expenditure and that waste is minimized. There is much evidence to suggest that present policies fail on this count also.

In terms of the prudent use of material resources, doubts must exist about policies aimed at keeping pace with the output of the motor industry. It appears wrong to encourage dependency on petroleum based travel at a time when there are 500 million starving or undernourished people in the world and petroleum products are so basic to the needs of agriculture.[14]

However, it is in the area of motorized transport and road building that current policy needs to be examined, for expenditure has risen sharply and relentlessly since the Second World War, both in real terms and as a proportion of national expenditure, as ever greater priority has been given to transport. In the past twelve years alone, consumers' expenditure (at constant prices) on the purchase and running costs of motor vehicles has almost trebled.[15]

Yet the meeting of this demand as more vehicles flow from factories onto the roads imposes an obligation on central and local government to accommodate the additional traffic. This entails heavy public expenditure; in the nine years up to 1973 a 5% increase in mileage has been achieved at an expenditure of over £3000 million on new road construction and major improvement.[16] It is apparent too that government policy on investment in the motor industry exacerbates this problem, for it will inevitably lead to renewed pressures on the Department of Environment (DoE) to expand the road building programme.

It is often argued, however, that unless a substantial road building programme is maintained to match the growth in traffic, congestion will increase, environmental quality will drop, roads will be less safe and industry will not be encouraged to invest in areas with poor road access. Moreover, it is stated that additional costs will be incurred in loss of travel time and higher vehicle running costs which will in turn be reflected in increased costs of goods in the shops. No doubt there is some truth in these arguments – new roads have generally increased the mobility of their users, there has been a reduction in local road conges-tion and in time savings on trips previously made, and goods in the shops are no doubt slightly cheaper.

One of the main consequences of this expenditure on roads and the accompanying private expenditure on transport, however, has been an escalation in the average mileage travelled by each person on the roads of Britain; for instance, in 1962 the annual motorized mileage was 3300 (62% by car); by 1972 it had climbed to 5200 (79% by car).[17] People have been encouraged to live far from their place of work, and industry has moved steadily to more dispersed locations away from railheads, ports and waterways, responding to the freedom and new opportunities that road transport has opened up for it.

Improvement of social and physical environment

The sixth social goal is concerned with environmental quality. In this connexion few will deny that the factor most responsible for its deterioration is the growth of traffic. The extent of noise and fumes from traffic has been revealed in numerous surveys, and is regarded as an intrusive nuisance by a rising proportion of the population.[18]

These aspects of transport were firmly identified in *Traffic in towns* where they were classified as 'environmental',[19] but the social conse-quences have received little attention. High volumes of traffic do not just lower the quality of the environment of people living or working nearby. In many urban situations traffic may intrude to the extent that it can alter behaviour and attitudes. Reference has been made earlier to children's loss of freedom. Traffic can also effectively dictate the allocation of rooms in a dwelling, with those overlooking noisy routes not being used as bedrooms even if it were intended that they should be; traffic can oblige people to keep their windows closed, and to double glaze them if they can afford it. Moreover, noise affects people's efficiency at work in factories and offices, and can prevent deep sleep.[20]

It may be that the deleterious effect of traffic on the quality of urban life is in some measure responsible for encouraging migration to more spacious suburbs and rural areas. This residential mobility, however, has undesirable features: the congenial surroundings in these places can only be enjoyed by incurring additional traffic costs for those left behind.

More generally, the substantial rise in traffic and its ubiquity have had other adverse consequences. Wide roads and streams of motor vehicles destroy the function of the street as a locus for social interaction and break community ties. The significance of this has been recently brought to light in research establishing the inverse relationship between traffic levels and social activity.[21] The increasing separation of home, work-place and recreation, encouraged by the planning process, threatens basic human needs of identity: people are far less likely to be concerned about their local environment if they spend most of their time outside it.

Nowadays walking as a social activity is less satisfying because it is difficult to converse against a background of traffic noise – which is not experienced in a closed car travelling at moderate speed – and heavy traffic makes it impossible for two people to cycle abreast in safety. The residential street used to be the traditional play space and social milieu for children and provided an introduction for them to a world beyond their family, without their needing to be accompanied to reach it. Now children are confined to the home or have to be taken to a playground which rarely provides the same freedom and unpredictability which are essential parts of the process of informal learning.

From the design viewpoint, urban motorways and road widening schemes can rarely be claimed as improvements to the appearance of a town. Generally the flow of traffic along them interrupts the urban form of linked views, while the size of new roads and of road signs and lighting standards on them is visually intrusive and out of scale with human beings.

It is clear that transport policies reflect the attachment of low values to these rather intangible elements of the quality of life. As a result, the social and physical environment could decline markedly were traffic to double by the end of the century, as the official forecasts predict.

Pursuit of social goals in transport policy

In my judgement, the only practical approach to the pursuit of the social goals which are the subject of this Paper is to call a halt to rising mobility by the adoption of phased policies aimed at reducing the need and incentive for motorized travel.

The benefits derived from the pursuit of social goals are clear: the attainment of a society with freedom to get around and freedom from traffic nuisance more fairly shared – and with more people alive and well to share it – a more moral life style, less wasteful of resources and more considerate of people as yet unborn, and a better social and physical environment. The further virtue of an approach which starts by defining social goals is that its pursuit would be far less dependent on economic growth. It should therefore appeal to policy makers inhibited by financial constraints. The goals may well be further advanced by slower rather than faster growth if the consequences of their adoption would bring about a society based less on the consumer.

Notes

1. Hillman, M. *Inquiry on urban transport planning*. Memorandum to House of Commons Expenditure Sub-Committee, HMSO, London, 1972, paras 8–16.
2. Hillman, M. with Henderson, I. and Whalley, A. 'Personal mobility and transport policy'. *Political and Economic Planning*, London, 1973, Broadsheet 542.
3. Hillman, M. and Henderson, I. 'Better environmental areas', *New Society*, 1973, **25**, 12 July, 75–77.
4. Hillman, M. and Whalley, A. 'Is the car cheating your child?' *J. Advis. Centre Education (Where)*, 1975, Apr., 94–97.
5. Hillman, M. with Henderson, I. and Whalley, A. *Mobility and accessibility in the outer metropolitan area*. Unpublished report to the Department of the Environment, 1974.
6. National Travel Survey, 1972–73. Unpublished data.
7. Office of Population Censuses and Surveys. *Census 1971 England and Wales*. HMSO, London, 1974, Table 2, Availability of cars.
8. Department of the Environment. *Road accidents in Great Britain 1973*. HMSO, London, 1974.
9. Metropolitan Police District. Unpublished data on road accidents 1966–73.
10. Maddox, J. 'Why North Sea Oil will only give us a breathing space in the drive for more energy', *The Times*, 2 July, 1975.
11. Price, J. *Dynamic energy analysis and nuclear power*. Earth Resources Research, 1974.
12. Lovins, A. *Nuclear Power: technical bases for ethical concern*. Earth Resources Research, 1974.
13. Buchanan, Sir C. 'The viewpoint of a planner', *J. Instn. Highw. Engrs*, 1975, **22**, Feb., 45.
14. Boerma, A. World Food Council, Rome, 25 June, 1975.
15. Department of the Environment. *Highway Statistics 1973*. HMSO, London, 1974, Table 48.
16. British Road Federation. *Basic Road Statistics 1973*. British Road Federation, 1974.
17. Department of the Environment. *Passenger Transport in Great Britain–1973*. HMSO, London, 1974.
18. Fielden, A. 'Alfred Bossom Lecture', *J. Roy. Soc. Arts*, 1975, Mar.
19. Working Group Appointed by Minister of Transport. *Traffic in Towns*. HMSO, London, 1963.
20. Burns, W. *Noise and Man: a summary of medically researched facts*. John Murray, London, 1968, 113–134.
21. Appleyard, D. and Lintell, M. 'Streets, people and traffic', *New Society*, 1975, **33**, 3 July, 9–11.

Social goals for transport policy: a retrospective commentary

My 1975 paper sought to put broader societal concerns onto the political agenda by setting out six objectives which had not yet featured as prominently as they clearly should do in policy formation. It is salutary to look back over the last two decades in order to evaluate what progress has been made in furthering these objectives. Perhaps, surprisingly in this 'soft' social scientific field generally judged not to be amenable to quantitative assessment, it is possible to do so from published statistical sources and thereby to compare the figures for 1990 with those for 1970.[1]

When attention is paid to four of the objectives – improving the quality of the environment, conserving fossil fuels in view of their finite nature, economising on spending for transport purposes, and reducing the gap between the ease of access and mobility of people with and without cars – the figures reveal an alarming outcome. We are far worse off: by 1990, the volume of most air pollutants from traffic had risen substantially, much in line with a three-quarters increase in petroleum consumption; personal expenditure on transport had almost doubled in real terms; and the quality of the environment for walking (and cycling) upon which people without cars are particularly reliant had deteriorated sharply, largely owing to the doubling of vehicle mileage.

Only in one respect could an improvement be observed, for the number of road deaths and the fatality rate per motorised mile travelled had fallen appreciably. However, closer examination of this apparent success in reducing danger on the roads indicates that, even in this respect, there has been failure: the number of road casualties has declined not, as government claims, because our roads have become 'much safer' but because they have been allowed to become much more dangerous. The findings of Policy Studies Institute (formerly Political and Economic Planning) surveys in 1990, which replicated ones conducted in 1971 among schoolchildren around the country, revealed a dramatic increase in parental restrictions on children's independent travel. The primary reason given by the parents for this was the fear that their child would be involved in a road accident.[2]

If is clear that if the objectives set out in the 1975 Paper are to feature prominently in transport policy many branches of government which make decisions affecting transport behaviour need to be involved. For instance, patterns of travel are directly influenced by the size and local of schools, shops and hospitals, the extent of concessions in the form of company-assisted motoring, the degree of traffic law enforcement, and no doubt in the near future, the scale of the inevitable carbon tax required as part of a package on combating global warming.[3]

It is becoming ever more obvious that the conclusions of that paper were correct in advocating that the objectives can only realistically be met by reversing the process whereby our lifestyles are increasingly oriented around the motor vehicle. Priority must be given to walking and cycling, with land use, planning control, and other policies affecting transport decisions, deployed to reduce the need for and attractions of motorised travel. There is *still* no other way.

Notes

1. Department of Transport (1991) *Transport Statistics Great Britain 1991*, London, HMSO.
2. Hillman, M., Adams, J. and Whitelegg, J. (1991) *One False Move . . . a study of children's independent mobility*, London, Policy Studies Institute.
3. Hillman, M. (1992) 'Reconciling transport and environmental policy objectives', *Public Administration*, Summer.

26

The Public Health Implications of Private Cars*

SONJA M. HUNT

The current vogue for targeting individual behaviour as a major factor in the aetiology of disease and disability can be seen as an interesting example of the creation of social problems and the manipulation of public awareness. Primarily four types of behaviour receive a disproportionate amount of attention. These are smoking, dietary habits, exercise and alcohol consumption. Why these four should have been 'chosen' in preference to other, perhaps more pertinent, human activities is, of course, related to the fact that powerful groups, whether medical, educational or commercial have the capacity to influence the flow of information and debate on matters affecting the public health. Directing attention to some issues rather than others can be seen as part of the social construction of 'problems' whereby certain groups have the power to act collectively to define a problem and then initiate attempts to relieve, change or eliminate the problem (Kitsuse and Spector, 1975).

The implications of private car ownership for the public health have thus largely escaped serious attention, principally because there have been few people with any interest in raising it as an issue. This may be related to the fact that those people with the power to do so are themselves likely to have a 'lifestyle' in which the motor car plays a prominent role. There are political and economic reasons too. The road lobby is very powerful and enormous amounts of revenue are raised from taxes on petrol. The attention given to car driving as a major hazard to the public health can be judged by the fact that the World

---

*This is an abridged version of a chapter that was first published in Martin, C. and McQueen, D. (1989) *Readings for a New Public Health*, Edinburgh University Press, pp. 100–115.

Health Organisation document on Health Promotion devotes 12 lines to it (WHO, 1982). These concentrate solely on alcohol, drugs and seat-belt use. This comparative lack of interest not only creates the impression that hazards associated with motor cars are trivial relative to, say, lack of exercise, but simultaneously conveys the idea that it is a few irresponsible 'maniacs' who tank up themselves as well as their vehicles, drive carelessly and refuse to wear seat belts who are to blame for any hazards associated with cars. Thus attention is diverted from the enormous impact of car use on disease, death, disability, quality of life, the integrity of the environment, social intercourse, social inequalities and from the huge financial cost to the public purse.,

Every private car should carry a government health warning.

Car driving kills or maims over 40,000 people every year in Britain

The dictionary definition of accidental is 'occurring by chance; unexpected or unintentional; non-essential; incidental; without apparent cause'. In all these senses, except perhaps unintentional, the major proportion of incidents on the road are not accidents at all, but the foreseeable outcome of a combination of speed, carelessness, insensitivity, poor judgement, aggressive behaviour and egocentricity, sometimes aggravated by alcohol.

In total there are about one and a half million *reported* 'accidents' on the roads every year in Britain, and last year there were about 12 million world-wide. The number of deaths resulting from these 'accidents', at around 6,000, is undoubtedly an underestimate, since deaths from, say, heart attack, which may have been triggered by the event are not included in the statistics. Moreover, injuries and conditions which are a consequence of road accidents and which result in death more than 30 days later are also not recorded as due to a road accident. Although the vast majority of 'accidents' involve private cars, half the people who die as a consequence are either pedestrians or cyclists (Hamer, 1985).

Most accidents to children occur in deprived urban areas where there is little play space. Boys in Social Class V are seven times more likely to be in an accident than those in Social Class I. Interestingly enough, the responsibility for this has usually been placed upon the child or upon his mother. The former for lack of road sense, impulsive behaviour or carelessness and the latter for lack of control or stress (Brown and Harris, 1978). Thus ameliorative measures have focused upon safety education for the children, or counselling and parental education for the mothers; a wonderful example of those who 'own' a problem trying to place responsibility for it onto less powerful groups, getting them to acknowledge the problem as belonging to them and urging them to change *their* behaviour accordingly (Gusfield, 1975).

Recent studies have shown that, in fact, children spend relatively small amounts of time in impulsive activities such as ball games; rather, for most of the time, they simply stand around or walk about (Chapman *et al.*, 1980). The association between stress in mothers and road accidents involving their children is probably an artefact of living in disadvantaged circumstances. Children from the lower social classes are less likely to have gardens or other play space and, therefore, spend more time in the streets. The real vulnerability of the children stems from their frequent daily exposure to risky situations, not their behaviour (Chapman *et al.*, 1980). Cars and other vehicles are allowed to pass through crowded urban streets which may even be widened and have obstacles removed to ensure traffic flow, leading to increased speed. Nicholas Ridley said in 1986, 'The motorist should not be hampered by petty rules and unnecessary restrictions of his liberty'. Is it an 'unnecessary restriction of liberty' to require that motorists drive slowly in urban areas if this will save the lives of several hundred children every year?

Studies of driving in urban areas have shown that no allowances are made by drivers for the presence of a child at the kerb (Chapman *et al.*, 1980). Most motorists maintain or increase speed, rarely do they slow down or move over to the crown of the road in anticipation. The 'jumping' of designated pedestrian crossing areas is not uncommon. Many drivers seem to assume that a car has the right to unimpeded progress.

It has been suggested, ironically enough, that measures pertaining to driver safety, for example seat-belts, padded fascia, better braking, improved acceleration, have resulted in increased accidents to other road users. Protecting car drivers from the consequences of their own follies can encourage careless driving and certainly faster driving (Adams, 1984).

Death is, of course, not necessarily the worst that can happen; injuries are more frequent and infinitely more distressing to the recipient. Front-seat passengers, who are more likely to be women than men, are injured more often and more severely than drivers. The consequences of this 'passive driving' are likely to be lacerations to the face. About 8 per cent of people involved in road accidents end up with permanent disabilities, including brain damage. World-wide, this means about one and a half million individuals, who, since they are mainly young, constitute a long-term drain on the energy, emotions and resources of their loved ones as well as on health and social services.

In spite of the very real dangers, however, few road users with the possible exception of cyclists, regard themselves, in the terms of Wordsworth, as 'travellers betwixt life and death'. The personal and financial cost has little impact on professionals or the lay public and most people are more afraid of flying even though it is much safer than car travel.

Public health economists have paid little attention to cost factors associated with motor vehicle accidents. In Scotland the estimated cost of *one* fatal accident is over £160,000 and last year the cost of all road accidents was in excess of £200 million. In Great Britain the total cost was £2,370 million (Plowden and Hillman, 1984).

Measures taken to reduce the burden of road accidents have generally focused on the convenience of the motorist and are designed to cause maximum inconvenience to others. Feeble old ladies and women with prams must struggle up steps and over bridges or scurry through stinking underpasses. Children unlucky enough to have no garden must confine themselves to the indoors or play at their peril. All such measures ignore the evidence that the main aetiological factor in deaths and injuries from road accidents is car driving itself.

Driving can damage your health and your environment

In towns and cities the foul and pestilent congregation of vapours which make up what is known as 'air' contains a large measure of car exhaust emissions. The most abundant of these is carbon monoxide, which is released in highly localised concentrations, especially in urban areas. High levels of this gas can hang in the air for extended periods of time. Levels as high as 100 parts per million (ppm) have been recorded at rush hours, reaching 350 ppm at peak times (Walker, 1978). These levels are sufficient to cause headache, lassitude and dizziness in normal people, since carbon monoxide interferes with the ability of the blood to carry oxygen due to its combination with haemoglobin. For susceptible people, for example, those who suffer from anaemia, have low haemoglobin levels, smokers and cardiovascular patients, the effects may be serious.

Internal combusion also results in elevated levels of hydrocarbons. Photochemical oxidation creates derivatives from hydrocarbons which become secondary pollutants producing photochemical smog composed of ozone and other toxins. These cause eye irritation and plant damage, but the main problem is that they augment the effects of sulphur dioxide and nitrogen oxides (Duffus, 1980). Sulphate concentrations as low as two parts per billion have been found to adversely affect people with chronic respiratory problems, including asthmatics. This concentration is often exceeded in urban areas (Walker, 1975).

Nitrogen oxides occur as nitric oxide and nitrogen dioxide. While nitric oxide mainly affects plants by interfering with photosynthesis, nitrogen dioxide penetrates mucus membranes and can affect breathing especially in susceptible people.

Recent attempts to eliminate lead from petrol in Britain have been delayed by the government, under pressure, no doubt, from powerful lobbies. Currently, there is about 400 mg of inorganic tetraethyl lead in every litre of petrol which, upon combustion, sticks to dust. Lead dust is washed by rain into drains or sewers contaminating water supplies and agricultural land, resulting in irreversible and cumulative poisoning of the earth. Children are most at risk because they absorb up to 50 per cent of the lead in the food they consume whereas adults take in only 5–10 per cent. A recent study in Edinburgh by Fulton *et al.* (1987) found that blood lead levels were significantly associated with children's scores on reading, attainment and ability tests, when 33 possible confounding variables had been taken into account.

The lead content in British food is so high as to contravene international regulations largely as a consequence of vehicle emissions. It has been estimated that, for those vegetables with a high surface area, such as lettuce and broccoli there are few places where the crops are fit for consumption by infant humans (Russell Jones, 1981).

Diesel fuel may be even more harmful, in so far as thousands of chemicals, many of which are carcinogenic are breathed in from diesel fumes, exposure to which over a prolonged period results in a 42 per cent greater chance of developing lung cancer. It is predicted that diesel car ownership will grow in Europe from 5.8 million in 1986 to 15.5 million by 1995.

Continual exposure to traffic noise has been found to increase heart rate, blood pressure and adrenalin output, which if added to other strains may culminate in chronic hypertension and damage to heart function (Andren, 1982; Ising *et al.*, 1980). In addition, uncontrollable and unpredictable noise has a clear stressing effect, especially when it is intermittent. Decreases in work performance are associated with traffic noise and there is some evidence that it accentuates failing hearing with age (Rossi, 1976).

There are other indirect health effects of car use. At a time when the populace are being urged to take more exercise, the cheapest and possibly best forms of activity, walking and cycling are discourged by motor traffic. Surveys have indicated that many more people would walk to work, to the shops and for leisure, if the roads were less noisy, dirty and dangerous (Morton-Williams *et al.*, 1978). In addition, the perception of danger effectively distorts the travel of others by deterring their own excursions. The elderly and disabled may prefer not to go out at all rather than cope with the roads. Likewise an old person or a child may require someone to accompany them to ensure their safety.

A study by Waldman (1977) found that the main deterrents to cycling were hills, danger from traffic and rain. The expected level of cycling in a flat but dangerous town was 6 per cent of all traffic, while in a safe town it was 43 per cent of traffic. This has been confirmed by studies in Holland (Dutch National Travel Survey, 1978). When facilities are provided huge increases of 40 per cent and more occur in the use of bicycles for journeys to school, work and the shops (Kolks, 1981). In Sweden and Japan where car use has been discouraged in favour of other means of transport, especially cycling, there has been a 25 per cent decrease in accidents to cyclists and a 31 per cent decrease in accidents to pedestrians, in addition to substantial reductions in noise and pollution. Cycle use, as well as being a source of exercise and enjoyment, requires only 7 per cent of the total energy required by a car, including fuel, repairs, maintenance and production. The increase in car ownership over the last few decades appears to have influenced exercise levels. Since there has been very little change in per capita energy consumption over this time it is tempting to speculate that car ownership has played a part in the increase in the number of people who are overweight. We have now reached a ludicrous situation where physical exercise requires special provision, jogging suits, time set aside and designated sports areas instead of being built into the flow of daily activity. People may drive 3 miles to work and then have to use the time they 'saved' taking exercise.

A car appears to engender a feeling of privacy, even though it is in the public domain, and a feeling of urgency, even though none exists. The speed limit is now routinely broken and the Highway Code is often disregarded.

Certain aspects of irresponsibility in motorists are officially encouraged. A driver who has been drinking and subsequently kills someone can be and often is accused of careless driving, fined a paltry sum or receives an endorsement on their licence, in spite of the fact that the decision to take alcohol and then take charge of a lethal weapon, must be regarded as criminal in moral, if not legal, terms.

Private cars or public transport?

Public transport, especially in Britain, has, in the past few years, been dramatically reduced, whilst road-building to cope with car traffic has proceeded at unprecedented rates.

As well as being convenient, bus travel is safer than any other form of transport. In addition, buses are more energy efficient and take up an infinitesimal amount of space per passenger mile as compared to a car.

Rail travel is also relatively safe and allows travelling time to be used for other pursuits.

Unfortunately, a vicious cycle has arisen whereby the decline in the availability of public transport has led to an increase in the use of the private car, thus justifying the decline in public transport at severe inconvenience to poorer rural and urban dwellers, the elderly, women and children, whose freedom of mobility is increasingly curtailed. Recent reports have highlighted the extent to which women in particular are discriminated against in transport policy. In the last ten years spending on road construction and maintenance has risen by 30 per cent. However, only one-third of women possess a driving licence and far fewer have access to a car on a daily basis. Schemes that are designed to speed up and facilitate traffic flow hinder the mobility of women by reducing or slowing down public transport or forcing them, literally, underground. The location of supermarkets, hospitals, schools and clinics, where women form a majority of visitors may require a long and involved trip by bus, as opposed to a short and simple journey by car (London Strategic Policy Unit, 1988; Transport 2000, 1988). Incidentally, one little remarked upon effect of the building of peripheral super-markets is an increase in the prices in local shops whose share of the available trade is inevitably diminished.

Conclusions

The dominance of the car in the landscape, the spoilation of towns, villages and countryside continues to go almost unquestioned, except by a few cranks. Far from being regarded as anti-social, the private car has been elevated to a status symbol, a cause for pride, a target of devotion. Even people who are aware of the problems associated with car owner-ship will plead that a car is a necessity rather as others might argue that they need a cigarette or a drink to help them cope with the exigencies of daily life.

The encouragement of car ownership is just as much a product of powerful lobbies as is smoking or alcohol use. Industrial societies subsidise motorists to a large extent (Bouladon, 1975). The car and oil industry, motoring organisations and road contractors exert their influence in the interests of private profit at enormous cost to the public purse. The drain on the public sector is not due solely to the cost of accidents and disability, hours lost at work or health services provided, but includes noise, vibration, congestion, damage to buildings, loss of time, waste of space, high energy consumption, pollution and incon-venience to others, especially those already at a disadvantage by virtue of age, sex or infirmity. In addition to the cost of 'accidents', congestion alone is estimated to cost the country £3,000 million in lost time and wasted fuel (GMCP, 1987).

The risks to life, limb and environment associated with cars are either ignored or treated as an acceptable price to pay (acceptable to motorists that is). Yet the number of people who will be killed on the roads between now and 1990 will far exceed the projected number of AIDS victims, and the number of people disabled for life will be many times greater; yet the resources and time devoted to this serious public health problem are far, far fewer. We have reached the ludicrous situation in Britain where the success of transport policy is measured by the number of vehicles that can travel at high speed to the detriment of everything else, a criterion comparable to measuring the success of health policy by the number of people who pass through hospitals.

Smoking, alcohol and drug use, dietary habits and lack of exercise are constantly targeted as 'unhealthy' and responsible for major diseases and disabilities, in spite of only meagre supporting evidence. Car use, on the other hand, is indisputably 'unhealthy' in a variety of ways, but as a 'risk factor' it is rarely cited. The perception and selection of risks is not independent of selectors. Cars are an unpopular target for the new public health reformers because they themselves are often car owners. The middle classes are less likely to smoke, but regard a car, even two, as essential.

If there is a recognition of risk, it is assumed that a combination of road and car design coupled with driver education will minimise the danger. However, the first merely transfers the problem to put other members of the public at risk and the second is as naïve a concept as health education in relation to, say, exercise, since it ignores the social context within which car driving is seen as a desirable behaviour and the complex pressure from interested parties.

The traditional way of dealing with car accidents has been to try to contain the number and severity in relation to a given volume of traffic (Plowden and Hillman, 1984). It would, however, make more sense to encourage alternative means of travel and, by creating more public awareness of the totality of hazards associated with private cars, encourage a demand for a more comprehensive and responsive public transport system.

References

Adams, J. (1984) *Sneed's Law, Seat Belts and the Empower's New Clothes*, London, Department of Geography, University College.

Bouladon, G. (1975) 'Costs and benefits of motor vehicles', in *Urban Transport and the Environment*, OECD, 277–319.

Brown, G. and Harris, T. (1978) *Social Origins of Depression, a Study of Psychiatric Disorder in Women*, London, Tavistock.

Chapman, A. J., Foot, H. and Wade, F. (1980) 'Children at play', in D.J. Osborne and J.A. Levis (eds) *Human Factors in Transport Research*, Vol. 2, London, Academic Press.

Duffus, J.H. (1980) *Environmental Toxicology*, London, Edward Arnold.

Dutch National Travel Survey (1978), the Hague.

Fulton, M., Raab, G., Thomson, G., Laxen, D., Hunter, R. and Hepburn, W. (1987) 'Influence of blood lead on the ability and attainment of children in Edinburgh', *The Lancet*, No. 8544, 1221–6.

Greater Manchester Cycling Project (1987) Stop the Child Slaughter, G.M.C.P., Occasional paper No. 2, August, Manchester.

Gusfield, J. (1975) 'Categories of ownership and responsibility in social issues: alcohol-abuse and automobile use', *Journal of Drug Issues*, **5**(4), 285–303.

Hamer, M. (1985) 'How speed kills on Britain's roads', *New Scientist*, 21st February, 10–11.

Ising, H., Dienel, D., Gunther, T. and Markert, B. (1980) 'Health effects of traffic noise', *Int. Arch. Occup. Env. Hlth*, **47**, 179–90.

Kolks, A. (1981) 'Bocholt – a town for cyclists', in *Proceedings of the 1st International Bicycle Congress VELO/CITY*, Bremen, West Germany Federal Ministry of Transport, April.

Kitsuse, J. and Spector, M. (1975) 'Social problems and deviance: some parallel issues', *Social Problems*, **36**, 584–94.

London Strategic Policy Unit (1988) *Women's Safe Transport in London*, London, LSPU.

Morton-Williams, T., Hedges, B. and Fernando, E. (1978) *Road Traffic and the Environment*, London, Social and Community Planning Research.

Plowden, S. and Hillman, M. (1984) *Danger on the Road: The Needless Scourge*, London, Policy Studies Institute.

Rossi, G. (1976) 'Urban traffic noise: auditory and extra auditory effects', *Acta Oto-Laryncology*, Suppl., 339.

Russell Jones, R. (1981) 'Lead poisoning: why the government must act now', *World Medicine*, February, 73.

Transport 2000 (1988) London.

Waldman, J. (1977) *Cycling in Towns: a quantitative investigation*, LTRI Working Paper No. 3, London: Department of Transport.

Walker, H. (1981) 'Is lead the key to perinatal mortality?' *World Medicine*, **16**(22), August 25, p. 20.

World Health Organisation (1982) *Lifestyles Conducive to Health. Regional Strategy for attaining HFA by year 2000*, Copenhagen, WHO, Regional Office for Europe.

27

Sex, Drink and Fast Cars*

STEPHEN BAYLEY

I had breakfast with a friend the morning after he had celebrated his fortieth birthday. He had that sense of regret coupled with the fairly profound wisdom of those who have celebrated over-well. He said to me, morosely pushing a morsel of poached haddock around his plate:

You know, Stephen, as I get older I've had to reconsider the priorities in life.

I struck the pose of a credulous martyr, but inside I was resigned to a homily about the virtues of pastoral poetry, family life, experimental communion with the Godhead and 'philosophy'. Instead my friend said to me:

And I'm more than ever certain that they are sex, drink and fast cars.

The fantasies and aspirations and appetites of most of the world are summarized in that one bathetic sentence . . .

My breakfasting friend was a North American. They are people with a peculiarly strong attachment to cars. I asked a Canadian why his continent bred a specially intense kind of car freak and he explained that, with no depth of culture and with no public transport and with an economic system which encouraged *consumption*, cars were a form of display. Every part of American life allows for more mobility than its European equivalent and it is a sort of mobility which is both real and metaphorical: money moves more freely in America. You can buy, rent, lease, hire or acquire things on credit. It is not unusual to drive 120 miles

---

*This is an abridged extract from Bayley, S. (1988) *Sex, Drink and Fast Cars*, Faber and Faber, pp. 1–8.

to see friends for dinner, at least in California. In a continent of shifting values, the coast-to-coast franchised trademarks provided fixed points, heraldry which consumers can readily identify. The cars provided the costumes.

It is a poetic truism that the pioneer American automobile manufacturers were farmboys who knew at first hand the crushing loneliness and mindless drudgery of life in the rural mid-West. Henry Ford wrote in his autobiography, *My Life and Work* (1922), 'It was life on the farm that drove me into devising ways and means to better transportation.'

In American literature cars frequently appear as symbols of material success, but also as machines capable of producing sensations of power and control. For their drivers, loosely located in a world of uncertain values, the possession of a car is a gratifying experience. Sinclair Lewis describes it in *Dodsworth* (1929):

> To-night he was particularly uplifted because he was driving his first car. And it was none of your old-fashioned 'gasoline buggies' . . . The engine bulked in front, under a proud hood over two feet long, and the steering column was not straight but rakishly tilted. The car was sporting and rather dangerous, and the lights were powerful affairs fed by acetylene gas. Sam sped on, with a feeling of power, of dominating the universe, at twelve dizzy miles an hour.

In his 'Ballad of Faith' William Carlos Williams wrote 'No dignity without chromium/No truth but a glossy finish . . .' Two spare lines that suggest the poignancy of new cars, a bitter-sweet sensation of universal experience. For some people, owning a new car is the nearest they will ever get to perfection in an otherwise flawed and soiled life. The journalist, Eric Larrabee, caught the mood perfectly in an article he wrote in *Industrial Design* magazine in 1955:

> Stand at night, on a corner in a strange town, and watch the cars go by. What is there so poignant in this? A sense of private destinies, of each making his own choice, of being independent of everything but statistics. The car owners choose – or think they do – when to stop and start, where to go. The automobile offers a vista of escape: for the adolescent, from parental planning; for the Negro, from Jim Crow; and for others, from less formal restrictions on their freedom of movement. Thus they are liberated to the loneliness (and perplexity) of their independence, and thus travel on the highway at night acquires its own tones of adventure and sorrow.

This same sense was expressed with less implied tragedy by Chuck Berry:

> Ridin' along in my automobile,
> My baby beside me at the wheel,

> I stole a kiss at the turn of a mile,
> My curiosity running wild–
> Cruisin' and playin' the radio,
> With no particular place to go

European attitudes to the car have been altogether more courtly. Perhaps because the car was never quite so *necessary* in Europe (where, states being smaller and distances being shorter, public transport is more effective), it has been treated neither with such exaggerated respect nor with such shocked repugnance as in North America. Nonetheless, the potential of the car as both a means and a symbol of freedom influenced European artists, as well as American citizens.

In Europe, always some way behind America in terms of prosperity, the car remained an important symbol longer. The Parisian savant, Roland Barthes (who met a poetic death under the wheels of a laundry truck) caught the mood exactly in his heroic (if ironic) comparison of the modern car with the medieval cathedral:

I think that cars today are almost the exact equivalent of the great gothic cathedrals; I mean the supreme creation of an era, conceived with passion by unknown artists, and consumed in image if not in usage by a whole population which appropriates them as a purely magical object . . .

Yet, despite its darker side, first seen and described by Ilya Ehrenburg in *The Life of the Automobile* (1929) and echoed by environmentalists and conspiracy theorists ever since, the allure of cars is indestructible. The freedom and the beauty and the power of a well-wrought machine evidently touches a universally sensitive part of the human soul.

Perhaps the single most significant aspect of man's relationship with his car is the element of power. Henry Kissinger once said, to an unfortunate journalist who had asked him what he saw in his job, 'Power is the greatest aphrodisiac'. A fast car has reserves of power. The very suggestion of power has in itself a strong erotic content. Designers, stylists, the creative people in advertising agencies, marketing men, all find their various ways of expressing that power in the appearance of cars and in the software that surrounds their promotion and their sales. It can be mechanical power or fiscal power. It doesn't matter, but the state of the world proves that people find it arousing and attractive.

Just look at Guernsey. This tiny island, where the speed of motor cars is limited to 35 mph probably has more Porsches per capita than anywhere else in the UK. They can never be driven at a fraction of the dynamic potential which engineers have struggled to build into them. These powerful cars are not transport, they are aphrodisiacs. They are sold as costumes and worn for sexual display.

28

The Changing Boundaries of Health

ALAN BEATTIE

Multiple voices for health

Since the mid-1970s an increasing volume of social research has been devoted to documenting the many different ways in which people explain health in contemporary society. And with gathering momentum health researchers appear to be making a 'paradigm shift' of the sort that has been seen in wider areas of social inquiry (Gerhardt, 1989). Increasingly, the focus is on explanations of health as 'forms of talk', on the narrative structures these reveal, and on how meanings are negotiated within conversational exchanges. Such a focus has many attractions: it can identify some of the commonsense meanings of health that are taken for granted in everyday life, and can show how competing narratives of health are in play in personal decision-making and in the 'micropolitics' of negotiation. It can capture much of the immediacy and vividness of the stories that people tell about health – and the complex and diverse scope of these stories (Stainton Rogers, 1991).

But this paradigm is itself only one way of 'explaining health explanations'; and as is the way with paradigms, there are some questions that it neglects. In particular it has little to offer in explaining what it is that influences people to select particular accounts. To do this we need another approach to social inquiry, one that seeks to identify the links between what people believe and what social worlds they inhabit (Dawe, 1970). While responding to the compelling human interest that flows through the multiple and diverse tales of health portrayed by recent research, we need to attend also to the sources and consequences within society of different health narratives. We need to exercise 'the sociological imagination' in an effort to see the accounts of health that people give as 'minute points of the intersections of biography and history in society' (Mills, 1959). In this article, I want to make the case for attempting to 'map' the cultural landscape within which the interplay between different voices for health is unfolding. I will present three different maps, each of them bringing to light a different feature of the cultural landscape, but all of them intended to illustrate the insights that come from a broadly 'structuralist' standpoint (Mepham, 1973).

Ways of knowing

Questions of health in contemporary Western culture have been inescapably connected to the growth of the life sciences and the human and social sciences. Because of this, it is not surprising that often the conflict and competition between accounts of health reflects disputes that are basically epistemological in origin – they revolve around differences of view about what counts as 'reliable' or 'true' knowledge (Wright and Treacher 1982). Two dimensions stand out in such disputes.

First, there is an opposition between different *modes of thought*. Within the professions and institutions of medicine, 'mechanistic' approaches to analysis are still dominant: they are seen as 'hard', and in keeping with the canons of the natural science tradition. In contrast, 'humanistic' approaches are given a place at the margins, but are seen as 'soft', and associated with the less prestigious traditions of sociological or literary inquiry. When lay views on health are in contention with expert views, a similar distinction commonly prevails, in which professional knowledge is seen as rational (and therefore 'serious'), in contrast to the 'pre-rational' (and therefore 'trivial') status of lay or popular health beliefs.

Secondly, there is dispute about *focus of attention*: whether health inquiry should take as its object individuals (the human organism, the person), or collectivities (the group, the community, the locality).

In Figure 28.1, I have used these two dimensions to chart different 'ways of knowing about health'.

Within this chart I have given titles to each of the four quadrants, in an effort to identify four distinctive 'ways of accounting for health'. Table 28.1 sets out some further characteristics of each of the four.

This analysis highlights some basic dimensions of social thought around which disputes about different kinds of health knowledge unfold: some models being assigned high status, and some low status, in particular social contexts – and the reverse in other contexts. It gives us some useful bearings on one of the major sources of conflict between different accounts of health.

262

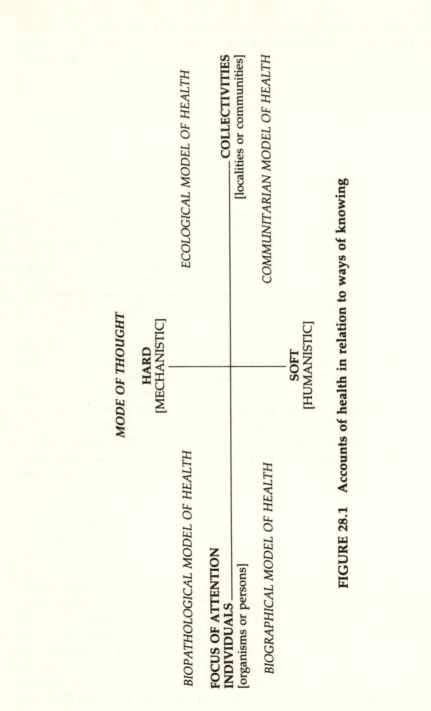

FIGURE 28.1 Accounts of health in relation to ways of knowing

TABLE 28.1 Four ways of accounting for health

	Biopathological model	Ecological model	Biographical model	Communitarian model
Knowledge base (= main source of legitimacy)	Biomedical sciences	Human ecology	Developmental and abnormal psychology	Self-accounts by autonomous social groups
Focus of attention	Human organism as a mechanism	Organism–environment interaction	Persons and their private troubles	Persons in their social relationships
Key appraisive criterion	Abnormalities Defects Sickness states	Fit–misfit in human habitats: risks, hazards	Failures of coping	Belonging or alienation
Typical expertise	Nosography Pathology Chemotherapy Surgery	Epidemiology Hygiene Social Engineering	Biography Case history Personal Counselling	Autobiography Oral history Discussion work
Typical agents	Clinicians Paramedics	Public health Doctors Health inspectors and engineers	Psychotherapists Counsellors Social workers	Advocates Community workers Rights campaigners

Sociopolitical philosophies

Frequently, however, different approaches to health are contested on grounds that are less to do with different 'ways of knowing' than with different political positions. So a further aspect of the cultural landscape that invites exploration is how far particular models of health are found congenial within particular political perspectives (and vice versa). Numerous attempts have been made to chart the diversity of social and political philosophies, and they are all quick to point out that this takes us well away from simple and familiar 'party political' labels. Analyses of social policy persistently identify two fundamental conflicts (e.g. Hardy, 1981; Walker, 1984; Hill and Bramley, 1986). One is the tensions in policy-making between 'paternalist' (or 'top-down') and 'participatory' (or 'bottom-up') approaches. The other is the divide in social planning between an emphasis on 'individualised' problems and solutions (located in the private domain) and a view of problems and solutions as 'collective' (in the public domain).

Figure 28.2 charts these two dimensions of conflict. In each quadrant I have identified a distinct sociopolitical philosophy, and attempted to summarise its characteristic features (drawing freely from the work of

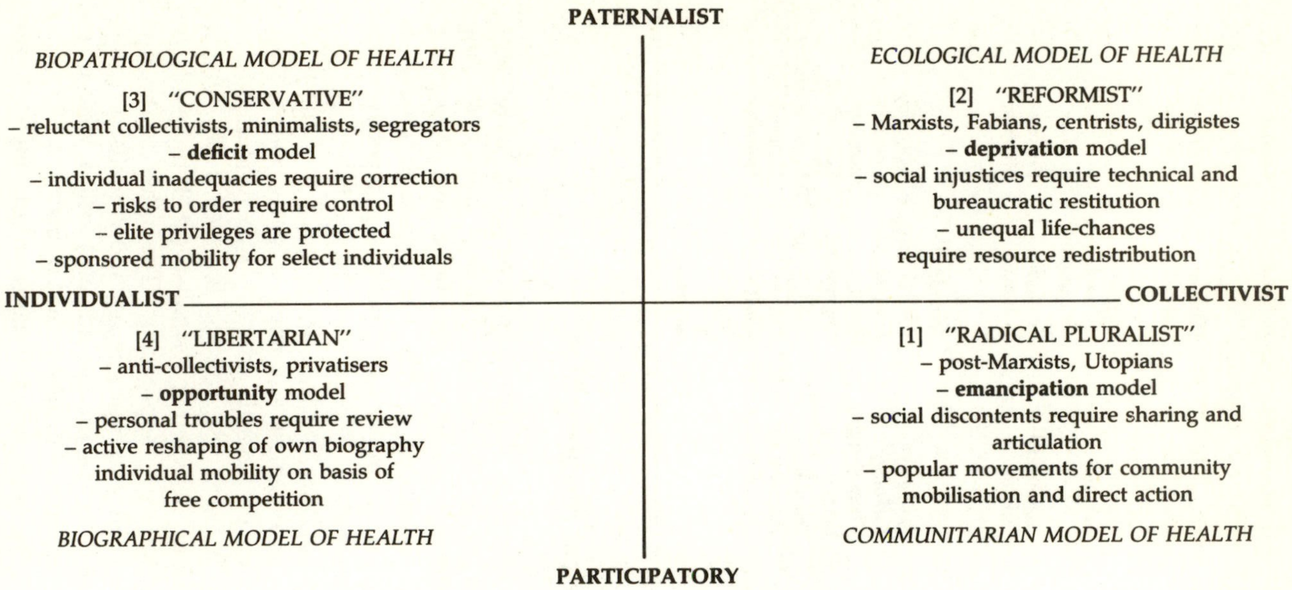

ECOLOGICAL MODEL OF HEALTH

[2] "REFORMIST"
– Marxists, Fabians, centrists, dirigistes
  – **deprivation** model
– social injustices require technical and
  bureaucratic restitution
  – unequal life-chances
  require resource redistribution

COLLECTIVIST

[1] "RADICAL PLURALIST"
– post-Marxists, Utopians
  – **emancipation** model
– social discontents require sharing and
  articulation
– popular movements for community
  mobilisation and direct action

COMMUNITARIAN MODEL OF HEALTH

PATERNALIST

PARTICIPATORY

BIOPATHOLOGICAL MODEL OF HEALTH

[3] "CONSERVATIVE"
– reluctant collectivists, minimalists, segregators
  – **deficit** model
– individual inadequacies require correction
  – risks to order require control
  – elite privileges are protected
  – sponsored mobility for select individuals

INDIVIDUALIST

[4] "LIBERTARIAN"
– anti-collectivists, privatisers
  – **opportunity** model
– personal troubles require review
– active reshaping of own biography
  individual mobility on basis of
  free competition

BIOGRAPHICAL MODEL OF HEALTH

FIGURE 28.2 Health accounts in relation to sociopolitical philosophies

several authors: George and Wilding 1976; Taylor-Gooby and Dale, 1981; Lee and Raban, 1983; Lawton, 1988). Lee and Raban commend a two-dimensional typology along these lines as a means of identifying what they call the 'strategic disputes' about welfare, and as a means of showing the 'loose, fragmented and often contradictory' mix of ideas in British political life. They argue that a framework of this sort 'facilitates an analysis of the internal disputes that are endemic to *all* of the traditions' in British political thought. They point to tensions within British socialism between the two traditions whose philosophies are summed up in quadrants 1 and 2 (along with a tendency to enter quadrant 3); while (they suggest) 'modern British conservatism clearly owes much of its vitality to an 'unholy alliance' between the philosophies of the third and fourth quadrants'.

This scheme can prompt analysis of the different political standpoints that are often undeclared but influential in 'strategic disputes' about health, as I have tried to show in locating within Figure 28.2 the four 'models of health' identified earlier. For example (Beattie, 1991) the ecological model of health is seen in recent calls to revive legislative and environmental action for public health, which have in the main come from 'old left' ('reformist') groupings, frequently located in Local Authority contexts, and demanding more systematic planning by the State, both centrally and locally. Communitarian models of health have arisen in close association with 'single issue' political activism since the late 1960s, and are connected with broadly 'new left' groupings, very heterogeneous in their makeup ('radical pluralist'). One obvious manifestation of the biopathological model of health is in persuasion campaigns directed at changing individual behaviour, which find particular favour with a traditionalist (broadly 'conservative') political ideology. This no doubt sees such campaigns as an acceptable 'minimal' intervention by the State: giving people information 'for their own good', so that if they don't act upon it, that's 'their bad luck'. The biographical model underpins the proliferation of services which offer personal counselling for health, whose political philosophy is more ambiguous – indeed such services are often claimed to be 'a-political'. It is a model that is colonised by those moderates, liberals, democrats, and fractions of the 'new left' who approve of its anti-authoritarian and humanistic style; and is simultaneously annexed and co-operated by the 'new right' – who see in its anti-collectivist stance the promise of privatisation and individual self-help: staking-out the curious common ground of 'libertarian' ideologies.

Cultural bias

The work of the anthropologist Mary Douglas offers another means of exploring the ways in which the categories in which we think may reflect major features of social structure and cultural context. She asks the question: how do the ways in which boundaries are drawn in society determine what 'dangers' people select as significant, and what 'explanations of misfortune' they find convincing? She calls this 'cultural bias' – the way that the structure of social environments shapes people's views of the world (Douglas, 1970; 1978; 1982); and she sets out her analysis in terms of the twin concepts of 'grid' and 'group', summarised in Figure 28.3.

'*Grid*' refers to the total system of rules and constraints which a culture imposes on its people: how far a person's behaviour and view of the world are ordered and prescribed by social distinctions and statements of authority. It is about the degree of formality and hierarchy in a social system. '*High grid*' is seen where roles and statuses are defined very precisely, and where distinct roles are kept separate and fixed: for example, where the boundaries between different kinds of knowledge (high status and low status) are kept clear and are patrolled and defended vigorously. '*Low grid*' is a state of affairs in which everything is negotiable, nothing is fixed in advance or permanently: status and value are judged on merit, and can be conferred (or taken away) on a fast-changing basis.

'*Group*' refers to the extent to which an individual is pressured or coerced through being a member of a bounded face-to-face unit; it is a measure of the strength (or weakness) of people's association with one another in a particular context, or of the boundary that people have erected between themselves and the outside world. It is about the degree of social cohesiveness in a social setup. '*High group*' means that people have a strong sense of belonging to a well-defined social group with whom they have much in common. They have a commitment to seeing the interests and survival of their group as more important than individual interests and survival. The individual tends to interact with the same people in different phases of their work and leisure, their public and private life. '*Low group*' is the situation in which groups exert little moral coercion over individuals, and the distinctiveness of individuals is paramount. Self-interest and competition are dominant, and individuals move through separate spheres of interaction in different phases of their private and public lives.

These features define what Douglas calls the 'boundaries of the moral economy': what it is that people value most, what it is that shapes their motives and desires, beliefs, tastes, and behaviours. Features of the four

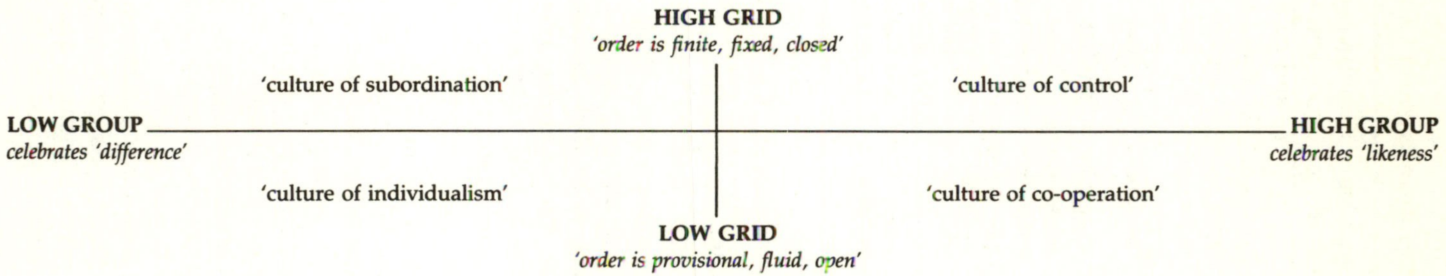

HIGH GROUP
celebrates 'likeness'

'culture of control'

'culture of co-operation'

HIGH GRID
'order is finite, fixed, closed'

LOW GRID
'order is provisional, fluid, open'

'culture of subordination'

'culture of individualism'

LOW GROUP
celebrates 'difference'

FIGURE 28.3   Four main types of cultural bias

TABLE 28.2   Four main types of cultural bias

	Culture of subordination	Culture of control	Culture of individualism	Culture of co-operation
Social order	Defensive traditionalism	Structured, four-square system	Zero structure, zero control	Multiple collaborative matrices
Preferred virtues	Conformity, compliance	Loyalty, honour	Personal success	Truth, honesty
Cardinal sins	Disobedience	Disloyalty	Guilt	Lack of sympathy
Notion of self-hood	Internally differentiated, complex	Passive, undifferentiated, part of whole	Subject acting alone: private, spontaneous	Active with others within own groups
Dominant beliefs or doctrines	Fortune favours the select few	Individual stores can be raided for group purposes	All taboos can be broken; adventurism and enterprise	Priority is to protect the borders of the social unit
Form of economic base	Feudal or family economy	Steered economy	Capitalist economy	Multiple twilight economies

ised in Table 28.2.

Although there are difficulties in assigning an empirical meaning to the two terms 'grid' and 'group', and the way Douglas herself defines them is not unambiguous (Wuthnow *et al.*, 1984; Oldroyd, 1986), many social researchers have used grid/group analysis in attempts to chart changes in ways of thinking in relation to changing social contexts (e.g. Bloor, 1982; Thompson, 1979; Caneva, 1978, 1981; Martin, 1981; Rudwick, 1982; Mars and Nicod, 1984; Schwarz and Thompson, 1990). Figure 28.4 represents my own attempt to use the Douglas four-fold matrix to identify the cultural foundations of the 'four models of health' (enumerated earlier).

Like other researchers who have used the grid-group framework, I find the merit of an analysis based on this kind of cultural theory is that it helps us to compare in a systematic way the different sorts of rationalities and doctrines that are in play in a field of social controversy. In the case of strategic disputes about health it can identify the different kinds of institutional values and social interests that define issues and shape agendas. It helps to reveal the 'social choices' that are embedded in different accounts of health, and to show how those choices – which may be argued for in terms that are sometimes epistemological, some-times political, sometimes ethical – reflect fundamental configurations in the moral economy. It raises intriguing questions about how far different protagonists may remain 'locked' within a particular 'cultural

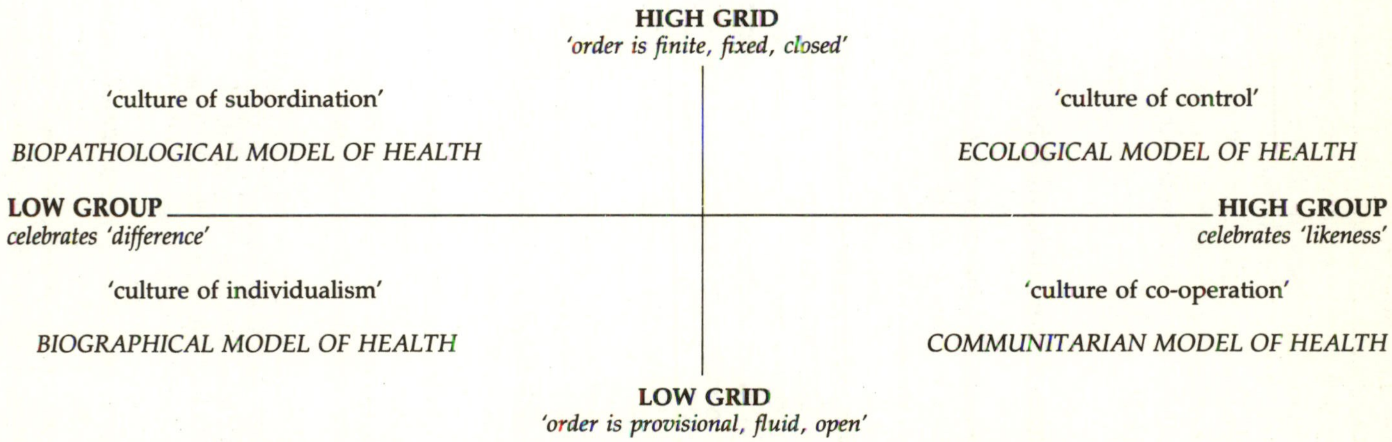

HIGH GRID
'order is finite, fixed, closed'

'culture of control'
ECOLOGICAL MODEL OF HEALTH

HIGH GROUP
celebrates 'likeness'

'culture of co-operation'
COMMUNITARIAN MODEL OF HEALTH

LOW GROUP
celebrates 'difference'

'culture of subordination'
BIOPATHOLOGICAL MODEL OF HEALTH

'culture of individualism'
BIOGRAPHICAL MODEL OF HEALTH

LOW GRID
'order is provisional, fluid, open'

FIGURE 28.4   Health accounts in relation to types of cultural bias

bias' in their reasoning, or how far they may 'change stories' and switch between different kinds of explanation; and how readily they may move into alliances with those other stakeholders whose ways of accounting for health are 'structurally' closest to their own.

In short, it offers a picture of the moral order that lies behind different views of health. By sketching the foundations of a 'psychosociology of knowledge', it provides a provocative means for tracing the ways in which health narratives are intertwined with wider cultural mandates in contemporary society.

Alternative maps of the cultural landscape

As new voices for health are increasingly heard, the three frameworks I have presented here help us to chart the shifting boundaries of ideas about health, and the grounds on which they are being attacked and defended. They show how changes in thinking about health connect up to other movements, other gradients, other fissures, in the post-modern cultural landscape. Of course the maps that I have devised in this search for the deeper structures beneath current disputes are simplifications, and they leave out much of the passion and poignancy of the contest between alternative visions of health. But if they challenge 'the sociological imagination' to find more convincing ways of depicting this highly turbulent and complex terrain, they will serve their purpose.

References

Beattie, A. (1991) 'Knowledge and control in health promotion'. In Gabe, J., Calnan, M. and Bury, M. (eds) *The Sociology of the Health Service*. London, Routledge.

Bloor, D. (1982) 'Polyhedra and the abominations of Leviticus: cognitive styles in mathematics'. In Douglas, M. (1982).

Caneva, K.L. (1978) 'From Galvanism to electrodynamics: the transformation of German physics and its social context', *Historical Studies in the Physical Sciences*, **ix**, 63–159.

Caneva, K.L. (1981) 'What should we do with the monster? Electromagnetism and the psychosociology of knowledge'. In Mendelsohn, E. and Elkana, Y. (eds) *Sciences and Cultures*. Boston, Dordrecht.

Dawe, A. (1970) 'The two sociologies', *British Journal of Sociology*, **21**, 207–18.

Douglas, M. (1970) *Natural Symbols: Explorations in Cosmology*. Harmondsworth, Penguin.

Douglas, M. (1978) *Cultural Bias*. London, Royal Anthropological Institute, Occasional Paper 35.

Douglas, M. (ed.) (1982) *Essays in the Sociology of Perception*. London, Routledge.

George, V. and Wilding, P. (1976) *Ideology and Social Welfare*. London, Routledge.

Gerhardt, U. (1989) *Ideas about Illness: An Intellectual and Political History of Medical Sociology*. London, Macmillan.

Hardy, J. (1981) *Values in Social Policy: Nine Contradictions*. London, Routledge.

Hill, M. and Bramley, G. (1986) *Analysing Social Policy*. Oxford, Blackwell.

Lawton, D. (1988) 'Ideologies of education'. In Lawton, D. and Chitty, C. (eds) *The National Curriculum*. London, Institute of Education, Bedford Way, Paper No. 33.

Lee, P. and Raban, C. (1983) 'Welfare and ideology'. In Loney, M., Boswell, D. and Clark, J. (eds). *Social Policy and Social Welfare*. Milton Keynes, Open University.

Mars, G. and Nicod, M. (1984) *The World of Waiters*. London, Allen and Unwin.

Martin, B. (1981) *A Sociology of Contemporary Cultural Change*. Oxford, Blackwell.

Mepham, J. (1973) 'The structuralist sciences and philosophy'. In Robey, D. (ed) *Structuralism*. London, Cape.

Mills, C.W. (1959) *The Sociological Imagination*. London, Oxford University Press.

Oldroyd, D.R. (1986) 'Grid/group analysis for historians of science', *History of Science*, **24**, 145–171.

Rudwick, M. (1982) 'Cognitive styles in geology'. In Douglas, M. (1982).

Schwarz, M. and Thompson, M. (1990) *Divided We Stand: redefining politics, technology and social choice*. London, Harvester Wheatsheaf.

Stainton Rogers, W. (1991) *Explaining Health and Illness: An Exploration of Diversity*. London, Harvester Wheatsheaf.

Taylor-Gooby, P. and Dale, J. (1981) *Social Theory and Social Welfare*. London, Arnold.

Thompson, M. (1979) *Rubbish Theory*. London, Oxford University Press.

Walker, A. (1984) *Models of Social Planning. Social Planning: a strategy for socialist welfare*, Chapter 3. Oxford, Blackwell.

Wright, P. and Treacher, A. (eds) (1982) *The Problem of Medical Knowledge: examining the social construction of medicine*. Edinburgh University Press.

Wuthnow, R., Hunter, J.D., Bergesen, A. and Kurzweil, E. (1984) 'The cultural anthropology of Mary Douglas'. Chapter 3 in *Cultural Analysis*, London, Routledge.

29

The Impact
of Industrialization
on World Health*

J. POPAY, J. GRIFFITHS, P. DRAPER and J. DENNIS[†]

Industrialization is, of course, an extremely complex phenomenon. On the one hand, it has clearly been accompanied by numerous benefits. In health terms, the older industrialized nations have certainly seen a reduction in the massive toll of suffering, disease and death associated with the infectious epidemics such as cholera, polio and tuberculosis which ravaged populations in the earlier stages of urbanization. Equally, it cannot be denied that life expectancy improved around the turn of the 19th century and for the next 50 years or so in countries like Britain. On the other hand, it must also be acknowledged that many industrialized countries have recently been experiencing an unfavourable change in the burden of disease from infections to conditions such as coronary heart disease and the cancers. Some of these justify the description of 'modern epidemics', and their origins lie at least in part in the very process of development that has brought so many blessings.

The Greek myths of Hygieia and Asclepius symbolize contrasting philosophies of health which, though well over 2000 years old, are very much alive today and of direct relevance to any discussion of industrialization on health. At the risk of oversimplification, contemporary followers of Asclepius can be said to be concerned with the relief of suffering and the treatment of disease. The doctor is seen rather as a

---

*This article was first published in Feather, F. (ed.) (1980) *Through the '80s: thinking globally, acting locally*. Washington, World Future Society.
†At the time of writing the authors were with the Unit for the Study of Health Policy, Department of Community Medicine, Guy's Hospital Medical School, London, England. Two former members of the unit, Gordon Best and James Partridge, also contributed to the development of this article.

mechanic repairing and occasionally servicing a machine. Followers of Hygieia, in contrast, are concerned more with the effects of the immediate and wider environments on the health of individuals and societies. Concern here is with preventing unnecessary suffering, disease and death. The debate, however, is not about choosing between Hygieian or Asclepian approaches; rather it is about whether and how advanced industrial societies can strike a more appropriate balance between the two. It is a central thesis of this article that, at present, most countries have the balance sadly wrong – even those that extol 'prevention.'

Despite powerful criticisms about the costs and effectiveness of modern medicine, it is still widely believed that progress in health will be achieved in the main by the provision of more and more hospital-based health services. Hats are occasionally doffed towards primary care and the caring and residential services in the community, but current preventive policies, at least in the United Kingdom, are emaciated and unrecognizable descendents of Hygieia. They contrast with the public health activities of the past which have paid serious attention to the effects of the wider environment on health – from sewage in the drinking water to a concern with 'unwholesome trades.' An equivalent movement today would need to look very seriously not so much at the health implications of industrialization per se, but at the largely indiscriminate nature of present economic growth – that is, at much of what is ironically termed wealth-creation. (See Table 29.1.)

Enemies of Hygieia: 'health versus wealth'

To pursue social and economic policies that largely neglect a variety of health hazards, and often actually increase such hazards, is to pursue a form of development that is in total conflict with the Hygieian idea. Yet in advanced industrial societies today, this is in many ways exactly what we seem to be doing. More specifically, apart from attempts to control inflation, the pursuit of social progress in industrialized societies is often reduced to the pursuit of a single goal: economic growth. And despite the fact that increasingly this goal is not achieved, the pursuit in itself conditions a number of critically important economic and social policies and practices. Indeed, many of our prevailing ideas of social progress can be seen to reflect a fundamental desire to effect what can fairly be called indiscriminative increases in the total output of material goods and marketed services. Typically, for example, industrial, agricultural and trade policies make no distinction between measures that might increase the production of socially useful products (such as nutritionally wise foods) and measures likely to increase the output of socially damaging and health-damaging products such as cigarettes. Our goal

TABLE 29.1   Economic conventions, health, and wealth

	Convention or assumption	Principle	Example
Indices of economic value	1. In general, the economic value of a good or service produced in the economy is equated with the price it fetches in the market place.	If one good or service is sold for X and a second is sold for 2X, then the contribution of the second to society's economic 'welfare' is conventionally taken to be twice that of the first.	In terms of national accounts, if £1m is spent on anti-smoking educational measures and £83m is spent on advertising and promoting tobacco, then tobacco advertising is viewed as over eighty times as valuable.
Indices of economic progress	2. In general, the health of the economy is seen to depend in part on increases in the aggregate sales value of the goods and services that exchange in the market place.	Measures such as GNP or national income measure the *level* of economic activity: that is, they increase (or decrease) as the total (price-corrected) sales value of goods and services increases (or decreases).	£1,000 spent on frozen vegetables has a positive effect on GNP; £1000 'worth' of home-grown vegetables that are consumed (or informally exchanged) by the growers do not enter national accounts (and therefore GNP).
Indices of welfare	3. In general, many unintended side effects of market activities (e.g. noise, pollution) are omitted from measures of economic welfare. Moreover, measures of economic welfare are often confused with measures of social or general welfare.	The production and consumption of goods and services are conventionally viewed as the *primary* activities of the economy: the unintended 'production' of, for example, air or water pollution or occupational 'stress' or accidents are viewed as 'external effects,' the costs of which are rarely reflected in measures such as GNP. Indeed, they sometimes are viewed as benefits.	'Defensive' expenditures such as those incurred in cleaning up the air or water, or in 'repairing' people following preventable accidents, are added to rather than subtracted from measures such as GNP. Many 'external' outputs of the economy for which no 'defensive' arrangements exist do not enter national accounts at all. Measures of economic welfare can increase therefore even in situations where general welfare may be in decline.

TABLE 29.1   (*Continued*)

	Convention or assumption	Principle	Example
Distinctions between productive and non-productive	4. In general, the production of many 'public' goods and services is viewed as a 'drain' on the wealth-producing (marketed) sector of the economy.	The economic value of many goods and services that are central to the quality of life (e.g. health, education, etc.), they are viewed as 'non-productive' uses of productive (i.e. marketed) resources.	Marketing health, education, etc., renders them productive in terms of national accounts.
Distinctions between economic and non-economic	5. Many essential productive activities that are important not only to the economy but to social welfare are not counted as contributions to society's economic welfare.	Much work that is undertaken without monetary remuneration has no economic value.	Child-rearing, housework, voluntary activities (e.g. blood donations) and any other charitable or benevolent activities, the outcomes of which do not enter into national accounts, have no economic value and therefore do not contribute to economic welfare.

Source: From a paper by members of the Unit for the Study of Health Policy, Royal Society of Health Journal, June 1977.

seems to be purely quantitative – increased productive output: what we produce, how we produce it and how we distribute it are of secondary importance.

There is a fundamental conflict between the 'production of wealth' – as it is commonly defined – and the promotion of health. For example, the higher the level of transport activity, the greater the number of cars, trucks and lorries which can be sold, the more fuel will be consumed and so in economic terms (at least on paper) things will be better: but other things being equal, the more transport, the more accident and emergency resources that will have to be devoted to traffic accidents. Similarly, cigarettes and alcohol production are 'wealth producing' from an economic perspective, but from a health perspective they are 'ill-health producing.' It is not only the nature of the products, however; the ways in which they are produced, marketed, distributed, and consumed can also generate health problems.

TABLE 29.2   Conflicts between health and wealth: a grouping of accidents and diseases (mainly as experienced in the United Kingdom in the 1980s) by economic, rather than biological, categories

Economic category	Examples: source of risk	Specific diseases, problems of risk
Production		
i Conditions primarily related to the *nature* or *organization* of production	The use of various chemical and other toxic materials in mining, industry and agriculture.	Occupational diseases and injuries, e.g. asbestos diseases; numerous skin, lung, bladder and other cancers; radiation diseases.
	Increases use of human beings in passive, repetitive or machine-like roles.	Obesity; industrial accidents; cigarette diseases; alcoholism; boredom and stress-related diseases and conditions.
	Multinational operations in the Third World.	Malnutrition resulting from cash cropping and distortion of the agricultural base.
ii Conditions primarily related to the *level* of production	Pressures leading to damaging rapidity in the production process.	Increased risks of accidents, e.g. diving accidents; executive stress leading to cigarette diseases, road accidents, alcoholism and over-eating (obesity).
	Pressures to utilize new and inadequately tested forms of energy inputs.	Nuclear power radiation hazards and deaths.
Consumption		
i Conditions primarily related to the *nature* or *organization* of consumption	The consumption of disease and accident linked products.	Cigarette diseases; dental caries obesity and some diabetes; road accidents secondary to alcohol, hypnotic or tranquilizer consumption; poisoning from week-killers and pesticides; aerosol sprays.
	Waste pollution hazards.	Poisoning from heavy metal or other chemical and radioactive wastes, e.g. to workers on waste tips or to others through water contamination, etc.
	Bottle-feeding of babies in the Third World.	Increased nutritional and infectious disease problems in infancy.
ii Conditions primarily related to the *level* of consumption	Pressures to consume more in an absolute sense, e.g. advertising of the form 'eat more, drink more.'	Advertising which contributes to over-eating and therefore to our major nutritional problem, obesity and assocated diseases, e.g. heart disease.

TABLE 29.2   *(Continued)*

Economic category	Examples: source of risk	Specific diseases, problems of risk
Distribution		
i Conditions primarily related to the maldistribution of economic opportunities or resources	Global inequalities.	Persistence of diseases of poverty in the Third World; diseases of affluence in the West.
	Chronic persistence of shortages and inadequacies in housing and basic amenities despite ever increasing levels of productive output and energy consumption.	Hypothermia; respiratory and gastro-intestinal conditions which arise from grossly inadequate housing and sanitation, overcrowding and homelessness; accidents to children from the lack of safe and attractive play facilities, e.g. the special problems of high-rise flats.

Source: Adapted from a paper by members of the Unit for the Study of Health Policy, *Royal Society of Health Journal*, June 1977.

To be critical of the pursuit of simplistically-measured economic growth is not, however, to argue that considerations of health should be paramount in our quest for social progress. Rather, it is to argue that a more reasonable balance between Asclepian and Hygieian approaches cannot be struck if the very processes whereby our society produces 'wealth' are at the same time a significant source of the conditions that jeopardize health. To clarify the issues we are raising, we have attempted to group such conditions and their associated accident, disease and health problems in relation to a broad classification of many of the economic processes involved in the pursuit of indiscriminate economic growth (Table 29.2).

A practical implication of this kind of classification is that attention is focused on the diverse range of causal – or conditioning – influences that originate in the functioning of the economy and that contribute to what René Dubos and others have called 'diseases of civilization.' Such an economic grouping (as opposed to the more conventional biological classifications) suggests directions for fruitful research and action.

A second set of problems, however, is at least equally important to the development of a better understanding of the health-versus-wealth conflict. Essentially, this second set of problems relates to the various linguistic and conceptual conventions that characterize most practical discussions of economic and social policy objectives and that serve to obscure or mark many of these conflicts. Table 29.1 has attempted to illustrate the nature of these conventions by giving examples of them and illustrating some of the ways in which they tend to conceal important health (and other social) questions in the consideration of national policies.

These examples and illustrations of the health-versus-wealth conflict suggest that the thoughtless pursuit of indiscriminate economic growth can best be understood as a contemporary *religion*, the worship of the god Economic Growth. Ironically, the very idea of health has also been conditioned by the growth imperative. The activities undertaken to ameliorate this situation constitute a significant proportion of what we call 'health services' and these services have come to be equated with the idea of health. We need, it is argued, to create more 'wealth' in order to be able to afford more 'health services.' But is that really how we make progress in health?

We need to get out of the habit of thinking that treatment service policies constitute adequate health policies. We must develop economic policy, social policy and health policy in an integrated way rather than putting economic considerations first and thus creating health and social problems. Industrial and transport policies, for example, are partly health (or anti-health) policies. We need to make sure that prevention is directed at underlying causes. Apparently desirable preventively-oriented activities can mistakenly focus on symptoms and amount to useless exhortations. For example, the essentially moralistic and puritanical appeals to the individual – 'pull yourself together, change your personal lifestyle, stop smoking, stop overeating, take regular exercise, drive carefully' and so on – achieve little and distract attention from the policies and practices that mould lifestyles and that generate the stresses and risks. As the tables suggest, attention has to be directed to removing or reducing the conditions that pressure people to lead unhealthy lives.

The solutions to many of these problems lie, for example, in the creation of appropriate technology rather than technology which so often squanders energy and creates unemployment as well as pollution. They lie also in a biological and ecological, rather than a narrowly chemical and engineering, approach to agriculture, nutrition and medicine. Most important, we must recognize that current economic behavior, whether for industrialized or developing countries, is generating accidents, illnesses and deaths on a massive scale as well as creating resource and pollution problems. With these points in mind, Table 29.3 gives examples of the health implications of a much more selective form of economic growth in the UK. But is there a good chance that such strategic objectives will find wide support?

It is worth noting that there is a remarkable and encouraging consistency between economic policies that are sound in environmental and ecological terms and economic policies that promote public health. There may also be support for such policies in industrialized countries

TABLE 29.3   Some specific policy areas: the health implications of a more selective form of growth

Area of policy	Strategic objectives	Examples of policy measures	Typical health implications
1 Energy	i *Overall reduction in energy consumption* including the use of less wasteful and more efficient forms of electricity generation.	Incentives to develop and invest in more energy-efficient forms of technology and production.	Less risk of serious industrial accidents (e.g. mining accidents, nuclear accidents, etc.).
	ii *Shift away from capital-intensive, extractive forms of energy production* toward lower technology, 'income' forms of energy.	Investment in research into alternative energy sources.	Less risk of climatic and other unknown changes due to over-heating of the atmosphere.
	iii *Less energy-related pollution* and waste disposal.	Stricter pollution and waste disposal regulatons.	Less air, water and other forms of pollution (e.g. sulphur).
2 Nutrition and agriculture	i *Greater national, regional and local self-reliance* in food production; more employment in agricultural production.	Import restrictions on animal food grains and incentives to 'local holdings.' Incentives to producer of 'home-grown' cereals, vegetables and fruits.	Better diet and fewer diet-related health problems (e.g. less diverticulitis and obesity). Less land and water pollution risks (e.g. nitrate pollution of water).
	ii *Less reliance on capital-intensive, high energy forms of agricultural production* (e.g. reduced utilization of nitrogen fertilizers, herbicides and pesticides and intensive animal rearing).	Pricing and subsidy policies to favor home-produced foods as above. Consumer nutritional education.	Less exposure to fertilizer and pesticide products and by-products.

Source: From work done at Unit for the Study of Health Policy by Gordon Best, John Dennis, and Peter Draper.

from those who are concerned about the division of resources between North and South. Thus, those whose primary concerns are health, the ecosphere and the Third World might find themselves sharing a global perspective on the process we call 'industrialization.'

Resources for a Journey of Hope*

RAYMOND WILLIAMS

There is now a growing body of detailed professional research, most of it dependent on the still expanding scientific community, in the key areas of ecology, alternative technologies and disarmament. There is also a rapidly growing movement of specific campaigns, most visible in the peace movement and in ecological initiatives but also extending over a very wide social and cultural range. Here, certainly, are actual and immediately potential resources for radically new kinds of politics.

Yet it has to be recognised that in some ways these are two very different groups of people. In some of their forms of activity they are quite distinct and unconnecting. Thus much of the most useful scientific work is directed, as if it were still orthodox research, at existing political leaders or generalised public opinion. Because by current definitions much of it is 'not political', but rather an objective assessment of physical facts, there is a tendency to resist its involvement with the simplifications of politics or with the street cries and emotionalism of demonstrations. Again, by their own best values, many of the campaigns are concerned primarily with forms of public witness and protest, with direct personal involvement in opposition to some evil, or with the growth of immediate relationships of an alternative kind. They can then be generalised, by some of their representatives, as movements of conversion, analogous to early religious movements, and as such disdainful both of what is seen as mere intellectualism and of the whole system of organised politics.

These differences have to be recognised. Yet the most remarkable fact about both the peace and the ecology movements of recent years has

---

*This is an abridged extract from Williams, R. (1983) *Towards 2000*, Penguin.

been their relative success in combining scientific information, at quite new levels of practical development, with the direct action, in witness and exposure, of both small-group protests and huge public demonstrations. This is never either an easy or a stable combination, but in the degree it has practically reached, in many countries, it is already a new political factor.

A similar kind of combination has been evident in the most recent phases of feminism. There is now a remarkable and growing body of distinctively feminist scholarship and argument, shifting our intellectual perspectives in many fields, while at the same time there has been a major expansion of supportive groups and initiatives, as well as sharp public and private challenges to old dominative and subordinating habits. This degree of combination is relatively stable, resting as it does on more immediate identities and bondings than are available in the peace and ecology movements. At the same time, the specific directions of what is called 'the women's movement', are still being formed and are subject to crucial interactions with others forms of political organisation, many of these not yet resolved.

It would be possible to project, from these humane and growing movements – peace, ecology and feminism – an immediately potential and effective political majority. Yet the general situation is not really like that. The potential cannot reasonably be doubted. It is the immediacy that is the problem. There is now a major risk that there will be a jump from this sense of potential, centred in the reasonable belief that these movements represent the deepest interests of large human majorities, to an option of indifference towards all other organised and institutionalised political and social forms. The jump seems irresistible, time and again, as we look from these dimensions of concern and possibility to the mechanical thinking and manoeuvring practice of most of these forms for most of their time. Yet this is still not a jump that can be reasonably made, especially by some loose analogy with early religious movements or with heroic minorities whose objective time will come. That option should already have been rejected in the experiences of the sixties, even if there were not such clear intellectual arguments against it.

For it is not only in the movements of peace, ecology and feminism that the shift has begun. It is also in the vigorous movement of what is called an alternative culture but at its best is always an oppositional culture: new work in theatre, film, community writing and publishing, and in cultural analysis. But what has been learned very clearly in all this work, and in new kinds of political and ideological analysis, is that the relations between small-group initiatives and potentials and a dominant system are at the very centre of the problem. It is there that we have learned how new work can be incorporated, specialised, labelled:

pushed into corners of the society where the very fact that it becomes known brings with it its own displacements. It is possible here also to persist as a minority, but in the cultural system as a whole it is soon clear that the central institutions are not residual – to be disregarded, for their often residual content, until the emergent minority's time has come – but are dominant and active, directing and controlling a whole connected process towards which it is impossible to be indifferent. And if this is true of the cultural system, it is even more strongly true of the general social and political system which the institutionalised forms control and direct.

At the practical centre of this problem are the existing political parties. For it is clear that at all effective levels it is towards such parties that the system now directs us. Yet it is equally clear that the central function of these parties is to reproduce the existing definitions of issues and interests. When they extend to new issues and interests, they usually lead them back into a system which will isolate, dilute and eventually compromise them. If there is one thing that should have been learned in the years since 1945, it is this. Indeed in Britain, where in the early 1960s the popular cause of nuclear disarmament was entrusted to an apparently welcoming Labour Party, only then to sink without trace, for some fifteen years, at either effective popular or institutional levels, the lesson has been very sharp and should be unmistakeable. Moreover, it is not of a kind that can be reversed by the now systematic apologias for such events, assigning merely local and proximate causes and assuring everyone that it is bound to be different next time. In their present forms the parties are practically constituted to be like this. They absorb and deflect new issues and interests in their more fundamental process of reproducing and maximising their shares of the existing and governing dispositions.

It need not stay like this. For comparable in importance to the growth of new issues and movements is a steady withdrawal of assent to orthodox politics by what is in all relevant societies a sizeable minority of a different kind, and in some societies an already practical majority. Thus except in conditions of unusual stablity, which are not going to be there, the pressures on existing political forms and institutions will in any case become irresistible. It is because one likely outcome of these pressures is a harsh movement beyond the now familiar forms, into new and more open kinds of control and repression, that there can be no jump to any kind of indifference to the institutions. On the contrary, just because there will be so many pressures of a negative, cynical and apathetic kind, it is essential that the carriers of the new and positive issues and interests should move in on the institutions, but in their own still autonomous ways.

This point has special reference to the institutions of the labour movement. It is clear that these began, in all or most of their original impulses, beyond the terms of what were then the governing definitions. They were genuine popular responses, slowly built over generations, to changes in the social and economic order which were at least as fundamental as those which we are now beginning to experience. Yet any comparative measure of degrees of change has to be assessed also in two further scales. First, the relative speed of current transfers of employment beyond the societies in which the institutions were shaped, and the interaction of this with internally generated structural unemployment. Second, the basic orientation of the institutions to predominantly male, predominantly stable, and above all nationally-based and nationally-conceived economic processes.

In both these respects the existing institutions have become not only insufficient but at certain key points actually resistant to new kinds of issue. The new issues of peace and of feminism have been included in certain ways: the former as a commitment to nuclear disarmament, but characteristically of a 'unilateral', nationally-based kind; the latter as a limited responsibility to women workers as trade unionists, but largely omitting, in theory and especially practice, response to the wider critique of hierarchy and dominance. The relative indifference of the institutions to the new cultural movements is notorious. Their confidence in their sets of received ideas – keeping new kinds of thinking at a distance ratified by the disdain for 'intellectuals' and 'academics' which they share with their capitalist masters – has ensured that at the broadest public levels they have been losing the decisive intellectual arguments. In relation to the ex-colonial world, the political affiliations of an earlier epoch have been sustained but there has been a radical unwillingness to face the consequences of the contemporary domination of the international economic order by capitalist trading forms within which, from positions of advantage, their own 'labourist' economic policies and assumptions are still based.

It is possible and necessary to believe that substantial changes can be made, in the general direction of the existing institutions. Yet by their nature this cannot be done by any form of intellectual affiliation to them. On the contrary, the only relevant approach is one of challenge. This is especially important in what is often the most urgent practical area, that of elections. There is an orthodox electoral rhythm in the society as a whole. But there is also a rhythm of radical thought, in which periods of intense activity on the decisive long-term issues are punctuated by silences, compromises, evasions, expressions of meaningless goodwill and artificial solidarity, which are thought appropriate because an election is imminent. It is not only that much of this is in any case vanity.

What a radical minority does or does not do in these large spectacular events, dominated by the deployment of competitive leaderships, is not in practice very important. But what is much more serious is the practical surrender of the real agenda of issues to just that version of politics which the critique has shown to be deceptive and is offering to supersede.

There are some elections which are genuinely decisive: especially some which it is important not to lose, with all the evident consequences of some reactionary or repressive tendency being strengthened. Specific decisions to be electorally active in these terms are entirely reasonable. There are also some rarer occasions when an election can be much more positively worked for, because it contains the probability of some coherent advance. But even in these cases there can be no intellectual affiliation to the adequacy of the processes themselves, and no defensible temporary pretence that they are other than they are. The challenging move towards the existing institutions, which can be effectively made only if there are already alternative institutions and campaigns on a different issue-based orientation, is in no way reducible to elections, or even to party programmes and manifestos. The central approach is always to the actual people inside them, but then on the same terms as the much wider approach to the significant number of people who are at their edges or who are leaving or have left them.

This approach, by definition, has to be in good faith, candid, open to learn as well as to teach: in all those real senses comradely. But we should now have reached the end of a period in which campaigners and intellectuals acquired the habit of going as petitioners or suppliants, touched by guilt or by an assumed deference to so much accumulated wisdom. There is hardly anything of that kind to go to any longer, and any of it that is genuinely wise will not require deference or sidelong flattery. If it is indeed the case, as now seems likely, that the most the existing institutions can do, in their fixed terms, is conduct losing defensive battles, then much deeper loyalties are in question, in the survival and welfare of actual people.

It is understandable that people still trapped in the old consciousness really do see the new movements of our time – peace, ecology, feminism – as primarily 'emotional'. Those who have most to lose exaggerate this to 'hysterical', but even 'emotional' is intended to make its point. The implied or stated contrast is with the rational intelligence of the prevailing systems. In reactions to this there is often a great business of showing how rational and intelligent, in comparable ways, the campaigns themselves are. Moreover, and increasingly, this is true. But a crucial position may then be conceded. For it is in what it dismisses as 'emotional' – a direct and intransigent concern with actual people – that the old consciousness most clearly shows its bankruptcy. Emotions, it is true, do not produce commodities. Emotions don't make the accounts add up differently. Emotions don't alter the hard relations of power. But where people actually live, what is specialised as 'emotional' has an absolute and primary significance.

This is where the new broad concept most matters. If our central attention is on whole ways of life, there can be no reasonable contrast between emotions and rational intelligence. The concern with forms of whole relationship excludes these specialised and separated projections. There are still good and bad emotions, just as there are good and bad forms of rational intelligence. But the habit of separating the different kinds of good from each other is entirely a consequence of a deformed social order, in which rational intelligence has so often to try to justify emotionally unacceptable or repulsive actions.

The deformed order itself is not particularly rational or intelligent. It can be sharp enough in its specialised and separated areas, but in its aggregates it is usually stupid and muddled. It is also, in some of its central drives, an active generator of bad emotions, especially aggressiveness and greed. In its worst forms it has magnified these to extraordinary scales of war and crimes. It has succeeded in the hitherto improbable combination of affluent consumption and widespread emotional distress.

Informed reason and inquiry can explore these complex forms, but it is not surprising that the strongest response to them has appeared at the most general 'emotional' levels. Before any secondary reasons or informed intelligence can be brought to bear, there is an initial and wholly reasonable reaction, carrying great emotional force, against being used, in all the ways that are now possible, as mere raw material. This response can develop in several different directions, but where it is rooted in new concepts, now being steadily shaped, and in many kinds of relationship – forms of genuine bonding which are now being steadily renewed and explored – it is already generating the energies and the practical means of an alternative social order.

It can then make a difference that this alternative is being clarified theoretically. The central element is the shift from 'production' to 'livelihood': from an alienated generality to direct and practical ways of life. These are the real bases from which co-operative relationships can grow, and the rooted forms which are wholly compatible with, rather than contradictory to, other major energies and interests. They are also, at just this historical stage, in the very development of the means of production, the shifts that most people will in any case have to make.

It is reasonable to see many dangers in the years towards 2000, but it is also reasonable to see many grounds for hope. There is more eager and constructive work, more active caring and responsibility, than the official forms of the culture permit us to recognise. It is true that these are shadowed by the most general and active dangers. They are shadowed also by the suspicion – which the official culture propagates but which also comes on its own – that as the demonstration disperses, as the talk fades, as the book is put down, there is an old hard centre – the reproduction of a restricted everyday reality – which we have temporarily bypassed or ideally superseded but which is there and settled and is what we have really to believe.

Two things have then to be said. First, that the objective changes which are now so rapidly developing are not only confusing and bewildering; they are also profoundly unsettling. The ways now being offered to live with these unprecedented dangers and these increasingly harsh dislocations are having many short-term successes and effects, but they are also, in the long term, forms of further danger and dislocation. For this, if we allow it, will be a period in which, after a quarter of a century of both real and manufactured expectations, there will be a long series of harshly administered checks; of deliberately organised reductions of conditions and chances; of intensively prepared emergencies of war and disorder, offering only crude programmes of rearmament, surveillance and mutually hostile controls. It is a sequence which no active and resilient people should be content to live with for long.

Secondly, there are very strong reasons why we should challenge what now most controls and constrains us: the idea of such a world as an inevitable future. It is not some unavoidable real world, with its laws of economy and laws of war, that is now blocking us. It is a set of identifiable processes of *realpolitik* and *force majeure*, of nameable agencies of power and capital, distraction and disinformation, and all these interlocking with the embedded short-term pressures and the interwoven subordinations of an adaptive commonsense. It is not in staring at these blocks that there is any chance of movement past them. They have been named so often that they are not even, for most people, news. The dynamic moment is elsewhere, in the difficult business of gaining confidence in *our own* energies and capacities.

It is only in a shared belief and insistence that there are practical alternatives that the balance of forces and chances begins to alter. Once the inevitabilities are challenged, we begin gathering our resources for a journey of hope. If there are no easy answers there are still available and discoverable hard answers, and it is these that we can now learn to make and share. This has been, from the beginning, the sense and the impulse of the long revolution.

31

Possible Futures for Work*

JAMES ROBERTSON

A post-industrial age?

At times of uncertainty like the present, different people perceive the future in different ways. There are at least three distinct views about the future of work. The keyword for the first is employment. The keyword for the second is leisure. The keyword for the third is ownwork. They are based on three distinct perceptions of the future of industrialised society. I call these Business As Usual, HE (Hyper-Expansionist) and SHE (Sane, Humane, Ecological). Business as Usual assumes that the society of the future will not be very different from late industrial society as it is today. HE and SHE are contrasting visions of a post-industrial society which, in either case, will be distinctly different from the society we have today.

Two visions of post-industrial society[1]

One vision of post-industrial society – the 'HE' vision of the future – might more accurately be described as superindustrial. It is a vision of a future based on big science, big technology and expert know-how. Its dominant drives and features would be those of industrial society accentuated and writ large.

By contrast, the 'SHE' vision of the future foresees, not an acceleration along the same path of development we have followed during the industrial age, but a change in the direction of development. According

---

*This is an abridged extract from Robertson, J. (1985) *Future Work*, Gower/Temple Smith, pp. 3–16.

to this view, the industrial revolution marked a huge advance in the capacity of human beings to control and harness the material world.

So, as the industrial age comes to an end, a comparable transformation may be in prospect – a post-industrial revolution which could bring about an advance no less far-reaching than the industrial revolution did. This time, however, the breakthrough will be primarily psychological and social, not technical and economic. It will enlarge the human limits to human achievement. It will amplify our capacity to develop ourselves as human beings, together with the communities and the societies in which we live. Not only will it bring fundamental social and personal change, as the industrial revolution did, but that is what will be its main motive force.

These two contrasting visions of post-industrial society have emerged quite clearly in the last few years. Some of their main values and tendencies are shown in these two columns.

HE	SHE
Quantitative values and goals	Qualitative values and goals
Economic growth	Human development
Organisational values and	Personal and inter-personal values and goals
Goals	Real needs and aspirations
Money values	Mutual exchange relationships
Contractual relationships	Intuitive, experiential, empathetic
Intellectual, rational, detached	Feminine priorities
Masculine priorities	All-round competence
Specialisation/helplessness	Self-reliance
Technocracy/dependency	Local
Centralising	Country-wide
Urban	Planetary
European	Ecological
Anthropocentric	

These two visions of a post-industrial future provide the two poles, and the two clusters of ideas and possibilities, around which serious discussion of the future, including the future of work, is likely to revolve from now on. Table 31.1 outlines some of the practical differences between them and 'Business As Usual'.

Three futures for work

The Business-As-Usual view of the future of work is still voiced, though with diminishing conviction, by politicians and economists of all mainstream persuasions, and by most business leaders and trade union

TABLE 31.1   Three possible futures

Business As Usual	HE	SHE
Work Full employment can be restored, and employment will remain the dominant form of work. Other activities (e.g. housework, family care, voluntary work) will continue to have lower status. Sharp distinctions will continue to exist between education for the young, work for adults, and retirement for the old; and between work and leisure.	Full employment will not be restored. All necessary work will be done by a skilled elite of professionals and experts, backed by automation, other capital-intensive technology, and specialist know-how. Others will not work. They will merely consume the goods and services provided by the working minority – including leisure, information and education services. Society will be split between workers and drones.	Full employment will not be restored. Work will be redefined to include many forms of useful and valued activity in addition to paid employment. Paid and unpaid work will be shared around more equally, e.g. between men and women. Part-time employment will be common. Many different patterns of working will be possible, according to people's circumstances and preferences. Households and neighbourhoods will become recognised work-places and centres of production. Young and old will have valued work roles. Work and leisure activities will overlap.
Money incomes Paid work will continue to be the primary source. Society will continue to provide a basic income to people who fall outside this norm, but such people, if of 'working age', will continue to be stigmatised as exceptions.	The skilled working elite will be highly paid. Proponents of this scenario have not yet worked out through what channels everyone else will receive an income. From dividends, after nationalisation of all production? Or from benefits financed by high taxation? Or as wages from menial jobs?	Society will pay everyone a basic income as of right, enabling them to choose how they will divide their time between paid and unpaid activities. People who do not need this extra income because they earn more on top of it will have it taxed back automatically.
Technology New technologies will continue to be developed for their own sake, because scientists and design engineers find them challenging, and because industries and governments hope they will prove profitable and that people can be	Even more effort and resources than at present will be channelled into the development of new technologies. It will be accepted that all problems have technical solutions, and that top priority should always be given to the technical approach,	The development and diffusion of certain types of new technologies and new skills will have high priority. These will be technologies and skills which enhance the capacities of people to do more for themselves and one another, and reduce

TABLE 31.1   (*Continued*)

Business As Usual	HE	SHE
persuaded to use them. There will also continue to be opposition to many new technologies on the grounds that they may be dangerous, exploitative, wasteful, polluting and socially undesirable or unnecessary.	including the development of new forms of expertise and reliance on the decisions and advice of experts. Opposition to this approach will become weaker. Technology will be master.	their dependence on outside systems, organisations and professional expertise. This scenario is not anti-technology. Technology will have an important role, but as servant.

Economy

Business As Usual	HE	SHE
Economic growth can be restored. Creation of wealth by industry and commercial services can continue to support publicly financed social services. Industrialised economies will remain centralised, and big business and publicly owned corporations will retain their dominant role. Formal economic activity will continue to be the only kind of economic activity that really matters.	Economic growth will only be achieved by concentrating on high technology production and by marketing highly professionalised services. The wealth thereby created will meet society's needs. Formal economic activity will become even more dominant. Multinational business will have an even more dominant role.	The most important areas for economic growth and social progress will be in the informal economy. People's energies will be released to create wealth and welfare for themselves and one another in their own households, neighbourhoods and localities. Within the formal economy, local small-scale enterprise will be the main growth sector. Localities will become more self-sufficient economically and less dependent on outside employers and suppliers.

Planning and housing

Business As Usual	HE	SHE
Urban industrialised patterns of lifestyle, employment and movement will continue to be the norm. Residential and work locations will remain in separate zones. Planning regulations will continue to assume that people use their homes for leisure and consumption activities only. Houses will continue to be designed that way. The land, premises and equipment tha people need for their work will continue to be provided by employers.	The coming of the leisure society and the information age will help to reshape the built environment. People will have more leisure time to spend at home, at local leisure facilities (swimming pools, sports centres, etc.), and on trips away from home. The provision of new leisure facilities (including education) will make big new demands on space. What precisely this will mean, for example in old inner city areas, is not yet clear.	Today's house designs, zoning arrangements and planning regulations will become inappropriate. More people will participate in planning and building their own houses and environment. There will be more shared, multi-family households and clusters of houses, including housing co-operatives. Residential densities will fall, in the old city centres as elsewhere, and the tendency will be toward more dispersed patterns of settlement country-wide.

TABLE 31.1   (*Continued*)

Business As Usual	HE	SHE
Transport Traffic and transport patterns will continue much as they are today.	A decline in travel between homes and places of work will be matched by a rise in travel for leisure.	A decline in travel between homes and places of work will only be partly matched by a rise in travel for leisure.
Energy Patterns of energy use and energy development will continue much as at present. Changes will mainly be prompted by adjustment to price changes and the balance of supply and demand.	Demand for energy will continue to grow. Dependence on capital-intensive, centralised, high technology sources of energy (e.g. nuclear power) will grow.[2] A few centres of energy production will supply the whole populace of energy consumers.	Less energy-intensive patterns of working, living and transport, coupled with conservation and more efficient ways of using energy, will reduce demand for energy.[2] Energy production will be more decentralised. There will be a tendency to greater energy self-sufficiency in regions and localities and even, to some extent, in households.
Food Patterns of food production, processing, distribution and consumption will continue to be dominated by agribusiness farming, industrial manufacturing, and the distribution of processed and packaged foods through supermarket chains to standardised consumers.	As for Business As Usual, but with more emphasis on new agricultural and nutrition technology. For example, more productive strains of animals and crops will be developed; beneficial elements (e.g. vitamins) will be added and harmful ones (e.g. fats) will be removed as a normal aspect of food-manufacturing and processing. People will eat out more often; fast-food chains will be part of a food service industry expanding in response to the growing 'leisure market'.	There will be, as for energy, a tendency to greater food self-sufficiency. More people will grow food, either as small farmers, part-time farmers and smallholders, or (for themselves) in their own gardens and allotments. Food production will be more decentralised and food distribution chains will be shorter. Food co-operatives will become more numerous. Home cooking will be the norm. Multi-family purchasing and feeding arrangements may become more common.
Education and learning As at present, education will take place in educational institutions at the hands of professional	Education will divide into two main branches. The first will qualify a person for a high status job as a	Education will be for capability. It will help people to learn life-skills of all kinds – physical,

TABLE 31.1   (*Continued*)

Business As Usual	HE	SHE
educators. It will continue to be primarily for young people, before they enter the age bracket in which they will be expected to have a full-time job. Its main aims will be to provide them with the credentials to get and hold down a job, and to socialise them into what will remain a mass-employment, mass-consumption society. Main criteria of a good education will continue to be the certificates and diplomas that one can show for it, and the jobs which it opens up.	member of the technochratic and professional elite. The second branch will teach people how to use their leisure. Its status will be somewhat lower. Both types of education will, in principle, be life-long. In the high technology, leisure society of the information age, education will be one of the biggest growth industries. Openings for professionally qualified, expert educators will greatly expand.	intellectual, inter-personal, emotional. It will be geared to a pattern of living in which most people expect to have part-time employment and also to undertake a good deal of useful, rewarding activity for themselves and their family and neighbours. It will recognise that people often learn better from doing things with experienced people than from receiving class-room instruction from professional educators.

Health

Individuals and society will continue to give lower priority to the promotion of health than to the treatment of sickness. 'Health services' will continue to be primarily sickness services, and people's perception of themselves as consumers of those services will continue to dominate their perception of health. The main debate will continue to be whether sickness services should be provided commercially or at public expense.	Medical technology will solve most health problems. Genetic screening, organ transplants, new drugs, computer monitoring and computer records will eliminate or control congenital diseases and handicaps, enable the body to be maintained in good operating order, and enable expert physicians to deal more quickly and effectively than today with their patients' problems – a widening range of which, such as bereavements, losses and failures, will become subject to medical treatment. Health promotion and sickness prevention may increase somewhat. But the increased dominance of medical experts and technologists will ensure that today's remedial bias remains strong.	Greater personal responsibility for health will lead people to the positive cultivation of their health and to the positive promotion of a healthy physical and social environment. Higher priority wil be given to nutrition, public health and the psychosomatic aspects of health than is given today. Personal self-help and co-operative mutual aid in matters of health and sickness will be more highly rated than dependence on the expertise of health professionals. People will learn to manage the health hazards and stressful transitions in their lives. Nurture and care will be emphasised, in contrast to the 'heroic' interventionism of the HE future.

TABLE 31.1 *(Continued)*

Business As Usual	HE	SHE
Principles		
Mass employment, mass consumption. Dependence on institutions for work and for goods and services. Obligation to be employed. Organisational values, masculine values, anthropocentric values. Interventionist, instrumental mode of action. Analytical, reductionist mode of thought.	Mass leisure, mass consumption. Continued dependence on institutions. Increased dependence on technology and experts. A schizophrenic society: the working elite will be hard-working, responsible, and highly motivated; the masses will enjoy leisured irresponsibility. Technocratic values dominant, including even greater emphasis on organisational, masculine, anthropocentric values, etc.	A shift towards self-help and decentralisation in production of goods and provision of services. Reintegration of people's work with other aspects of their lives. This will bring new meaning to life. Personal values, feminine values, ecological values. Experiential mode of action. Intuitive mode of awareness.

leaders, in all the industrial countries. They do not question, at least not in public, that employment will remain the dominant form of work and that full employment ought to be restored. They suggest that it can be restored if the particular policies which they support are adopted. For some this means bringing back high levels of employment in conventional manufacturing industry. For others it means replacing jobs lost in manufacturing by a great increase of jobs elsewhere: in information services like computing and telecommunications; in sectors of the knowledge industry like research and consultancy; in social services like education and health; and in leisure industries and services like sports, entertainment, and travel. Some hope that, by making the economy internationally competitive, the resulting creation of wealth will automatically generate enough jobs for all. Others, by contrast, hope that by insulating the national economy from international competition and by planning it centrally, they will be able to organise enough jobs for all.

Because we have become so accustomed to these various expressions of the Business-As-Usual view, we have tended to forget how much they take for granted and, until quite recently, we have often failed to notice how large an element of utopian wishful thinking they contain.

The HE view of the future of work appeals to many scientists, technologists, industrialists and business commentators who, as most people do, see the future primarily from their own point of view. They expect the existing polarisation between skilled and unskilled workers, employed and unemployed, to continue to the point where all the important work is done by a minority of highly skilled and highly responsible people. These people will be putting the space colonies into orbit, installing and monitoring the automated factories, managing the nuclear power stations, running the psychiatric institutes and genetic laboratories, operating the communications networks, and carrying out all the other highly skilled tasks on which a super-industrial society will depend. The rest of us will be living lives of leisure. As in past societies, the prevailing pattern of work in the HE future will reflect a division between superior and inferior members of society. But the division will no longer be between masters and slaves, lords and serfs, employers and employees. This time it will be between workers and drones. The working minority will monopolise all the important work and exclude the rest of the population from it – at best permitting them to undertake marginal, menial tasks.

Because we have become accustomed to accept the authority, in their own specialist fields, of those who support the HE view of the future of work, we have sometimes tended to forget the political, social and psychological realities which it ignores, and have failed to notice how large an element of utopian, 'mad scientist' fantasy it contains.

The SHE view of the future of work, by contrast, sees the historical progression from masters-and-slaves to lords-and-serfs and then to employers-and-employees as an unfinished progress towards greater equality. It now envisages a further step in that direction. As hopes of restoring full employment fade away, the dominant form of work will not longer be seen as employment but as self-organised activity. In other words, many more people will take control of their own work. They will work on their own account, to meet their own needs, to achieve their own purposes, in their own households and local communities, on a personal and inter-personal basis, to a very much greater extent than the prevailing pattern of work in the industrial age has allowed them to do. The direction in which work will develop in the SHE future will represent a reversal of some of the dominant trends of the industrial age. Thus, the informal economy will become one of the main areas for further economic growth and social progress. A fulfilling, well-balanced life will be regarded as one that offers a flexible choice of work patterns; and part-time work in the formal economy and part-time work in the informal economy will come to be seen as the norm.[3] Ownwork will be the characteristic form of work in the new work order.

Notes

1. Robertson, J. (1983) *The Sane Alternative: A Choice of Futures*. Revised edition. London, Robertson.
2. Amory Lovins (1977) *Soft Energy Paths*. London, Penguin.
3. For example, David Bleakley (1983) *Work: The Shadow and the Substance*, SCM Press, argues for alternative approaches and employment and unemployment which will transcend the conventional work ethic.

32

Towards a Green and Healthy Future

DAVE GEE

Introduction

Campaigning for the environment is often portrayed as the ultimate altruistic cause – 'not for you, or for me, but for the planet'. But our own well-being and survival depend on our environment, now more than ever before. One hundred and fifty years ago environmental influences on health were highlighted by Edwin Chadwick and the public health movement, and they have been underlined recently by the World Health Organisation[1]. If we are to create a green future for ourselves and our children then we must re-establish the links between our health and our environment and reorientate our societies towards preserving and enhancing these most precious of our assets.

Resources for health

The Universal Declaration of Human Rights (1948) gives everyone the right to live and work in an environment that is conducive to physical and mental health – that is, an environment that not only minimises disease but also maximises security, self-esteem and dignity. This environment must be one where we have access to fresh water, clean air, and good soil. We now also know that we need life support systems such as the ozone layer and a stable global climate.

None of this can be maintained if we are poor, for real poverty means that people have to destroy what little resources they have to survive until tomorrow. A poor world cannot protect its own health or that of the planet. But affluence and over-consumption can also destroy environments. What is needed is a basic income that is sufficient to allow both sustainable economic activity, and investment in the energy and waste treatment systems that underpin all economies. How far have we established these environmental conditions for a healthy future?

Fresh water

Nearly half of the world's population suffers from diseases associated with insufficient or contaminated water.

Most of this ill health strikes the urban poor in developing countries, but in developed countries pollution of water by agriculture and industry is on the increase. This, together with our profligate water use and shrinking supplies, is threatening our health.

Most of Britain's rivers and coastal waters do not meet the standards set by the EC Directive on Bathing Water, because of sewage and agricultural pollution. Overall river pollution is increasing, along with contamination of fish in many areas, and the UK Government is still refusing to apply the EC Directive on pollution monitoring to inland waterways.[2]

Clean air

More than 1,000 million people living in towns and cities are exposed to outdoor air pollution levels that are higher than those recommended by the WHO.[3] Whilst traditional pollutants from industry, households and power stations, such as sulphur dioxide, lead, hydrocarbons and particulates, have declined in OECD countries, nitrogen oxides and secondary pollutants such as smog and acid rain have increased.[4] Developing countries have poorly regulated traditional industries as well as cars, all pumping out pollutants, so the air quality in urban areas is worsening.

Air pollution from industry is a potent cause of health hazards to both employees and the public, either through accidental releases such as at Bhopal, India, where over 2000 died and over 50,000 were injured, or from long term low-level pollution. In Eastern Europe and developing countries limited pollution abatement, and 'double standards' by multinational companies have contributed to significant health hazards.[5]

We are now experiencing a new generation of problems which are the result of the environment's own reaction to chemicals – an 'indirect' pollution whose health effects are even more difficult to assess but which may be profound. Carbon dioxide, methane and nitrous oxide are all 'greenhouse gases', that are contributing to global warming and climate instability.

The loss of our ozone layer has been caused by reactions to chlorofluorocarbons (CFCs) in the atmosphere. The most recent measurements of ozone depletion over Europe show losses of around 10%, which is likely to cause an extra 8000 cases of skin cancer in the UK, and millions of extra cases of skin cancer and cataracts world-wide.[6]

Good soil

Over the last 20 years, the world's stock of cultivated land has declined due to soil erosion, salination, urbanisation and desertification.[7] Soil losses exceed soil formation on one-third of USA cropland; and agricultural areas as diverse as the Sussex Downs and Malaysia are losing 200 tons of soil per hectare per year from overintensive agricultural techniques.[8] The 'green revolution' in developing countries did lead to large increases in crop yields, but also to higher chemical and water inputs, which then caused increased salinity, waterlogging, soil erosion and pollution problems.[9]

However, if you get ill by not having enough to eat, it is usually because you are poor and have no access to land, rather than because of the low quality of that land. As the WHO report on 'Health and the Environment' concludes, 'chronic hunger is due more to lack of purchasing power or of land . . . than to the non-availability of food' (p. 67). This raises the general question of people's access to sufficient income to maintain both a healthy body and a healthy planet.

Income, poverty and overconsumption

Poverty is the main cause of ill health in most of the world, whilst in rich and poor countries alike, 'most of the differences in health status are determined by living and working conditions'.[10] If poverty is defined as inadequate access to food, fodder, water, shelter and basic health care then about 2000 million people live in poverty in the developing world.[11] Poverty is both a cause and an effect of high population growth and population pressure is a potent cause of environmental degradation, particularly when it is accompanied by the breakdown of traditional communal resource management, excessive tree clearance and inequality of access to land.[12] Overconsumption is the health hazard in the developed world.

In order to make ecological room for the 5–8 billion people expected in developing countries over the next few decades, the rich of the world will need to greatly reduce their consumption of the world's non-renewable resources (fossil fuels and minerals) and to reduce their use of both renewable resources (soils, water and vegetation) and of the planet's capacity to absorb wastes. In short, there needs to be a revolution in both the distribution and the use of resources if the health of people and the planet are to be preserved. How is this green and healthy future to be achieved?

Strategies for achieving a green and healthy future

It is a curious paradox that we place little or no economic value on our two most precious assets, our health and our environment. The preservation of these assets has rarely been the main objective of economic and social policies and consequently their fate has been the result of actions to achieve other policy goals. It is not surprising then to find that the state of the world's health and environment is poor, often irreversibly so, and looks set to get much worse unless we re-order our priorities.

We can start by putting economic prices on environmental resources such as soil, air and water, energy supplies, forests and biodiversity. Money reflects value, and we should use financial levers to ensure that our assets are protected. We must remove the subsidies which encourage overconsumption, and the squandering of resources, and redirect those subsidies toward conservation. When we count the cost of production, we should build into our calculations the cost of resource use and waste disposal – the full environmental costs, including those which are usually passed on to society, other countries or future generations. By raising the unit costs of such basic commodities as water, food, energy and transport we would increase the incentives to economise on their use. The combination of price increases and regulations to achieve efficiency targets would mean that we would pay, say, three times as much for our petrol or electricity but get three times as much use from it. The technology for trebling the efficiency of our washing machines and cars is already available, we just lack the market signals and regulations needed to make them widely available.

The practical consequences of re-orientating eco-nomics towards preserving our environment would be to increase the incentives to avoid waste, and to improve the efficiency of resource use, e.g. the 60% losses of energy from conventional coal power stations and the 20–60% losses of water from distribution systems in both the UK and the Third World would no longer be tolerated.

If we do raise the prices of basic goods we will put the costs of change more on to the poor than on to the rich but we can prevent that, and further refocus our economy on a green future, by shifting the burden of taxation from labour and profits to resource use and pollution. Why tax the things that are good for the economy such as work and investment, when we could tax the things that are bad for us such as profligate resource use and pollution? Studies in Germany and the USA have shown that perhaps one-third of the tax burden could be re-focused in this way. The revenue from 'green' taxes would be used to finance subsidies for eco-investments, benefits for the poor who may be below the income tax threshold, and for income transfers to the Third World as part of our ecological debt repayments.

The national income accounts and measures of gross domestic products (GDP) should be adjusted to account for the degradation of ecological capital and pollution. At the moment GDP rises more quickly if we pollute more rapidly and then spend money cleaning up the resulting mess. And the more quickly we squander our natural resources such as North Sea oil the faster our GDP rises. By removing the depreciation of natural capital from the GDP and subtracting the costs of pollution we will produce a more accurate measure of economic progress. We will also need to use additional measures of progress based on resources use, pollution, waste generation, housing and health conditions.[13] Such indicators, and the publication of Natural Resource Accounts and annual environmental reports from companies and governments, would help to steer us towards our green future.

The next step would be to put health and environmental objectives at the centre of policy-making so that the integration of effort across sectors which are usually isolated from each other such as housing, industry, forestry, agriculture, energy, and transport, could be achieved.

There would need to be large transfers of both resources and appropriate technology from rich to poor countries, via increased aid, debt cancellation and improved trade terms. This would need to be targeted on the type of community-managed projects that have been the success stories of aid programmes of recent years. These have been inspired by the principles of primary health care and have been designed to meet basic needs via optimal use of the environment through the mobilisation of local resources and people. Such examples of 'primary environmental care' have achieved success in improving water supply and sanitation, agricultural yields, natural resource management, health care and family planning, housing and employment.[14]

An example of primary environmental care is the Dodota water supply project in Ethiopia. This community of some 60,000 people in a drought-prone area, organised the construction and maintenance of their own water supply system, with the aid of the Swedish Development Agency, working through the local women's associations. For a total cost of $30 per person they achieved high levels of consumer satisfaction, better water resource management, improved health, especially amongst children, and improved economic activity. So much time was saved by not having to collect water that people could turn their energies to small-scale agriculture.[15] This success story is in marked contrast to much of the wasted development air spent on 'top down' large-scale construction projects.

Conclusion

It is possible to have a healthy planet and healthy people, all enjoying Western European standards of living, even if the population rises from the current 5.4 billion to 8 billion. But to do this requires more than was needed in Chadwick's day, when much of Britain's wealth came from exploiting the rest of the world. As Ghandhi remarked when asked if, after independence, India would attain British standards of living, 'It took Britain half the resources of the planet to achieve its prosperity; how many planets would a country like India require?' It is clear that a more radical approach is needed, involving fundamental shifts in values, resources and power, if a green and healthy future is to be possible. This poses huge political difficulties but already we have signed an unprecented international agreement on ozone protection, and there is a gradual greening of aid, public health, industry, economics and governments, in response to pressure from campaigning groups, the public, and scientists. This pressure can only increase if the link between the health of our environment and the health of ourselves is made as clear as it was in 1842. But more than the fear of ill health is needed to persuade people to change. We must also show that a society committed to development, rather than growth, to equity rather than gross disparities in wealth and income, to quality not quantity, and to participation rather than patronage or rigid central planning, would actually be a far better place to live than our current world.

Notes

1. 'Our Planet, Our Health' Report of the WHO Commission on *Health and the Environment*, March 1992.
2. 'Health risks associated with bathing in sea water', *British Medical Journal* 1991, 303, pp. 144–5; Balavan *et al.*, 'Bathing Water' Friends of the Earth Briefing 1991.
3. Our Planet, Our Health, p. 149.
4. *The State of the Environment*, Organisation of Economic and Cultural Development. Paris, 1991.
5. An investigation into pollution at the Ulsan/Onsan industrial complex in South Korea found nervous symptoms amongst residents and damage to local agriculture and fisheries. Foreign companies were applying local pollution controls that were 'less stringent than in their home countries' (p. 186, Note 2). Sulphur dioxide levels in East Germany over recent winters have been higher than in London in December 1952, which killed 4000 people ('Air Pollution I: From pea souper to photochemical smog' *British Medical Journal*, Vol. 3037, December, 91).
6. Russell Jones, R. (1989) *Ozone Depletion: Health and Environmental Consequences*, Wiley.
7. *State of the World 1991*, Worldwatch Institute, Washington, USA.
8. 'Off the Treadmill' FoE, 1992.
9. Conway, G. R. and Barbier, E. B. (1990) *After the Green Revolution: sustainable agriculture for development*, Earthscan Publications.
10. WHO 'Targets for Health for All'. See also Whitehead, M. (1987) *The Health Divide: inequalities in health in the 1990s*. London, Health Education Council.

11. Our Planet, Our Health, p. 41.
12. Our Planet, Our Health, p. 49.
13. A core set of indicators for these categories is being developed by the WHO and other UN agencies – see p. 229 of Ref. 2; and 'Alternative Economic Indicators' by Victor Anderson, 1991.
14. 'Operationalising sustainable development at the community level: primary environmental care,' by Pretty, J. and Sandbrook, R., IIED, 1991: See also *Lessons Learnt in Community Based Environmental Management* by Borrini, G., Instituto Superiore di Sanita, Rome, 1991.
15. *Concern and Responsibility: an evaluation of the Dodota Water Supply Project in Ethiopia*, Swedish International Development Authority, 1990.

33

The Return of the Spirit*

PATRICK PIETRONI

Man's initial attempts at understanding the workings of the universe entailed creating a panoply of Gods and Goddesses. These powerful figures of his imagination controlled the wind, the sea, the sun and all other aspects of his environment with which he came in contact. Man felt his insignificance in relation to the Gods and erected a whole edifice of belief and practice to enable him to communicate effectively with these powerful forces. Witch-doctors, shamans, priests were selected by man to become the mediators between him and the Gods. Elaborate rituals, sacrifices, incantations, ceremonies were developed as a means of both appeasing the Gods as well as demanding their favour, blessings and recovery from illness. The shaman or tribal religious leader is found in almost all cultures and is the *primogenitor* of all subsequent health-care practitioners. He combined the roles of both priest, doctor and social worker, and the religious nature of healing ceremonies formed an essential part of the ritual of health care. The shaman would enter into a trance either through the drinking of some hallucinogenic herb or after the performance of a repetitive chant or dance. Whilst in the trance he would engage with the evil spirits or offer sacrifices to the God who had been offended.

The illness that had entered the patient was seen to have been caused by some spiritual transgression, and it was only through the mediation of the priest/shaman that the illness could be transformed and the patient regain his health. The magical quality of the ritual was often accompanied by empiric interventions – drugs, herbs, poultices, enemas and physical manipulations. Study of the details of these empiric interventions suggest that the shamans were astute physicians as well as

---

*This is an abridged extract from P. Pietroni (1990) *The Greening of Medicine*, Gollancz, pp. 159–70.

magicians. Nevertheless, the early history of medicine and healing is linked strongly to the belief that man's spirit or soul formed an integral part of his being. Illness and health were inextricably linked to his spiritual nature and that powerful external forces directly determined the course of his life and death. The organised churches whether Jewish, Christian, Islam or Hindu were all concerned with health and healing and several of the earliest 'medical' text books are to be found in the great scriptures of the day. It was not only the religious leaders who were involved in determining the appropriate healing practices. Hippocrates is seen as having laid the foundation of modern Western medicine. But the three great philosophers who preceded him and followed each other – Socrates, Plato and Aristotle – all involved themselves in matters medical, and taught on the appropriate relationship between doctor and patient.

Hippocrates, who is seen as having inspired and collated the body of works that bears his name, helped to introduce an element of objectivity and empiricism in medicine. Nevertheless he was a firm believer, like Plato before him, that

> The cure of the part should not be attempted without treatment of the whole. No attempt should be made to cure the body without the soul and if the head and body are to be healthy you must begin by curing the mind, for this is the greatest error of our day in the treatment of the human body that physicians first separate the soul from the body . . .[1]

The mediaeval Christian church held firmly to the belief espoused by Plato and continued to exercise its power over doctors. The mediaeval practice of 'trial by ordeal' implied that as long as the soul was pure no harm could be done to the body even if it were plunged into boiling oil or burning brazier. With the advent of the earliest medical schools in Italy and France, the church still maintained a strong hold on the study of anatomy. Dissection of bodies was forbidden.

Thus the early church had a major influence in maintaining that mind, spirit and soul were all closely linked and helped determine the functioning of the body. This not only gave the church control over the study of the mind and body but allowed it to impose guidelines as to what the mind was allowed to think, feel and imagine. For the early church, a healthy mind meant believing in its dogma and an unhealthy mind meant allying oneself with the forces of evil.

The explosion that occurred during the Renaissance heralded a major shift in medicine as in all other areas. Copernicus, Galileo, Descartes, and Newton all helped to propel the study of man away from the narrow dictates of the church and towards the rational and scientific model that has held sway for the last three hundred years. This process of secularisation led to a division of the patient. The care of the soul became the legitimate focus for the church and its priests whilst the study of the mind and body was acknowledged as the basis of future medical developments. The spirit or soul with its immaterial and unknowable qualities became more and more difficult to incorporate within the developing framework of scientific medicine. Indeed it seemed as if the mind was also to be excluded from the proper study of medicine and it is not until the latter part of the nineteenth century that attempts to study the mind were made with any earnestness. We need only remind ourselves of the difficulty psychiatry has had as a discipline in establishing itself as a legitimate specialty in medicine to appreciate how much a problem the reintegration of 'the spirit' into the study of medicine may well prove to be. Precise definitions and clear statements regarding the spirit do not come easily. For many it is difficult to separate spirit from mind. Yet all the scriptures of whatever religion imply that the spirit is more than the sum of emotional and psychological states. Table 33.1 gives some of the more popular definitions of spirit.

It may still not be clear from these definitions how the spirit of a person is separate from his mental state and the nearest it may be possible to arrive at for a convinced materialist is that the spirit like the wind is a force you cannot see but which you know by its effects. In Christian terms the spirit has always had some association with death or rather life after death. The strong Christian belief in life after death came from its very beginning – the resurrection of Christ – and for many it is soul or spirit that lives on after death. It is this transcendent quality that helps to differentiate spirit from mind. It is seen, though not always, to involve a consideration of something greater than oneself. It is often associated with an experience, a sense of harmony or peace – a knowing from within, and many spiritual practices endeavour to encourage the development of these experiences.

TABLE 33.1   What is spirit?

• Immaterial part of man	• Inspired
• Religion/beliefs/conviction	• Emotional calmness
• Soul – vitality	• Everyday ecstasy
• Quintessence of various forms	• Sense of harmony
• Life force	• Sense of belonging
• Breath of life	• Knowing sure from within
• A possession	• Transcendent force
• Something higher	• Mystical experience

Source: P.C. Pietroni, 'Spirited interventions in a general practice setting' (1986) in *Holistic Medicine*, **1**, 253–262.

TABLE 33.2   **The role of priest and role of general practitioner**

Spiritual practice	General practice counterpart
1 Providing a sanctuary	Consulting room as a 'safe space'
2 Confessional	Active listening
3 Interpret tribulation	Give meaning to stressful life events
4 Source of ritual and ceremony	Repeat prescription
5 Provide support and comfort	Teamwork
6 Increase spiritual awareness	Give permission for spiritual discussion
7 Laying on of hands	Use of touch
Prayer and meditation	Relaxation and quiet time
8 Communion	Self-help groups/patient participation

Source: P.C. Pietroni, 'Spiritual interventions in a general practice setting'.

Another possible method of arriving at a definition of spirit that can begin to be integrated within a materialistic and causal world view is to examine the spiritual practices and interventions associated with priests', Rabbis' or Shamans' work and place them alongside possible similar interventions found in more secular settings. A comparison such as outlined in Table 33.2 may suggest that the idea that the general practitioner has taken over the role of the priest is not so far-fetched as it may seem. A brief description of a few of those interventions outlined will emphasise the difficulty of separating spiritual interventions from psychological and physical ones.

Sanctuary/safe space

Churches were built not only as places of worship but to serve as sanctuaries from invading forces. They were seen as protected territory providing the itinerant traveller with shelter and warmth. Spence describes the unit of medical practice as 'the occasion when in the intimacy of the consulting room a person who is ill or believes himself to be ill seeks the advice of a doctor whom he trusts'. The words 'intimacy' and 'trust' invoke the notion of the consulting room as a 'sanctuary' or safe space. Fry, in his book *Safe Space*, traces the use of this concept in medical settings and draws attention to the importance of architecture and colour in conveying an atmosphere where healing can be enhanced.[2]

Confessional/active listening

The act of unburdening oneself of troubled thoughts, feelings, resentments is an act as old as man himself. It formed part of all spiritual traditions: 'Give up what thou hast and then thy will receive' is translated in more popular words as 'Confession is good for the soul'. Since the notion of repression, the drama has moved from the confessional to the analytic couch, psychotherapist's chair or general practitioner's consulting room. The Greek word 'catharsis' or 'cleansing' is seen as the first stage of the psychotherapeutic process and Jung writes: 'The goal of the cathartic method is full confessional – not merely the intellectual recognition of the facts with the head, but their confirmation by the heart and the actual release of suppressed emotions.'[3] Many of the psychotherapeutic techniques developed in the first half of this century to aid the process of confessional, from free association to hypnosis and breathing exercises, have similar counterparts in shamanistic practices and, as pointed out by Sargant, are not dissimilar to the brain-washing techniques found in interrogation and counter-intelligence centres.[4] However, it is the emphasis on active listening within the consultation between doctor and patient that has been emphasised in clinical textbooks.

Laying on of hands/use of touch

Touching, laying on of hands and blessings have always formed part of spiritual practice and is validated within the Christian church from references to the scriptures. Christ in direct instruction to his disciples as described in Matthew (10.8) – Heal the sick, raise the dead, cleanse the lepers, cast out devils. For St Luke Jesus healed through touch – 'the power of the body'. European royalty, who claimed to rule by divine right, took on this power and by 1307 the public in need of healing were visiting Philip the Fair, the King of France. The English kings soon followed and touching for tuberculosis became a common practice; the condition became known as the King's Evil, and the royal touch and laying on of hands formed part of the accepted practice of spiritual healing. The claims made by many of these itinerant healers were challenged forcefully, much as today. Nevertheless the laying on of hands still remains the most popular of all spiritual interventions, and the scientific community has very reluctantly studied its secular equivalent of touch with some trepidation. Montagu points out, citing many examples from animal and human behaviour, how the skin and touching form an essential psychological first step in the proper development of the other sensory systems of the body.[5] Deprivation dwarfism is a well-recognised condition that occurs in institutions where children, in spite of good food and medical care, fail to thrive because they are not held, touched and hugged.

In its survey on *Alternative Therapy*, the BMA committee identified the use of touch as one of the contributory factors for the popularity of many such therapies.[6] Spiritual healers in an attempt both to quantify and validate the 'laying on of hands', or therapeutic touch, have conducted several experiments both with inanimate material, plants, human beings and complex electronic equipment. Several clinical trials are currently under progress, testing the claim that therapeutic touch will limit the growth of cataracts and eradicate intestinal parasites in horses.[7] Notwithstanding the claims made for therapeutic efficacy, the use of touch, massage, holding, laying on of hands etc. has increased in clinical and secular settings and in the most recent survey of alternative practitioners in the UK the largest group were found to be spiritual healers.[8]

Prayer and contemplation/relaxation and meditation

As outlined earlier, one of the ways in which 'spirit' has been interpreted is to separate it altogether from organised religion and a set of beliefs and link it to a 'special way of being'. Spirit and spiritual states are seen as something beyond the mundane and everyday. The notion of spirit is linked to the concept of life-force, a transcendent or mystical state of consciousness. It is this link to consciousness that has produced a reawakening of interest and study into matters spiritual. Like spirit, consciousness can be difficult to define but we can come nearer to studying and observing different states of consciousness through the use of electro-encephalograms and the measurement of brainwave activity.

It is the link with 'special states of consciousness' and the spiritual practices of prayer, meditation, contemplation, that have drawn millions of people back to some form of 'spiritual practice'. And it is the assumed link with positive health, a 'sense of well being', 'inner peace', 'harmony', 'balance' that has seen the growth of the consciousness therapies. By transforming one's consciousness it is believed that unwanted, unpleasant and unhealthy aspects of behaviour and emotions can be altered. Nearly all of the newer psychotherapies – mind–body therapies and humanistic therapies, work on the assumption that healing involves an alteration in consciousness and the development of awareness. 'Becoming aware' and 'maximising one's potential' are the buzz words of the growth movement that arose during the Sixties, and that form part of modern secular spiritual practice. It is easy to dismiss many of these approaches to health-care as signs of the narcissistic-culture and self-absorption linked to Western affluence. However, the end-point to many of these practices appears to be remarkably similar, and secular descriptions of these states of consciousness are almost identical to those found in Buddhist, Christian and Jewish literature. They have been described by poets and writers throughout time. They have in common elements which lift them out of ordinary emotional experiences one may have on a day-to-day basis. Their extraordinariness is often startling and for many may mark the beginning of profound changes, psychological as well as physical.

> ... that serene and blessed mood
> In which the affections gently lead us on–
> Until, the breath of this corporeal frame
> And even the motion of our human blood
> Almost suspended, we are laid asleep
> In body, and become a living soul;
> While with an eye made quiet by the power
>   of harmony, and deep power of joy,
> We see into the life of all things.[9]

It is these observable and measurable changes that have allowed for the introduction of meditation as a therapy into several orthodox medical centres. Meditation can be defined as a state of 'relaxed non-aroused physiological functioning' and the changes that have been identified with this state include:

1 Slowing of the pulse
2 Lowering of blood pressure
3 Reduction in breathing rate
4 Increase in blood flow to fingers and toes
5 Changes in oxygen and CO_2 concentrations in the blood
6 Reduction in lactate
7 Alterations in brainwave pattern:
   (a) increase in alpha brainwave activity
   (b) synchronisation of brainwaves (left and right hemispheres).

Some of these can be observed during the practice of meditation. Regular practice produces a 'carry-over' effect which has proved effective in the management of several clinical disorders, including migraine, high blood pressure, sleep disturbance, pain relief, anxiety and other stress-related disorders.[10] Far more commonly, however, is the use of meditation as a spiritual exercise and a technique for 'transforming one's consciousness'.

More recent developments have been to explore the link between mental states, the immune system and chronic disorders from arthritis to cancer.[11] Self-help interventions, including relaxation techniques, meditation and visual imagery form part of the therapeutic packages that are associated with 'new-age' therapies. The therapists involved in these interventions are clear that spiritual transformation and personal salvation form an integral part of the expected outcome.

Through this system a person is able to make contact with his Soul or Divine energies, literally rejuvenating his whole being. In this expanded state of awareness he is easily able to release deep-seated blockages. Not only from this life, early childhood traumas, etc., but also from other incarnations. This therapy also helps most physical-emotional-mental-psychic, and sexual conditions.[12]

It is these all-encompassing claims that have led some critics to warn against the returning to an era of religious superstition and the acceptance of a spiritual cause to health and disease. Let us not forget Hippocrates' admonition that 'too many use the divine as a screen for their inability to offer any assistance.'

It is, nevertheless, a fact that the process of mental imagery which is an accepted and legitimate focus of enquiry in cancer treatment is described in detail in the *Spiritual Exercises of Ignatius Loyola* published several centuries before. Whole-person medicine, with its emphasis on integrating body, mind and spirit has emerged in the latter part of the twentieth century as a health-care movement which challenges the bio-medical model of man that has held sway since the time of Descartes and Newton. Its emergence parallels the importance placed on 'man's relationship with himself' that forms an integral part of the Green movement. The wish to 'obey the laws of nature' and 'promises to achieve a higher reason' are pursued by 'Greens' and 'patients' alike through a process of spiritual practice which has been linked with the art of healing that transcends both centuries and cultures.

Notes

1. Plato, *Dialogues*.
2. Fry, A. (1987) *Safe Space*, Dent.
3. Jung, C. J. (1982) *Collected Works*, **16**, p. 59.
4. Sargant, W. (1960) *Battle for the Mind*, Pan.
5. Montagu, A. (1973) *Touching* Perennial Library, Harper and Row.
6. British Medical Association Board of Education and Science (1986) *Alternative Therapy*.
7. Ibid.
8. Fulder, S. (1988) *The Handbook of Complementary Medicine*, 2nd ed. OUP.
9. Wordsworth, W. *Lines upon Tintern Abbey*.
10. Pelletier, K. (1978) *Mind as Healer, Mind as Slayer*, Allen & Unwin.
11. Locke, Hornig-Rowan (1985) *Mind and Immunology*, Institute for Advancement of Health.
12. Coward, R. (1989) *The Whole Truth*, Faber & Faber.

34

The Space Crone*

URSULA LeGUIN

The menopause is probably the least glamorous topic imaginable; and this is interesting, because it is one of the very few topics to which cling some shreds and remnants of taboo. A serious mention of menopause is usually met with uneasy silence; a sneering reference to it is usually met with relieved sniggers. Both the silence and the sniggering are pretty sure indications of taboo.

Most people would consider the old phrase 'change of life' a euphemism for the medical term 'menopause', but I, who am now going through the change, begin to wonder if it isn't the other way round. 'Change of life' is too blunt a phrase, too factual. 'Menopause,' with its chime-suggestion of a mere pause after which things go on as before, is reassuringly trivial.

But the change is not trivial, and I wonder how many women are brave enough to carry it out wholeheartedly. They give up their reproductive capacity with more or less of a struggle, and when it's gone they think that's all there is to it. Well, at least I don't get the Curse any more, they say, and the only reason I felt so depressed sometimes was hormones. Now I'm myself again. But this is to evade the real challenge, and to lose, not only the capacity to ovulate, but the opportunity to become a Crone.

In the old days women who survived long enough to attain the menopause more often accepted the challenge. They had, after all, had practice. They had already changed their life radically once before, when they ceased to be virgins and became mature women/wives/matrons/mothers/mistresses/whores/etc. This change involved not only the physiological alterations of puberty – the shift from barren childhood to fruitful maturity – but a socially recognized alteration of being: a change of condition from the sacred to the profane.

*This story was published in *Dancing at the Edge of the World* (1989), Gollancz, pp. 3–6.

With the secularization of virginity now complete, so that the once awesome term 'virgin' is now a sneer or at best a slightly dated word for a person who hasn't copulated yet, the opportunity of gaining or regaining the dangerous/sacred condition of being at the Second Change has ceased to be apparent.

Virginity is now a mere preamble or waiting room to be got out of as soon as possible; it is without significance. Old age is similarly a waiting room, where you go after life's over and wait for cancer or a stroke. The years before and after the menstrual years are vestigial: the only meaningful condition left to women is that of fruitfulness. Curiously, this restriction of significance coincided with the development of chemicals and instruments that make fertility itself a meaningless or at least secondary characteristic of female maturity. The significance of maturity now is not the capacity to conceive but the mere ability to have sex. As this ability is shared by pubescents and by post-climacterics the blurring of distinctions and elimination of opportunities is almost complete. There are no rites of passage because there is no significant change. The Triple Goddess has only one face: Marilyn Monroe's, maybe. The entire life of a woman from ten or twelve through seventy or eighty has become secular, uniform, changeless. As there is no longer any virtue in virginity, so there is no longer any meaning in menopause. It requires fanatical determination now to become a Crone.

Women have thus, by imitating the life condition of men, surrendered a very strong position of their own. Men are afraid of virgins, but they have a cure for their own fear and the virgin's virginity: fucking. Men are afraid of crones, so afraid of them that their cure for virginity fails them; they know it won't work. Faced with the fulfilled Crone, all but the bravest men wilt and retreat, crestfallen and cockadroop.

Menopause Manor is not merely a defensive stronghold, however. It is a house or household, fully furnished with the necessities of life. In abandoning it, women have narrowed their domain and impoverished their souls. There are things the Old Woman can do, say, and think that the Woman cannot do, say, or think. The Woman has to give up more than her menstrual periods before she can do, say, or think them. She has got to change her life.

The nature of that change is now clearer than it used to be. Old age is not virginity but a third and new condition; the virgin must be celibate, but the crone need not. There was a confusion there, which the separation of female sexuality from reproductive capacity, via modern contraceptives, has cleared up. Loss of fertility does not mean loss of desire and fulfillment. But it does entail a change, a change involving matters even more important – if I may venture a heresy – than sex.

The woman who is willing to make that change must become pregnant with herself, at last. She must bear herself, her third self, her old age, with travail and alone. Not many will help her with that birth. Certainly no male obstetrician will time her contractions, inject her with sedatives, stand ready with forceps, and neatly stitch up the torn membranes. It's hard even to find an old-fashioned midwife, these days. That pregnancy is long, that labor is hard. Only one is harder, and that's the final one, the one that men also must suffer and perform.

It may well be easier to die if you have already given birth to others or yourself, at least once before. This would be an argument for going through all the discomfort and embarrassment of becoming a Crone. Anyhow it seems a pity to have a built-in rite of passage and to dodge it, evade it, and pretend nothing has changed. That is to dodge and evade one's womanhood, to pretend one's like a man. Men, once initiated, never get the second chance. They never change again. That's their loss, not ours. Why borrow poverty?

Certainly the effort to remain unchanged, young, when the body gives so impressive a signal of change as the menopause, is gallant; but it is stupid, self-sacrificial gallantry, better befitting a boy of twenty than a woman of forty-five or fifty. Let the athletes die young and laurel-crowned. Let the soldiers earn the Purple Hearts. Let women die old, white-crowned, with human hearts.

If a space ship came from the friendly natives of the fourth planet of Altair, and the polite captain of the space ship said, 'We have room for one passenger; will you spare us a single human being, so that we may converse at leisure during the long trip back to Altair and learn from an exemplary person the nature of the race?' – I suppose what most people would want to do is provide them with a fine, bright, brave young man, highly educated and in peak physical condition. A Russian cosmonaut would be ideal (American astronauts are mostly too old). There would surely be hundreds, thousands of volunteers, just such young men, all worthy. But I would not pick any of them. Nor would I pick any of the young women who would volunteer, some out of magnanimity and intellectual courage, others out of a profound conviction that Altair couldn't possibly be any worse for a woman than Earth is.

What I would do is go down to the local Woolworth's, or the local village marketplace, and pick an old woman, over sixty, from behind the costume jewelry counter or the betel-nut booth. Her hair would not be red or blonde or lustrous dark, her skin would not be dewy fresh, she would not have the secret of eternal youth. She might, however, show you a small snapshot of her grandson, who is working in Nairobi. She is a big vague about where Nairobi is, but extremely proud of the grandson. She has worked hard at small, unimportant jobs all her life, jobs like cooking, cleaning, bringing up kids, selling little objects of adornment or pleasure to other people. She was a virgin once, a long time ago, and then a sexually potent fertile female, and then went through menopause. She has given birth several times and faced death several times – the same times. She is facing the final birth/death a little more nearly and clearly every day now. Sometimes her feet hurt something terrible. She never was educated to anything like her capacity, and that is a shameful waste and a crime against humanity, but so common a crime should not and cannot be hidden from Altair. And anyhow she's not dumb. She has a stock of sense, wit, patience, and experiential shrewdness, which the Altaireans might, or might not, perceive as wisdom. If they are wiser than we, then of course we don't know how they'd perceive it. But if they are wiser than we, they may know how to perceive that inmost mind and heart which we, working on mere guess and hope, proclaim to be humane. In any case, since they are curious and kindly, let's give them the best we have to give.

The trouble is, she will be very reluctant to volunteer. 'What would an old woman like me do on Altair?' she'll say. 'You ought to send one of those scientist men, they can talk to those funny-looking green people. Maybe Dr Kissinger should go. What about sending the Shaman?' It will be very hard to explain to her that we want her to go because only a person who has experienced, accepted, and acted the entire human condition – the essential quality of which is Change – can fairly represent humanity. 'Me:' she'll say, just a trifle slyly. 'But I never did anything.'

But it won't wash. She knows, though she won't admit it, that Dr Kissinger has not gone and will never go where she has gone, that the scientists and the shamans have not done what she has done. Into the space ship, Granny.

Index